AN INTRODUCTION TO PRIMARY PHYSICAL EDUCATION

Physical education is a core component of the primary school curriculum. The primary years are perhaps the most significant period for motor development in children, a time during which basic movement competencies are developed and which offers the first opportunity for embedding physical activity as part of a healthy lifestyle. This is the first comprehensive introduction to the teaching of PE in the primary school to be written exclusively by primary PE specialists, with primary school teaching experience.

The book highlights the importance of PE in the primary curriculum and the key issues facing primary teachers today, such as inclusion, training needs and the development of creativity. Central to the book are core chapters that examine functional areas common to many primary PE syllabi – including games, dance, gymnastics, athletics and outdoor learning – and give clear, practical guidance on how to teach each topic. Rooted throughout in sound theory and the latest evidence and research, this book is essential reading for all students, trainee teachers and qualified teachers looking to understand and develop their professional practice in primary physical education.

Gerald Griggs is Senior Lecturer in Physical Education and Sports Studies at the University of Wolverhampton, UK. Dr Griggs trained as a primary teacher with a specialism in physical education, before teaching in several primary schools in the UK. He is a member of the British Educational Research Association, including the Special Interest Group for Physical Education, the Association for Physical Education and the British Sociological Association.

AN INTRODUCTION TO PRIMARY PHYSICAL EDUCATION

EDITED BY GERALD GRIGGS

 Routledge
Taylor & Francis Group

LONDON AND NEW YORK

First published 2012
by Routledge
2 Park Square, Milton Park, Abingdon, Oxon OX14 4RN

Simultaneously published in the USA and Canada
by Routledge
711 Third Avenue, New York, NY 10017

Routledge is an imprint of the Taylor & Francis Group, an informa business

British Library Cataloguing in Publication Data
A catalogue record for this book is available from the British Library

Library of Congress Cataloging in Publication Data
An introduction to primary physical education / edited by Gerald Griggs. -- 1st ed.
p. cm.
1. Physical education for children. 2. Movement education--Study and teaching (Elementary) 3. Education, Elementary--Activity programs. I. Griggs, Gerald.
GV443.I58 2012
372.86--dc23   2011050037

ISBN: 978–0–415–61308–8 (hbk)
ISBN: 978–0–415–61309–5 (pbk)
ISBN: 978–0–203–13188–6 (ebk)

Typeset in Optima and Eras
by Bookcraft Ltd, Stroud, Gloucestershire

MIX
Paper from
responsible sources
FSC   FSC® C004839
www.fsc.org

Printed and bound in Great Britain by
TJ International Ltd, Padstow, Cornwall

CONTENTS

FIGURES

TABLES

ACRONYMS

ADHD	attention deficit hyperactivity disorder
AOTT	adults other than teachers
CPD	continuing professional development
DofDPEG	Developmental Physical Education Group
EYFS	Early Years Foundation Stage
FMS	fundamental movement skills
HMI	Her Majesty's Inspector[s]
ITE	initial teacher education
ITT	initial teacher training
LDA	local delivery agencies
LEA	Local Education Authority
NCPE	National Curriculum for Physical Education
OAA	outdoor and adventurous activities
OEAP	Outdoor Education Advisors Panel
OSHL	out-of-school-hours learning
PDM	Partnership Development Manager
PEDPAS	physical education, physical activity and sport
PESSCL	Physical Education, School Sport and Club Links
PESSYP	Physical Education and Sport Strategy for Young People
PGCE	Postgraduate Certificate of Education
PLT	Primary Link Teacher
PPA	planning, preparation and assessment
PSA	public service agreement
QCA	Qualifications and Curriculum Authority
SCITT	School Centred Initial Teacher Training
SEN	Special Educational Needs
SSCo	School Sport Coordinator
SSP	School Sport Partnership
STEP	space, task, equipment and people
TGfU	Teaching Games for Understanding
UPES	Upper Primary and Early Secondary
WIIO	World Health Organisation

NOTES ON CONTRIBUTORS

Sue Chedzoy is a Senior Lecturer in Education at the University of Exeter. She was Head of Department in two large comprehensive schools before working as the only Advisory Teacher in Devon supporting non-specialist primary school teachers in the teaching of physical education in schools. Since 1990 Sue has been involved in the initial teacher training in physical education of specialist and non-specialist trainee teachers in primary education. She has written four books: *Fitness Fun* published by Southgate, *Physical Education in the School Grounds* published by Learning through Landscapes, *Physical Education for Teachers and Coordinators at Key Stage 1 and 2* and *Physical Education for All*, both published by David Fulton. Her research interests include health-related physical activity and primary school children, teachers' perceived confidence to teach physical education and transitions from primary to secondary school. She has published widely in peer-reviewed academic journals. She received the Ling Award from the Physical Education Association of the United Kingdom for her outstanding contribution to the association and the physical education profession. Sue is both a Fellow of the Higher Education Academy and an honoured member of UK Association for Physical Education (AfPE).

Gerald Griggs is a Senior Lecturer in Physical Education and Sports Studies at the University of Wolverhampton. Gerald trained as a primary teacher with a specialism in physical education at Edge Hill, before teaching in primary schools in both Suffolk and West Sussex. After gaining a scholarship to complete his MA at the University of Warwick, Gerald first entered higher education and taught at Newman University College, Birmingham, where his time was split between lecturing physical education, the sociology of sport and supervising trainee teachers in schools. Since his move to the University of Wolverhampton in 2006 he has published and presented increasingly widely on primary physical education and the sociology of sport, as well as completing his PhD. He is a member of the British Educational Research Association, including the Special Interest Group for Physical Education, the Association for Physical Education and the British Sociological Association. Gerald is also both a Fellow of the Royal Society for the Encouragement of Arts, Manufactures and Commerce and a Fellow of the Higher Education Academy.

Dominic Haydn-Davies is a Senior Lecturer in Physical Education at the University of Roehampton. His current responsibilities include managing the BA Primary Education route to QTS and he leads the Primary Physical Education specialist route. His previous experience includes primary teaching in both Key Stage 1 and 2 and he has also spent several years as a development manager of a School Sport Partnership. Dominic has been involved in the writing of several books and resources and is widely published in the area of primary physical education. He is an experienced professional development tutor, designing and delivering courses for a range of audiences. Dominic completed his MA in Education in 2008 focusing on the concept of physical literacy. He started his PhD studies in 2010 exploring perceptions of gender in early childhood movement experiences. He is a Fellow of the Higher Education Academy and received the Gerald Murray Primary Physical Education Award in 2005.

Kristy Howells is a Senior Lecturer in Primary Education at Canterbury Christ Church University, Canterbury, and specialises in primary physical education. She leads on the part-time Primary Education course, as well as the physical education for the BA Primary Education full-time course. She is also the partnership coordinator for the full- and part-time level 1 BA Primary Education programme, and is part of a workshop team that supports students whilst on placement within the Ashford and Ashford rural area. She has worked on the BA Primary Education programme in Malaysia. She also is currently completing a PhD within Sport and Exercise Science at Canterbury Christ Church University, which has focused on a longitudinal case study of one primary school across an academic year and has explored the contribution physical education lessons make to children's overall physical activity levels. She has also written for *Primary Physical Education Matters on several occasions, for* Literacy Today and for the *European Journal of Neuroscience*, she has also presented her PhD findings nationally at BERA and internationally at the AEISEP conference 2011 and at the PEPAYS forum.

Rachael Jefferson-Buchanan is a Senior Lecturer in the School of Education at Bath Spa University. Having gained a BEd (Hons) in physical education and Special Educational Needs, with a specialism in dance, Rachael began her physical education and GCSE dance teaching career at a UK secondary comprehensive. Two years later, she moved to Switzerland, to work as a physical education/GCSE dance teacher in the International School of Geneva. Following six years of teaching primary and secondary aged children, Rachael took sabbatical leave and embarked upon an MA in Dance Studies at the University of Surrey. On successfully completing this she returned to Switzerland and was appointed Head of Physical Education. Rachael began lecturing in Physical Education and Dance at Bath Spa University during January 2004, and the majority of her work is with primary PGCE students. She also teaches dance on various undergraduate modules. Beyond the university Rachael runs her own dance school, delivers Dance INSET regularly in the South West region and has been an executive member of the National Dance Teachers' Association (NDTA) for six years. Rachael has published many teacher resources and articles in the areas of physical education and dance, as well as a book on fundamental movement skills in August 2009. Presently, she is undertaking her PhD at the University of Birmingham.

Mike Jess has extensive experience teaching physical education in preschool, primary and secondary settings. He is currently coordinator of the physical education subject area and director of the Developmental Physical Education Group at the University of Edinburgh. He is also joint coordinator of the Scottish Primary Physical Education Project, a £6 million Scottish Government project running from 2006–2012. He is programme leader of the Postgraduate Certificate in 3–14 Physical Education and directs the Basic Moves programme which is currently being delivered to tens of thousands of children throughout the UK. His main research interests are in complexity theory, developmental curriculum and pedagogy innovation and teachers' professional learning. Mike has delivered over 100 conference presentations and CPD sessions and has written extensively on children's physical education, sport and physical activity.

Jeanne Keay is Dean of Education at Roehampton University and currently Chair of the Association for Physical Education for the UK. She was a teacher of physical education in secondary schools for 15 years and since then has been involved in leading and managing teacher education, both initial and continuing, in two universities. Her research work and publications have centred on continuing professional development, particularly in relation to teacher induction and high-quality development experiences.

Jim Lavin is Professor of Physical Education in the Department of Health and Physical Education at Eastern Connecticut State University, USA. He was formerly subject leader for physical education at the University of Cumbria. He has been involved in initial teacher training of physical education for over twenty-five years. His PhD focused on the perceptions of primary teachers in the delivery of physical education within the National Curriculum framework. Jim has been awarded a Winston Churchill Travelling Fellowship and looked at the teaching of exercise concepts in an international educational setting. In 2008 he was presented with a Main Level Award by the Association for Physical Education for 'having made a difference at local and national level to the promotion and development of physical education'.

Richard Medcalf is a Lecturer in Sports Studies and Leisure at the University of Wolverhampton. Richard studied for a BSc (Hons) in Sports Studies (First Class) at the University of Worcester. He has a PGCert in Research Methods (Distinction) and was awarded his PhD in 2010. Prior to his move to Wolverhampton, Richard taught for two years at Hartpury College, a Faculty of the University of the West of England, where he was a Lecturer in Sports Science, and Programme Leader for BSc (Hons) Sports Studies (Top-Up). Richard's research interests relate to the sporting and educational experiences of children and young people. He has worked with both quantitative and participatory qualitative methods, studying the perceptions of physical education and school sport for children with social, emotional and behavioural difficulties. He is also interested in social research methodology; particularly the use of multi-modal and visual methods that help to support the inclusion of vulnerable groups and special populations within research processes.

Ian Pickup is currently Director of Student Affairs at the University of Roehampton, having previously worked as Principal Lecturer and Subject Leader for Physical Education, Director of Sport and Wellbeing and Director of Student Development. Before joining Roehampton, Ian played and coached professional rugby union at Harlequins Rugby Club, taught in secondary and primary schools, within further education, and worked as a development officer for the Rugby Football Union in Surrey and South London. Ian is a passionate advocate for high-quality and inclusive sport and physical education experiences and is committed to working with teachers, coaches and young people. Ian is the founder of 'Move', an innovative sports-based social inclusion project which transfers life skills from sport and arts contexts to empower young people to engage with educational and vocational opportunities. His work is not limited to the UK – he has supported practitioners working in post-disaster contexts and was the UK partner in an EU-funded Early Years Physical Education project which brought together teachers and academics from Greece, Finland, Cyprus, Italy and England. Ian was awarded a National Teaching Fellowship by the Higher Education Academy in 2007 and was elected as a Fellow of the Royal Society for the Encouragement of Arts, Manufactures and Commerce the same year.

Lawry Price has spent a teaching career championing the importance of physical education as a vehicle not just for children's learning, but equally so as a motivational tool for personal enjoyment, expression and reward. An advocate of developmental approaches to learning, his commitment to highlighting the significance of providing children from an early age with valid and appropriate physical learning opportunities remains a guiding personal philosophy. He has taught the subject across the age span from toddlers to adults in a variety of educational settings and is widely published as an author in the area. He is currently Principal Lecturer in Physical Education at the University of Roehampton where he continues to teach on a variety of courses that contribute to the education of prospective and currently in-service teachers.

Jon Spence is Principal Lecturer, Subject Leader and Enterprise Manager for Physical Education at the University of Roehampton. He has been involved in the teaching of physical education for more than 20 years, initially as a teacher and head of department and for the last 8 years as a teacher educator. Jon manages the highly successful primary Physical Education Teacher Education Programme at Roehampton whilst also fulfilling other roles: training teachers, working with practising teachers, providing consultancy and researching issues in physical education and CPD.

Nalda Wainwright is a Senior Lecturer in Education at Trinity St David University, Carmarthen. Her previous experience includes teaching in primary schools, teacher in charge of a special unit and associate advisor for physical education. Her current responsibilities include delivery of all aspects of the BA Ed QTS programme and modules within the BA Physical Education and BA Outdoor Education degrees with particular focus on pedagogy, inclusion and health. She is also programme coordinator for the MA Physical Education. In addition to her university role, Nalda is a consultant for the Physical Education and School Sport (PESS) project in Wales, and lead on the Inclusion project, producing resources and training to support teachers

in their delivery of an inclusive programme of physical education. She is a tutor and trainer for several other PESS projects, and she also delivers training to teachers on the use of the Outdoor Learning Cards resource produced by the Outdoor Education Advisors panel (OEAP). Nalda's current research interests include the implementation of the new Foundation Phase in Wales, the physicality of children's learning and the implications of the greater emphasis on the outdoors in the new curriculum.

Gavin Ward is a Senior Lecturer in Physical Education at the University of Wolverhampton. Prior to this, Gavin taught physical education across Key Stages 1 and 4, including 6th form, for fourteen years at a range of educational institutions, serving contrasting communities both in the UK and abroad. Before joining the University of Wolverhampton Gavin worked as a Partnership Development Manager, based at Idsall School and Sports College in Shifnal, Shropshire. From 2003 to 2008, he commenced the strategic and operational creation of the East Shropshire School Sport Partnership and the implementation of the PESSCL and later PESSYP strategies. Gavin's academic education has encompassed a BA (Hons) in Human Movement Studies at the University of Wales Institute Cardiff. Following this he studied for an MSc in Adapted Physical Activity through the University of Northumbria at Newcastle. On successful completion of his MSc, Gavin undertook a Postgraduate Certificate in Education in Secondary Physical Education and Humanities through St Luke's School of Education, University of Exeter. He commenced his teaching career in Peterborough in 1994.

EDITOR'S PREFACE

Over the last decade or so, concerns have been raised by both those inspecting schools and academics alike regarding the preparedness of primary and junior school teachers to teach physical education. A key aspect underpinning such concerns has been the lack of time given to the subject during teacher training which has reduced significantly since an increased focus was placed upon the core subject training of English (literacy), maths (numeracy) and science. Furthermore there has been an erosion of available support for qualified teachers during this time and a significant reduction in the specialist advisory support service.

Consequently what has emerged in this landscape has been a boom of practitioners' guides focusing often on quick-fix 'how to do something' solutions. However, common sense leads to the inevitable question that if a teacher's quick fix does not work, what do they do next and why? Clearly these texts lack relevant theory and research in which good principles should be rooted. The key motivation for writing this text therefore is that it might in some way offer a clear direction across the current landscape of primary physical education which should empower practitioners to be able to develop their knowledge and understanding.

With expectations placed upon already less than confident staff to meet basic provision, pressure has been magnified by government policies to deliver more physical education and school sport. What has resulted to fill the void has been the proliferation of outside agencies plying their trade in primary schools. However, many have been widely condemned due to their lack of specific knowledge and understanding of primary physical education and primary-aged pupils. It is hoped that this book can also provide clear advice and support for all such groups involved in this delivery.

With most physical education specialists being trained in secondary education it is perhaps unsurprising that many authors to date who have written on the topic of primary physical education have had little actual experience in this sector. Because of this, much advice that has been given historically has often been watered-down secondary practice. When primary specialists have emerged they have thus tended to work in small teams not least because of a lack of willing or appropriate partners. What this book will provide is a congregation of the talents of those consistently writing, speaking and *specialising* in the delivery of primary physical education with trainees, teachers and outside agencies.

The book contains contributions in three broad areas, namely: a part introducing a vision for primary physical education, a part pertaining to curriculum and then finally a part exploring key issues. In the first part, the early chapters highlight how the foundations of motor development need to be secure in order to develop higher-level skills. The most significant periods of development in this respect take place almost entirely within the primary age range whereby children must pass through a 'proficiency barrier' of basic movement competencies in order to be proficient in more complex activities. The importance of primary physical education is stressed as it prepares the basic building blocks for all physical activity that follows. This book seeks to outline a vision for what these building blocks should look like and provide guidance for how they might be best delivered.

The second part concerning curriculum comprises the more complex activities which children should move on to. Irrespective of the fads and fashions of curriculum and policy in the UK, since 1933 the key areas within primary physical education have remained largely constant. Primarily these have concerned activity relating to games, gymnastics, dance, athletics, outdoor and adventurous activities (OAA) and swimming. We do not believe that imminent or future reviews will change this landscape significantly in practice and so it seems prudent that direction is given in these areas for trainees, teachers and outside agencies. The only omission here is that of swimming as now the majority of schools ask others to deliver this in local authority pools. Whilst in parts, some authors relate to specific curriculum or policy documents, they do so largely by means of illustration. The conceptual overview of each activity area in the curriculum part can easily transcend new curriculum orders and thus be applied when working with all primary-aged pupils.

The final part concerns itself with contemporary issues in primary physical education. In changing times in education, in an age where generalist primary teachers receive only a few hours' physical education training, where there is a well documented increase in child obesity and where aspects such as creativity and inclusion are being given greater priority across curricula in all sectors it is vital not only that such key areas are kept abreast of but that they are discussed in relation to the specialist field that primary physical education has become. In this book, such topics are discussed as separate issues by experts in the field informed by the latest research.

To assist in a wider understanding of each of the chapters discussed, key readings have been identified throughout. Furthermore, following the introduction, each chapter contains 'thought boxes' to highlight important aspects to reflect upon. It is hoped that, by engaging in the text fully, readers will feel that they been given a comprehensive introduction to primary physical education.

Gerald Griggs

ACKNOWLEDGEMENTS

Thank you to everyone who has been involved with this project. In particular, a huge thank you to each of the contributors for investing their time and efforts and believing in the collective vision that the book has become. In addition, thanks must also be given to the team at Routledge for their continued support and patience.

Part 1

INTRODUCING PRIMARY PHYSICAL EDUCATION

CHAPTER ONE

SURVEYING THE LANDSCAPE OF PRIMARY PHYSICAL EDUCATION

Gerald Griggs

INTRODUCTION

In 2000 a plethora of texts were published in the UK pertaining to primary physical education (see examples such as Bailey and MacFadyen, 2000; Hopper *et al.*, 2000; Williams, 2000). The reason for this sudden rush can largely be explained by the publication of the National Curriculum for physical education a year earlier (DfEE/QCA, 1999). Though no new orders have been published for primary physical education since that time, the surrounding landscape has continued to shift. During this period a number of individuals who are active teachers and researchers involved with primary physical education have gained prominence. This book brings together many of these talents in a bid to provide both a specialist and current viewpoint in what have been broadly changing times within education.

One of the most significant changes to the physical education landscape over the last decade has been the amount of interest and government investment in physical education and school sport. In October 2002 the Physical Education, School Sport and Club Links (PESSCL) strategy invested in excess of £1½ billion into physical education and school sport within the UK. With its overall objective to enhance the take-up of sporting opportunities by 5–16-year-olds, a public service agreement (PSA) pledged to engage children in at least two hours' high-quality physical education and sport at school each week. The strategy contained eight different strands (specialist sports colleges, sport coordinators, gifted and talented, investigating physical education and school sport, step into sport, professional development, school/club links and swimming) (DfES/DCMS, 2003). In more recent times, the expectation on staff to increase their delivery time was raised still further with the injection of another £¾ billion and the introduction of the Physical Education and Sport Strategy for Young People (PESSYP) which pledged to 'create a new "5 hour offer" for all' (DCSF, 2008b).

During the same period, the National Curriculum in England underwent significant change but strangely not as a joined-up and coordinated strategy but as isolated pieces of engineering at either end of the educational continuum. At the very earliest stage, May 2008 saw the introduction of the Early Years Foundation Stage (EYFS) framework, which provided the statutory requirements for setting the standards for learning, development and care for children from 0–5 years. The framework aimed at laying a secure foundation for future learning through learning and development that is planned around six areas: personal, social and emotional development; communication, language and literacy; problem solving, reasoning and numeracy; knowledge and understanding of the world; physical development; and creative development (DCSF, 2008a).

At the other end of the age range, a new secondary curriculum for England was published in 2007 and came into effect in September 2008, as part of a wider review of 14–19 education. As previously, a single-subject approach was advocated with the biggest change evident in the change of language. Out went activity areas and strands and in came a 'range of content' identified as outwitting opponents, accurate replication, exploring and communicating ideas, concepts and emotions, performing at maximum levels, identifying and solving problems and exercising safely and effectively. Through this range of content, 'key concepts' (competency, performance, creativity and healthy active lifestyles) and 'key processes' (developing skills in physical activity, making and applying decisions, developing physical and mental capacity, evaluating and improving and making informed choices about healthy active lifestyles) should be fostered (QCA, 2007). Importantly it shared little or no similarity in structure with the existing primary National Curriculum or the newly devised EYFS framework, leaving the landscape unclear as to where one might begin in conceiving any future primary curriculum.

Despite the lack of development with the primary National Curriculum, perspectives on how to approach a new vision for primary physical education existed close to home. Since devolution, Wales opted to produce its own curriculum (all previous iterations were written for England and Wales), the most recent of which was published in 2008. In many ways it remained similar to the current orders in England, being largely focused on skills and competencies and discretely taught in separate subjects. However, interestingly, there was a repositioning of the content, which was grouped into such themes as creative, health fitness and wellbeing and a showed greater commitment to cross-curricular links (DCELLS, 2008).

By contrast, to date, the curriculum is non-statutory in Scotland and so is not dictated by the Government. Responsibility for what is taught rests with local authorities and schools, taking into account national guidelines and advice. However, more recently through its strategy of Curriculum for Excellence a concerted effort has been made to provide a more coherent, flexible and enriched curriculum from 3 to 18. Rolled out in 2010/11, the curriculum is laid out in eight major areas, namely expressive arts; health and wellbeing; languages; mathematics; religious and moral education; sciences; social studies; and technologies. Of relevance here 'physical education, physical activity and sport' can be located in the area of health and wellbeing, along with five other topics, namely mental, emotional, social and physical wellbeing; planning for choices and changes; food and health; substance misuse; and relationships, sexual health and parenthood (LTS, 2009). What has been of interest in both Wales and Scotland has been the shift back towards a more holistic viewpoint and a child-centred approach, echoing HMI recommendations of the mid 1980s.

Beyond the developments of any curricula during this time is the specific concern high-lighted in a number of papers which strongly highlight the same conclusions, namely that primary physical education is being delivered ineffectively in primary schools (Davies, 1999; Revell, 2000; Speednet, 2000; Warburton, 2001; Wright, 2004; Caldecott et al., 2006; and Griggs, 2007). This concern is further reinforced by the Office for Standards in Education (Ofsted) reviews of the subject within primary schools during this same period, which continually highlight the same recurring themes: insufficient challenge in lessons, an over-concentration on performance, the delivery of an imbalanced curriculum (dominated by games), and poor assessment and recording (see Office for Standards in Education, 1999, 2005).

Over the last decade or so, concerns have continued to be raised regarding the prepar-edness of primary and junior school teachers to teach physical education (Caldecott et al., 2006). A key aspect underpinning such concerns has been the lack of time given to the subject during teacher training (Clay, 1999; Warburton, 2001), which has reduced significantly since an increased focus was placed upon core subject training (English, maths and science) (Ofsted, 1998). This can amount to as little as nine hours on a one-year Postgraduate Certificate of Education (PGCE) course and just five hours for those involved with School Centred Initial Teacher Training (SCITT) (Caldecott et al., 2006).

With a limited amount of training provided within non-core, or what were termed 'foundation subjects' such as physical education, concerns have been raised about the impact this has upon teacher confidence. Low levels of teacher confidence are apparent amongst non-specialists, common in the primary sector (DeCorby et al., 2005; Morgan and Bourke, 2005). Morgan and Bourke (2008) indicate that developing the confidence of the primary non-specialist is key to teacher avoidance in areas such as physical education and this has been illustrated in more recent research by Griggs (2010) who reports an active willingness of primary schools to give up delivery of curriculum phys-ical education. In many cases across England this responsibility is increasingly being handed to local sports coaches (Griggs, 2007, 2008, 2010; Blair and Capel, 2008a, b; Lavin et al., 2008).

This has been facilitated by two further contributory factors. Firstly in order to meet such ambitious PSA targets of engaging children in two hours' high quality physical education and sport at school each week, which has now been raised to five hours, the number of adults other than teachers (AOTTs) used in primary schools, such as sports coaches, has increased dramatically (Lavin et al., 2008). Secondly the imple-mentation of the 'National agreement for raising standards and tackling workload' (DfES, 2003) has begun to remodel and broaden the school workforce in England, 'designed to tackle the problem of workload, and the crisis in teacher recruitment and retention' (Gunter, 2007: 1). Consequently, since 1 September 2005, all teachers have had an entitlement to a guaranteed minimum of 10 per cent of their timeta-bled teaching commitment for planning, preparation and assessment (PPA). Many schools have opted to cover this 10 per cent shortfall in staffing by employing sports coaches for as little as £20 per hour rather than employ further qualified teaching staff (Griggs, 2010).

Systems to support and develop the delivery of primary physical education have come via the creation of the aforementioned Specialist Sports Colleges and the creation of School Sport Partnerships (SSPs). Within the programme, families of schools (including both secondary and primary schools) have built solid partnerships facilitated by specific role holders such as Partnership Development Managers (PDMs), School Sport Coordinators (SSCos) and Primary Link Teachers (PLTs). The PLTs have been recruited largely from existing primary staff (often the physical education subject leader in the school) and are released from teaching for twelve days per year in a role that requires them to advocate high-quality primary physical education and coordinate and support school sport opportunities (YST, 2008).

Findings, however, have shown that the role for some has become more logistical and administrative rather than hands-on pedagogical development and as such has created a seemingly unpopular role, which many teachers unintentionally 'inherited' or were pleased to pass on. A key objection stemmed from being on the bottom tier of a hierarchy, where they felt they bore the brunt of nationally driven targets, which gave little consideration for their local needs (Ward and Griggs, 2010). Clearly a better way forward needs to be found.

TOWARDS A CLEARER VISION

Such revelations present what at times might appear something of a bleak landscape for primary physical education, so it is more important than ever for those who value it and speak about it passionately that a vision for what it should look like can be clearly communicated. This therefore becomes the focus for the early part of this book and commences in Chapter 2, where Ian Pickup reminds us of the importance of primary physical education, and provides a clear rationale for a high status for physical education in today's primary schools. This rationale is based on the potential outcomes of a high-quality physical education provision within physical, social, affective and cognitive domains and is contextualised within prevailing debates and policy decisions concerning child development, curriculum change and children's health. Chapter 2 leads on from this opening introductory chapter, which will identify current issues within primary physical education teaching and learning and suggest steps that can be taken to ensure that both the status and quality of teaching and learning in the subject can be enhanced. This will not however be based on quick wins or on a generic 'template' approach to the subject, but will emphasise the importance of well thought-out, planned-for and assessed teaching and learning. Case study examples of practice in today's schools are included and serve to challenge readers to reflect on what may be considered 'best practice'.

In Chapter 3, Dominic Haydn-Davies sets out the view that the challenges and potential within primary physical education stem from the same starting point – the value that is placed on the subject within schools and society. It explains some of the key challenges that face the subject arise when its value to children's wellbeing is misunderstood or misrepresented. This includes a focus on curriculum provision and learning including time allocations, approaches and structure. Furthermore, issues relating to the delivery mechanisms including staffing and issues with professional development will be explored. The chapter also outlines the potential that primary physical education holds if it is valued and understood as set out in Chapter 2. This will focus on how current initiatives have managed to overcome the challenges and how innovative practice can minimise the potential effects of the subject being undervalued.

The future of primary physical education becomes the focus of attention in Chapter 4, where Mike Jess posits that if primary physical education is to help all children develop a foundation for an active life, then we really must take it more seriously. It is suggested that teachers need to develop a much better understanding of the developing children they work with, the core and authentic learning experiences that act as a foundation for future learning and the context in which physical education is being taught. By developing this understanding, teachers will be able to create primary physical education programmes that are developmentally appropriate, inclusive, connected and linked to children's lives. As such, they will be able to move beyond the direct, controlling teaching that has long dominated physical education and embrace a complex pedagogy that actively engages all children in the learning process and creates authentic experiences that connect with children's overall education and to their lives outside the school setting.

With the vision of what primary physical education could and indeed should be clearly outlined, the second part of the book consists of a series of chapters that consider key dimensions of curriculum content and its implementation. In an ever-changing policy world, locating physical education within the curriculum is not as straightforward as it may first appear. This becomes the focus of Chapter 5, where Sue Chedzoy considers how physical education's relationship to primary education has changed over time. This journey covers over a century of changes, numerous iterations of syllabi and curricula, many from competing agendas. However, the commonalities found here conclude that ultimately children benefit from experiences which help them to master fundamental motor skills such as locomotor and manipulative skills and to develop dexterity and confidence in themselves. Once these foundations have been laid through play and structured activities, programmes need to be developed to encourage children to integrate skills into simple phrases and more complex sequences of movement. It is at this stage that more recognisable forms of activity will be introduced. This leads on to the first of these forms, namely games.

Games has been one of the cornerstones of physical education teaching since its earliest inclusion in the school timetable. However, it is an area that is inherently complex and as such has often been delivered poorly or without real clarity of purpose. These issues are tackled head-on in Chapter 6 by Gavin Ward. A critical review is undertaken of the current approaches which aim to aid the teaching of games, in particular instruction models which aim to develop a better understanding and enhanced performance of outwitting opponents. A key feature of this evaluation is an analysis of frameworks which have attempted to aid teachers' comprehension of the core categories of games. The chapter concludes by presenting a model for primary school teachers which provides a clear holistic overview of games, their principles, tactics, skills and their inherent interrelationships. This seeks to enable practitioners to capitalise on the inherent value of using games as a medium to teach greater cognitive aspects.

A further core aspect of many physical education curricula is that of gymnastics. In Chapter 7, Lawry Price makes the case for providing children throughout the primary age range with opportunities to improve and enhance their body management skills. By stating firstly a rationale and baseline philosophy for the inclusion of this activity area in children's physical development, the chapter highlights a thematic approach to teaching the skills to be included in giving a worthwhile, meaningful and relevant gymnastic learning experience to all children in primary school settings. Further sections include an identification of fundamental skills that can be learnt in and through gymnastic activities; the transferability of knowledge, skill and understanding to other areas of learning; the planning, organisation and assessment of primary gymnastic activities; advocated teaching styles that promote learning in the area; and the relevance and importance of equipment and resources that support gymnastics learning. In essence the chapter highlights why gymnastics provides a unique contribution in helping children become more skilful and more controlled in their physical competence, and the personal confidence that accrues from those experiences.

Dance is a playful way to learn, offering children the opportunity to explore and become confident in the three processes of composing, performing and appreciating, whilst simultaneously contributing to their wellbeing. In Chapter 8 the teaching and learning of dance and its possibilities within the primary school context are discussed by Rachael Jefferson-Buchanan. Through an interrogation of the three processes outlined, key dance knowledge, skills and understanding will be drawn out, emphasising the importance of nurturing children's physical skilfulness and development, their accurate replication of actions, their creative play, and their creative problem solving in and through primary dance educational experiences.

Beyond areas of games, gymnastics and dance, opportunities for many pupils may remain limited. One such area that has remained largely neglected is that of athletics, with many schools taking the opportunity to 'drop it' altogether. Where delivered, the teaching of athletics involves activities which will most likely focus upon recognised adult techniques, measuring and improving performance and preparing for 'sports day'. What has been lost, however, in these adult conceptions of what athletics 'is', is sound development of running, jumping and throwing – core skills that permeate all other areas of physical education. In Chapter 9, Gerald Griggs explains how we should rethink primary athletics, celebrate its importance and outline how it might be done more effectively.

A further area of apparent neglect within schools is that of outdoor and adventurous activities but in Chapter 10 Nalda Wainwright presents a strong rationale for the use of the outdoors as a medium for learning. The chapter incorporates recent research that suggests interaction with natural environments improves physical and emotional wellbeing, enhances motor development, raises activity levels and facilitates the development of key skills. The chapter also explores the role of schools in providing opportunities that allow children to work collaboratively, to solve problems, make judgements and overcome challenges in a risk-averse society. It follows the progression of outdoor and adventurous experiences across the primary age phase and onto lifelong physical activity. It discusses the role of the outdoors and adventure in the curriculum, the contribution to the skills agenda, children's wellbeing, and links to other aspects of the curriculum. The chapter also includes the development of children's awareness of the physical landscape and how man has shaped, responded to, interacted with and impacted on the environment. The chapter concludes with examples of a range of activities and learning opportunities for schools. Activities are linked to existing resources that are available to schools and examples are given of how schools have used these and developed areas of work in response to their own setting and local environment.

As outlined earlier in the introduction, beyond the curriculum a complex network of related issues impact upon primary physical education provision. The latter chapters of the book explore some of the most pertinent of these issues. In Chapter 11 Jeanne Keay and Jon Spence tackle the thorny issue of addressing the training needs in primary physical education. Specifically, the chapter considers issues relating to the professional development of teachers and classroom assistants to deliver the primary physical education curriculum. The important links between the initial education phase and the need for progressive professional development are at the heart of the discussions. The chapter considers the subject knowledge and subject pedagogy requirements of both the physical education specialist and the primary generalist, both of whom need to provide a high-quality, developmental and safe learning experience for all pupils. Furthermore the barriers to and opportunities for professional development for teachers and classroom assistants during the initial, early career and continuing education phases are explored. The benefits and drawbacks of different types of development activities are also considered in order to promote the planning of personalised professional progression in the area of physical education.

In recent years, there has been an increasing level of attention paid to the nature of special educational needs (SEN) within the delivery of physical education and this area is explored in some depth by Richard Medcalf in Chapter 12. To date, much of this consideration has been upon the inclusion of (and planning for) children and young people with a physical disability of some kind. This focus somewhat lacks an appreciation of the wider concept of 'need' in primary physical education. A focus upon 'need' in the physical domain has negated the full range of difficulties which can be ascribed the label of SEN (i.e. profound and multiple learning difficulties; behavioural, emotional and social difficulties; and speech, language and communication needs). Each of these categories is born out of distinct variations of 'need', and, subsequently, the requirement for pedagogic and policy differentiation is apparent. This chapter considers a move towards a more inclusive provision in primary physical education, highlighting the need for a range of 'core learning' opportunities for all children and young people who are considered as being on the spectrum of special educational need.

Despite the media barrage of how unfit and unhealthy our young people are today, to date little importance has actually been placed on health and physical activity within primary physical education. In Chapter 13, Kristy Howells considers this very issue, defining first what we mean by physical activity and then exploring and examining the role of physical education lessons within a primary school setting. The chapter questions how physical education and physical development may contribute to the children's overall physical activity levels. Furthermore the chapter addresses these issues against UK Government policy considering a range of documents and strategies relating to obesity and physical activity. This includes Every Child Matters and considers whether teachers need to be taught how to 'be healthy'. It also considers theoretical claims relating to the social debate as to whether there is an impact from claims and moral panics relating to an 'obesity crisis' and how this is impacting on primary school settings. It then considers the local impact of obesity and how it is affecting community cohesion.

The book concludes with an exploration of one of the most topical areas to emerge within education in recent years, that of developing creativity. In Chapter 14, Jim Lavin introduces us to general notions of creativity in education. This establishes the key role of creativity in the primary curriculum and of the recent national developments that place creativity at the heart of the learning process. This is followed by a section on the unique contribution of physical education in terms of creativity. This includes notions of pupils being able to deepen and broaden their knowledge, skills and understanding of physical education. Pupils should use imaginative ways to express and communicate ideas, solve problems and overcome challenges. Pupils should explore and experiment with techniques, tactics and compositional ideas to produce physical education activities that are exciting, challenging and fulfilling. The relationship of activity areas to creative approaches to physical education is explored and developed. The chapter stresses the need for primary teachers to take a much broader and more innovative view of what could be offered to children in terms of the physical education curriculum.

KEY READINGS

A more in-depth view of the primary physical education landscape can be gained from reading Griggs, G. (2007) Physical Education: Primary Matters, Secondary Importance, *Education 3–13*, 35, 1, 59–69. Further to this, the continual publications by Ofsted (see http://www.ofsted.gov.uk/) which relate to primary physical education illustrate key issues raised in this chapter.

REFERENCES

Bailey, R. and MacFadyen, T. (eds) (2000) *Teaching Physical Education 5–11*, London: Continuum.
Blair, R. and Capel, S. (2008a) The use of coaches to cover planning, preparation and assessment time – some issues, *Primary Physical Education Matters*, 3, 2, ix–x.
Blair, R. and Capel, S. (2008b) The use of coaches to cover planning, preparation and assessment time – some issues, *Primary Physical Education Matters*, 3, 3, v–vii.

10

Gerald Griggs

Caldecott, S., Warburton, P. and Waring, M. (2006) A survey of the time devoted to the preparation of primary and junior school trainee teachers to teach physical education in England, *The British Journal of Teaching Physical Education*, 37, 1, 45–48.

Clay, G. (1999) Movement backwards and forwards; the influence of government on physical education – an HMI perspective, *The British Journal of Physical Education,* 30, 4, 38–41.

Davies, H.J. (1999) Standards in physical education in England at Key Stage 1 and Key Stage 2, past, present and future, *European Review of Physical Education*, 4, 2, 173–188.

DeCorby, K., Halas, J., Dixon, S., Wintrup, L. and Janzen, H. (2005) Classroom teachers and the challenges of delivering quality physical education, *The Journal of Educational Research*, 98, 4, 208–220.

Department for Children, Education, Lifelong Learning and Skills (DCELLS) (2008) *Physical Education in the National Curriculum for Wales*, Cardiff: DCELLS.

Department for Children, Schools and Families (DCSF) (2008a) *Early Years Foundation Stage*, London: HMSO.

Department for Children, Schools and Families (DCSF) (2008b) *Physical Education and Sport Strategy for Young People*, London: HMSO.

Department for Education and Employment/Qualifications and Curriculum Authority (DfEE/ QCA) (1999) *The National Curriculum in England: Physical Education*, London: HMSO.

Department for Education and Skills/Department for Culture, Media and Sport (DfES/DCMS) (2003) *Learning through Physical Education and Sport: A guide to the Physical Education, School Sport and Club Links Strategy*, London: DfES/DCMS.

Department for Education and Skills (DfES) (2003) *Raising standards and tackling workload: a national agreement.* London: DfES.

Griggs, G. (2007) Physical Education: Primary Matters, Secondary Importance, *Education 3–13*, 35, 1, 59–69.

Griggs, G. (2008) Outsiders inside: The use of sports coaches in primary schools in the West Midlands, *Physical Education Matters,* 3, 2, 33–36.

Griggs, G. (2010) For Sale – Primary Physical Education, £20 per hour or nearest offer, *Education 3 – 13*, 38, 1, 39 – 46.

Gunter, H. (2007) Remodelling the school workforce in England: a study in tyranny, *Journal for Critical Education Policy Studies*, 5, 1. Available online at http://www.jceps.com/index.php? pageID=articleandarticleID=84 (accessed 12 February 2009).

Hopper, B., Grey, J. and Maude, T. (2000) *Teaching Physical Education in the Primary School*, London: Routledge.

Lavin, J., Swindlehurst, G. and Foster, V. (2008) The use of coaches, adults supporting learning and teaching assistants in the teaching of physical education in the primary school, *Primary Physical Education Matters*, 3, 1, ix–xi.

Learning and Teaching Scotland (LTS) (2009) *Curriculum for Excellence*, Edinburgh: LTS.

Morgan, P. and Bourke, M. (2005) An investigation of preservice and primary school teacher perspectives of physical education teaching confidence and Physical Education teacher education, *ACHPER Healthy Lifestyles Journal*, 52, 1, 7–13.

Morgan, P. and Bourke, S. (2008) Non specialist teachers' confidence to teach physical education: the nature and influence of personal experiences in schools, *Physical Education and Sport Pedagogy*, 13, 1, 1–29.

Office for Standards in Education (Ofsted) (1998) *Teaching physical education in the primary school: the initial training of teachers*, London: HMSO.

Office for Standards in Education (Ofsted) (2005) *Physical education in primary schools*. London: HMSO.

QCA (2007) *The National Curriculum for Physical Education at Key Stage 3 and 4.* Available online at http://curriculum.qcda.gov.uk/ (accessed 10 November 2009).

Revell, P. (2000) Strategic moves, *Sports Teacher*, Spring, 14–15.

Speednet (2000) Primary school physical education – Speednet survey makes depressing reading, *British Journal of Physical Education*, 30, 3, 19–20.

Warburton, P. (2001) A sporting future for all: fact or fiction?, *The British Journal of Teaching Physical Education*, 32, 2, 18–21.

Ward, G. and Griggs, G. (2010) Cogs in the machine – Primary Link Teachers, *Primary Physical Education Matters*, 5, 1, 3–4.

Williams, A. (ed.) (2000) *Physical Education for the primary years*, London: Routledge.

Wright, L. (2004) Preserving the value of happiness in primary school physical education, *Physical Education and Sport Pedagogy*, 9, 2, 149–163.

Youth Sport Trust (YST) (2008) The school element of the 5 hour offer: Guidance notes on delivery roles and responsibilities, Loughborough: Youth Sport Trust.

CHAPTER TWO

THE IMPORTANCE OF PRIMARY PHYSICAL EDUCATION

Ian Pickup

INTRODUCTION

The letters 'P' and 'E', dropped casually into a dinner party or bus stop conversation, are guaranteed to evoke dim and distant memories which may include (depending on who your conversation is with) reference to knickers and vests, cold weather, cross country runs in the rain, indomitable teachers, personal injury (or worse, bearing witness to a major health and safety disaster which would see the toughest children running for cover) and of course being picked last for playground games. Occasionally, the conversation may err towards a critique of so-called liberal educational theories which are said to denounce competition (your own stance on this will be based on whether you were in fact picked last or not), the supposed evils of the 1980s teacher strikes or the government's stance on selling off school playing fields. If your conversation is with a parent of a primary-aged child, then expect a whole other can of worms to be agitated, usually with reference to the annual sports day.

At a time when the need for high-quality physical education in today's schools is more evident than ever before, it would seem that universal, real-world understanding of the nature, aims and outcomes of the subject is lacking, confused and oft conflated with perceptions and memories of sport. Primary physical education is said to be absent in practice, under-researched and therefore under-theorised (Hunter, 2006), with practitioners and researchers alike repeatedly pointing to a variety of problems inherent in the subject. In particular, children's experiences in primary school physical education are thought to be heavily influenced by the confidence, knowledge and disposition of their respective teachers (Morgan and Bourke, 2005) who are likely to have received little training in the subject (Caldecott et al., 2006), or at least progressed through professional learning experiences which paid scant attention to their own dispositions towards the subject (Garrett and Wrench, 2007). Primary physical education has also been blighted by a perceived low status in comparison to other subjects, a paucity of facilities, inappropriate curriculum content, fragmented delivery, and the teaching of physical education by non-qualified teachers (Kirk et al., 1988; Tinning and Hawkins, 1988; Graham, 1991; Curtner-Smith, 1999; Hardman and Marshall, 2001; Speednet, 2000; DeCorby et al., 2005; Griggs, 2007).

Despite such challenges, there remains a great potential for physical education to play a significant part in the lives and learning of all children; the unique blend of *learning to move* and *moving to learn* (BAALPE *et al.*, 2005) provides a powerful conduit for the educative process that is unique within the school curriculum and is one that can sit neatly within contemporary approaches to learning and teaching. However, school curricula that purport to be 'whole child' in approach are impostors without a meaningful, well planned and consistent focus on teaching and learning in the physical domain; high-quality physical education provides an inimitable and valuable contribution to children's learning and the time is now here for the state and status of the subject in primary schools to be protected, enhanced, celebrated and more clearly articulated. For primary teachers to be empowered to embrace such a vision, the various policies, curricula and teacher development structures must be re-shaped to ensure that physical education is afforded a heightened status. A clear articulation of the importance of the subject is therefore necessary; this chapter aims to provide just this, exploring the factors inherent in high-quality primary physical education and considering approaches to the teaching of physical education which capitalise on its unique ability to bring about particular learning outcomes.

THOUGHT BOX

Consider for a moment the possible outcomes of around 500 hours of high-quality physical education in the primary school where the dual focus is on developing motor competence and learning through physical experiences. What would 11-year-old children be able to solve, create or perform on entering secondary school? What would this mean for the secondary school physical education curriculum? What would this mean for the pursuit of lifelong physical activity or community sport and dance? What learning has been accrued in social, cognitive and affective domains in parallel to learning and applying a range of physical skills in different contexts? Do not limit your thinking or ambition for the subject with any thoughts about a lack of teacher knowledge, facilities or curriculum time.

THE UNIQUENESS OF PHYSICAL EDUCATION

Certain aspects of physical education are unique. Art, geography, history and all other classroom-based subjects are undoubtedly important components of the curriculum, each with their own place and standing in children's learning. However, these subjects will not help children to learn how to throw, dodge, roll, leap, dance, float or climb. The context in which physical education is taught undoubtedly provides unique challenges for the teacher more used to working within a classroom environment. The hall, field, playground or swimming pool are all physical education classrooms, environments rich with specific challenges and significant opportunities for creating interactive, dynamic, multi-sensory and enjoyable lessons. In articulating a justification for a height-ened status of physical education, then, this uniqueness must be acknowledged, as long as the learning which follows from such experiences is necessary, valuable and takes place within a high-quality environment. It is pertinent therefore to focus on the *unique learning content* that physical education provides in the primary school, in addition to exploring the subject's *unique medium for learning*. All primary school teachers must consider how this uniqueness can be best embraced in order to facilitate learning. It is, however, this uniqueness of both subject content *and* the teaching and learning envi-ronment which provides some teachers with significant challenges; put simply, without being adequately prepared or sufficiently confident, poor-quality teaching and learning experiences or a low status of the subject may follow.

STARTING FROM THE CHILD

The uniqueness of physical education must not be confused with being strange or unfa-miliar, at least not for the children we teach. If we explore the potential of the subject from a child's perspective then we see that movement already plays a significant role in child development. Early travelling, balancing and object control skills help pre-schoolers to engage actively with experiences, to construct their own views of the world, to interact with other children and to explore their environment. Long before starting school, most infants have progressed through a variety of rudimentary movement milestones, gained some control over the body and everyday objects. The body and an infant's developing physicality are central to a broad learning process, and movement in early childhood provides a well-placed vehicle for practitioners who want to 'start from the child' (Fisher, 2000). Embracing the seemingly natural desire to move, to play and to explore within interactive, collaborative, physical and multi-sensory approaches to learning is seen frequently within a thematic approach to learning in early years contexts. Many practi-tioners provide daily opportunities for young children to be physically active, to interact socially and to solve problems through movement experiences.

THOUGHT BOX

A group of Reception class children are using a variety of equipment in the play-ground. Some are balancing along the trim trail logs whilst others are playing 'chase'. A teacher begins to ask the children questions about what they are doing. How many different ways can you travel along the logs? Can you travel across the logs as well as along them? What different body parts can you use? Can you travel high and low? Four of the children begin to make up a game where the logs are the 'base' (i.e. where a tagger can't reach you). The teacher begins to ask the children how they can stay on the logs for longer and encourages the taggers to think of ways to keep others away from the base.

15

Where movement is happening through play, golden opportunities for skilful, well timed and age-appropriate teacher–pupil interaction present themselves. Such occasions are early opportunities for education *in* and *through* the physical domain. By viewing physical education as a progression from early movement experiences in this way, it becomes clear that primary physical education is not simply a means to an end, or a set of pre-determined activities planned in six-week blocks, defined by the parameters of teacher knowledge, facilities or relative status of other subjects. The subsequent section of this chapter considers the place of primary physical education within a lifelong approach to physical activity and emphasises the particular need for high-quality experiences in the early and later childhood age phases.

THE LIFELONG VALUE OF PRIMARY PHYSICAL EDUCATION

Education is increasingly seen as a lifelong process within a holistic view of education, so building on the natural propensity for movement in young children to promote learning in later childhood, adolescence and adulthood would appear to be a logical approach. For many children, school is the only context in which physical activity can be combined with structured learning (Telama *et al.*, 1997), at a time when it is thought that some children are becoming less active than ever before. Whilst some children are able to take advantage of the myriad of community-based sports and physical activity provision, many more will be excluded from 'optional' activities for a range of social or economic reasons which may include a lack of encouragement, money to facilitate attendance, or available opportunities within particular communities. Consequently, the most appropriate place for high-quality, motivational and individually relevant provision is within a fully inclusive, statutory curriculum to be experienced by all children regardless of socio-economic, familial or geographical factors. Within such a framework, it is clear that early experiences need to be positive, fun, motivating and focused on nurturing a lifelong love of physical activity.

A high-quality primary school physical education curriculum therefore builds on the culture of childhood, provides a bridge between unstructured play and structured physical activity and sport and affords all children an opportunity to develop a strong movement foundation from which future participation in and learning through the physical domain can follow. Effective practitioners view primary physical education within such a lifelong framework and take a well-planned approach to providing individually relevant, developmentally appropriate experiences.

A DEVELOPMENTAL APPROACH

The design of tasks in primary physical education need not, therefore, be limited by pre-conceived notions of what is appropriate for 3-, 5-, 7- or 11-year-old children, but should take account of biological, environmental and task factors that impact on each child's unique stage of motor development. This 'ecological perspective' (Bronfenbrenner, 1979) provides a useful focus for those seeking to promote motor development amongst

Ian Pickup

primary-aged children and ensures that lessons and curricula are positioned to maximise learning *in* and *through* movement. Such an approach to the teaching of physical education necessitates careful planning as a consequence of on-going assessment in physical education; knowing what children are able to do allows the teacher to plan learning episodes in order to bring about further learning at an appropriate level and pace for each child. By taking such an approach, teachers also acknowledge the need for tasks to be differentiated in accordance with existing abilities and the importance of providing appropriate challenge for all learners. Anecdotal evidence suggests that planning for primary physical education in today's schools is generally poor, at least when compared to the extensive planning evident for core curriculum subjects. Many teachers also appear unsure as to what the movement content of lessons should be and how such content can be differentiated, progressed or continued from lesson to lesson, year to year and key stage to key stage.

THOUGHT BOX

Assessment of children in physical education cannot take place without regular observation of movement. How often do you actually observe children's movements with the attention to detail required to determine the type of feedback you should be giving or to plan subsequent learning tasks? How do you know that the tasks you are planning in physical education are at an appropriate level for each of the children? Just as we wouldn't expect all children to complete exactly the same series of questions in maths, physical education tasks must be planned carefully to reflect different levels of ability. Without doing this how can we be sure that all children experience success and remain motivated to carry on learning in the physical domain?

BUILDING A MOVEMENT FOUNDATION

The primary years provide the most appropriate context for children to develop competence in a range of basic body actions, commonly referred to as fundamental movement skills. These are an organised series of basic movements that involve the combination of movement patterns of two or more body segments (Gallahue and Cleland-Donnelly, 2003). The fundamental movement phase of motor development is a critical time for children to build on the rudimentary movements of infancy. It is a key time for movement skill development within travelling, object control, balance and coordination categories of movement (sometimes called locomotion, manipulation and stability or non-locomotor skills). The development of fundamental movement skills can provide the foundation from which children move with increasing complexity, variety and versatility in a range of activity areas. Whilst developing these skills, children are also able to build on social, affective and cognitive learning opportunities.

17

For many years, a 'maturational' perspective advocated by Arnold Gessell (1928) led practitioners to believe that movement competence emerges naturally through play and physical activity; as a consequence, motor skill development has not traditionally been a key goal of early years 'physical development' syllabi. However, as Gallahue and Ozmun (1998: 84) argue:

> Although maturation does play a role in the development of fundamental movement patterns, it should not be viewed as the only influence. The conditions of the environment – namely opportunities to practice, instruction and the ecology of the environment itself – all play important roles in the degree to which fundamental movement patterns develop.

It is clear that today's children are living, playing and attending school in a very different world from that known by Gessell and his contemporaries. Technological advances and changes to the fabric of society have led some writers to note an increasing number of young children entering school without the core stability or spatial awareness to broadly function as learners in the primary classroom (Wainwright, 2006), let alone to access rich and varied sporting and cultural opportunity outside school. For such children, these crucial components of physical and perceptual motor development have not evolved naturally through a process of maturation. High-quality physical education in the primary years therefore underpins a child's ability to function as a learner and provides opportunities for all to build a movement foundation from which future participation can follow.

MOVEMENT DEVELOPMENT

Each category of fundamental movement includes a number of specific skills (see Table 2.1) which children appear to develop over a significant period of time from emerging (or 'initial') attempts to a transitionary (or 'elementary') phase through to a mature (or 'efficient') pattern of movement. The mature pattern is characterised by increased coordination, fluency, efficiency, accuracy and economy of action. At this stage of development, children appear less clumsy and are able to integrate a number of skills into flowing sequences. The mature mover is also one who is becoming physically stronger and whose skeleto-muscular system can produce greater force in movement; the result is faster, increasingly dynamic and varied actions. It is also important to note that this mature movement can also be increasingly applied to more complex challenges, whether in recognisable games contexts, dance choreography or aquatic challenges.

The early and later childhood age phases represent a period of steady physical growth and development and are considered by some to be the greatest window of opportunity for physical skill acquisition and development (Pickup and Price, 2007). The refinement of movement capabilities in the primary years provides a base from which all later physical activity and sport participation can follow throughout life (Gallahue and Ozmun, 1998; Malina, 1996), something that cannot be ignored if an objective for physical education is

18

Ian Pickup

Table 2.1 Examples of fundamental movement skills

Travelling (Locomotion)	Object control (Manipulation)	Balance (Stability)
Basic ■ Walk ■ Run Rhythmical ■ Gallop ■ Side slip ■ Skip Jumps Apparatus ■ Climb ■ Swing	Send ■ Throw ■ Kick ■ Punt ■ Ball roll ■ Static ball strike Receive ■ Catch ■ Trap/stop (feet/stick) Travel with ■ Dribble × 3 Receive and send ■ Volley ■ Strike	Postural ■ Upright posture ■ Ready position ■ Stopping ■ Landing Coordination ■ Cross laterality ■ Stretch/curl ■ Twist/turn ■ Spin ■ Sink/fall ■ Body roll ■ Dodge

Source: Adapted from Jess (2004)

to promote an enduring and lifelong love of physical activity and sport (whether for social or health reasons). In optimum circumstances, it is thought that most children are able to achieve a mature pattern of movement in fundamental skills around the age of transition to the upper primary years. Of course, for this to happen across all of the categories of skill, regular opportunities for practice must be matched by ample encouragement and feedback, a careful matching of tasks to the stage of development and use of appropriate equipment. The transition to 'maturity' is of critical importance if children are to access more complex activities in upper primary and early secondary age phases, yet it appears that a lack of focus on the physical aspect of learning is currently resulting in a 'proficiency barrier' hindering the progress of many children (Jess *et al.*, 2004).

THOUGHT BOX

To what extent is the content of the average primary school's physical education curriculum helping to foster movement proficiency in all children? Consider the experiences of a Year 6 class following a medium-term plan focused on games activities. Have those children who play regular sport in the community developed new skills, mastered existing ones or applied these in different contexts as a result of the physical education lessons? Have other children developed skill and understanding in order to enjoy participating and experience some success within the parameters of the games? Have all the children extended their conceptual understanding about tactics, use of space in attack or how to work well as part of a team? Think carefully about the full range of learning outcomes evident in this simple hypothetical example. Have all opportunities for learning been exploited?

LEARNING BEYOND THE PHYSICAL

A focus on the development of fundamental movement is not detrimental to the broader educational benefit of primary physical education. By asking children to work together to solve problems and to master new skills, the primary class teacher has a unique tool at her disposal for facilitating learning in social, cognitive and affective domains. Whilst there is a general lack of research evidence to support physical educators' intuitive feelings that the subject can contribute to broad learning outcomes (Bailey *et al.,* 2007) it would seem that the subject is well placed to supplement and, in some cases, for some children, strengthen learning that takes place in the classroom.

The use of a rich and varied movement vocabulary to describe movement encourages children to consider where, how and with whom actions will be carried out. 'Movement concepts' are ways in which a skill can be changed or progressed according to the requirements of a particular context or activity. This has a clear implication for the use of language across the curriculum and suggests that movements experienced in physical education can enrich vocabulary by using a range of verbs and adjectives to help children explore their own and others' actions. In addition to linking movement in physical education with language development, movement concepts also enhance the child's ability to adapt and be creative in movement, impacting positively on movement competence and improving access to lifelong physical activity. The pupil's body, when seen as 'the instrument of action' (Davies, 2003) can be given colour and form by 'playing' the instrument in different ways, through changing the dynamic quality, space and relationships between people and objects. The development of movement concepts alongside fundamental movement skills gives children opportunities to solve problems for themselves, to plan their own actions and to evaluate their work. This has clear relevance to the aims of current curricula for physical education, for the aspirations of policies that aim to encourage creativity amongst children and for the primary teacher who utilises problem-based and broadly constructivist approaches to learning.

ENJOYMENT, MOTIVATION AND INTER-ACTION

International studies have repeatedly shown that the majority of children and young people have positive feelings towards physical education, with younger children in particular most likely to say that they 'love' physical education and school sport. This enjoyment factor should not be underestimated; enjoyment experienced during physical activity is thought to reinforce self-esteem, in turn leading to enhanced motivation to participate further (Sonstroem, 1997), a key consideration for those wishing to encourage children to become more physically active. Structured play and physical education programmes therefore have the potential to contribute to the development of self-esteem in children (Fox, 2000) whilst it has also been suggested that self-esteem is influenced by one's perception of competence or ability to achieve (Harter, 1987). This has a clear implication for the design of tasks in physical education and it is possible that primary physical education can provide a wealth of positive, motivational experiences for every child during an optimum time for motor development. The need for positive and motivating experiences in physical education is also evident in the secondary school and a key challenge is for successive learning to be integrated with what has gone before, building on learning accrued from Reception to Year 6 and continuing the learning process into adolescence and beyond.

Recent trends in the primary classroom have included the introduction of 'Brain Gym' and similar packages (such as 'The Class Moves' in Scotland and Wales) which claim to strengthen neurological pathways through a variety of actions (Dennison and Dennison, 1989). Whilst the scientific base for such claims is not particularly strong, it would appear that teachers and pupils respond positively to such activities. The links between mind and body are areas of significant potential for a subject where a dual focus is on physical and cognitive processes. More importantly, if teachers in the primary years are aware first-hand of the broad benefits of a physical, activity-based curriculum, then with appropriate ITT (initial teacher training) and CPD (continuing professional development) in the subject, the true potential for physical education can be realised.

BRINGING LEARNING TO LIFE

Physical education in the primary years can support all dimensions of learning within an appropriate pedagogical structure for the benefit of all children. The development of fundamental movement skills should not take place within a sterile, command-style (Mosston and Ashworth, 2002), teacher-led approach to learning, and practitioners must be encouraged to plan creatively, to seek out links to other areas of learning and to engage children in collaborative activities. These are hallmarks of a primary teacher's everyday work in the classroom and in many ways the primary class teacher is ideally placed to create an environment that can promote learning in the physical domain. There does, however, appear to be a teacher proficiency barrier that undermines this position, largely due to a lack of knowledge about the development of fundamental movement skills. If all teachers knew what to look for, what to say as feedback and 'feed forward' and how to facilitate subsequent learning, then they would surely be in a stronger position to capitalise on the tremendous resources they have at their disposal. The primary class teacher has a wealth of understanding about the children in her care and is well placed to engage all children in developmentally appropriate and much-needed activities.

CONCLUSION

It is clear that primary physical education, when structured effectively with quality learning experiences at its core, can have a tremendous impact on the lives of all children and young people. The time spent in primary physical education can enable young people to continue to engage, enjoy and achieve throughout secondary school years and to make informed choices about their health and active lifestyles throughout life. The primary years provide the optimum window for the development of these areas of knowledge, skills and understanding and are far too important to be left to chance.

If physical education is ever to realise this exciting potential as a conduit for learning for all children in the primary school, then the readers of this text must join with others who care, who understand the importance of physical education as an educational experience, to work collectively to raise its status within school curricula, ITT and amongst the general public. It is here, most worryingly, that personal biography often serves to reinforce the negative stereotypes of the subject. The true value of physical education is so much greater than the oft reported experiences alluded to in the introduction of this chapter, yet broad understanding and acceptance of this continues to be lacking. For primary physical education to achieve its true potential, the teaching profession must fully embrace the possibilities alluded to in this chapter. Paying lip service to the subject without a consistent focus on high-quality and well planned teaching and learning will do little to impact on the experiences of all children. Without action, pre-published schemes of work, ad hoc approaches welded to teachers' levels of confidence and the low status of physical education in relation to classroom-based subjects will continue to weaken the potential impact of the subject. The time is now here for a re-think of the nature, content and style of the primary school physical education curriculum centred on clear, planned-for, developmentally appropriate and individually relevant learning experiences.

KEY READINGS

Understanding how fundamental movement patterns develop is vital to underpinning all work in physical education. A very good point of reference here is Gallahue, D.L. and Ozmun, J. (1998) *Understanding Motor Development – Infants, Children, Adolescents, Adults*, Duboque, Iowa: McGraw-Hill. A coherent exemplification of the developmental approach to physical education advocated here can be found in Pickup, I. and Price, L. (2007) *Teaching physical education in the primary school: a developmental approach*. London: Continuum.

REFERENCES

BAALPE, CCPR, PEAUK and Physical Education ITT Network (2005) *Declaration from the National Summit on Physical Education*, London, 24 January 2005.
Bailey, R., Armour, K., Kirk, D., Jess, M., Pickup, I. and Sandford, R. (2007) *The Educational Benefits Claimed for Physical Education and School Sport: An Academic Review*, Research Papers in Education.
Bronfenbrenner, U. (1979) *The Ecology of Human Development*, Cambridge, MA: Harvard University Press.
Caldecott, S., Warburton, P. and Waring, M. (2006) A survey of the time devoted to the preparation of primary and junior school trainee teachers to teach physical education in England, *British Journal of Teaching Physical Education 37*, 1, *Physical Education Matters 1*, 1.

Ian Pickup

Curtner-Smith, M.D. (1999) The more things change the more they stay the same: factors influencing teachers' interpretations and delivery of national curriculum physical education, *Sport, Education and Society*, 4, 1, 5–97.

Davies, M. (2003) *Movement and Dance in Early Childhood* (2nd ed), London: Paul Chapman Publishing.

DeCorby, K., Halas, J., Dixon, S., Wintrup, L. and Janzen, H. (2005) Classroom teachers and the challenges of delivering quality physical education, *The Journal of Educational Research*, 98, 4, 208–220.

Dennison, P.E. and Dennison, G.E. (1989) *Brain gym, teacher's edition: simple activities for whole brain learning*, Ventura, CA: Edu Kinesthetics.

Fisher, J. (2000) *Starting from the child, teaching and learning from 3 to 8* (2nd ed), Buckingham: Open University Press.

Fox, K. (2000) The Effects of Exercise on Self-Perceptions and Self-Esteem, in S. Biddle, K. Fox and S. Boutcher (eds) *Physical Activity and Psychological Well-being*, London: Routledge.

Gallahue, D.L. and Donnelly, F.C. (2003) *Developmental Physical Education for All Children*, Champaign IL: Human Kinetics.

Gallahue, D.L. and Ozmun, J. (1998) *Understanding Motor Development – Infants, Children, Adolescents, Adults*, Duboque, Iowa: McGraw-Hill.

Garrett, R. and Wrench, A. (2007) Physical experiences: primary student teachers' conceptions of sport and physical education, *Physical Education and Sport Pedagogy*, 12, 1, 23–42.

Gesell, A. (1928) *Infancy and Human Growth*, New York: Macmillan.

Graham, G. (1991) An overview of TECPEP, *Journal of Teaching in Physical Education*, 10, 4, 323–334.

Griggs, G. (2007) Outsiders Inside: The use of sports coaches in primary schools in the West Midlands, poster presentation at the Annual Conference of the British Educational Research Association, 5–8 September, University of London.

Hardman, K. and Marshall, J.J. (2001) World-wide survey on the state and status of physical education in schools, in G. Doll-Tepper (ed.) *Proceedings of the world summit on physical education, Berlin, 3–5 November 1999*, Berlin, International Council of Sport Science and Physical Education, 15–37.

Harter, S. (1987) The Determinants and Mediational Role of Global Self-worth in Children, in N. Eisenberg (ed.) *Contemporary Topics in Developmental Psychology*, New York: Wiley.

Hunter, L. (2006) Research into elementary physical education programs, in D. Kirk, D. Macdonald and M. O'Sullivan (eds), *Handbook of Research in Physical Education*, London: Sage, 571–586.

Jess, M. (2004) *Basic Moves*, Edinburgh: The University of Edinburgh.

Jess, M., Dewar, K. and Fraser, G. (2004) Basic Moves: developing a foundation for lifelong physical activity, *British Journal of Teaching Physical Education*, Summer, 24–27.

Kirk, D., Colquhoun, D. and Gore, J. (1988) Generalists, specialists and daily physical education in Queensland, *The ACHPER National Journal*, 122, 7–9, 36.

Malina, R.M. (1996) Tracking physical activity and physical fitness across the lifespan, *Research Quarterly for Exercise and Sport*, 67, 3, 48–57.

Morgan, P.J. and Bourke, S.F. (2005) An investigation of preservice and primary school teachers' perspectives of PE teaching confidence and PE teacher education, *ACHPER Healthy Lifestyles Journal*, 52, 1, 7–13.

Mosston, M. and Ashworth, S. (2002) *Teaching Physical Education* (5th ed), London: Benjamin Cummings.

Pickup, I. and Price, L. (2007) *Teaching physical education in the primary school: a developmental approach*, London: Continuum.

Sonstroem, R.J. (1997) Physical activity and self-esteem, in W.P. Morgan (ed.) *Physical activity and mental health*, Washington, DC: Taylor & Francis.

Speednet (2000) Primary school physical education – Speednet survey makes depressing reading, *British Journal of Physical Education*, 30, 3, 19–20.

Telama, R., Yang, X., Laakso, L. and Viikari, J. (1997) Physical activity in childhood and adolescence as predictor of physical activity in young adulthood, *American Journal of Preventive Medicine*, 13, 317–322.

Tinning, R. and Hawkins, K. (1988) Montaville revisited: a daily physical education program four years on, *The ACHPER National Journal*, 121, 24–29.

Wainwright, N. (2006) Accessing learning through effective physical education, *Physical Education Matters*, 1, 3.

CHAPTER THREE

THE CHALLENGES AND POTENTIAL WITHIN PRIMARY PHYSICAL EDUCATION

Dominic Haydn-Davies

INTRODUCTION

In 2007 I wrote on this subject with colleagues (Haydn-Davies *et al.*, 2007) and expressed a view that primary physical education faced a number of significant challenges. The argument put forward stemmed from a perception of primary physical education having a low and marginalised position. The article focused primarily on two areas of challenge, curriculum (timing and structure) and staffing. Critics (Carney and Winkler, 2008: 13) argued that the paper did 'not confront all of the issues'. I would have to agree with this criticism. This chapter offers the possibility to address this. Whilst the initial challenges put forward will be further explored in this chapter, as time has progressed, different arguments have surfaced and a more fundamental challenge is put forward.

It will be argued that this 'hidden' challenge is in part the cause of the practical and organisational challenges that the subject faces. It will be argued that until this challenge is overcome, progress towards clarification about *what* should be taught *how*, and *who* is best positioned to provide this cannot fully be resolved. It is from an educational perspective that this chapter is written and from this 'point of view it may not matter so much *what* is taught but *how* it is taught' (Wright, 2002: 38).

Primary physical education as a subject faces numerous problems. Contemporary textbooks consider issues such as gender, ability, access and inclusion (Doherty and Brennan, 2008) or workforce, preparation and the effect of educational policy (Pickup *et al.*, 2008) as the challenges facing the subject. On the surface the most prominent challenges might appear to come from not having enough balls to go around a class, or that the balls are constantly flat. It might also be a concern that teachers and children do not know the rules of the game they are supposed to be playing. These are real challenges but do not get to the root of the problem.

In addition to those above, any challenge that faces *primary* education must by definition also be a challenge for primary *physical education*. As it is a subject that contributes to the curriculum for primary aged children it will share these problems. This chapter sets out those challenges which may be more specific to physical education or may require a different type of response from those relating to more classroom-based subjects.

Physical education is a practical subject. It takes place in halls or gymnasia, on the playground, the field and in swimming pools. The logistics and practicalities of organising learning in these different environments is a fundamental challenge. physical education is a subject where children express their understanding through action and movement rather than through the written word. This makes recording assessments a challenge. These issues are also what makes physical education what it inherently is. They are at the root of any definition of the subject. They are an integral part that should be valued and seen not as a challenge but as the essence of what primary physical education is about. The most significant challenge can be to ensure that the subject is understood and valued enough to make this possible.

THE HIDDEN CHALLENGE FOR PRIMARY PHYSICAL EDUCATION

When attempting to determine how to overcome and solve problems and challenges it is easy to rush and grasp at the most obvious solution or quickest 'fix'. Primary physical education does face many challenges and the profession has made some significant steps towards overcoming or reducing these. However, it could be suggested that this has avoided or missed the 'elephant in the room'.

The aims and values of physical education have been much debated (for example, Whitehead, 2000; McNamee, 2005; Morgan, 2006) and there is still no consistent agreement within, or between, theory or practice as to what is trying to be achieved. Different stakeholders will perceive the subject differently, not for the subject's own 'good' but for how it may serve, sometimes cynically, their particular aims. Why does a teacher believe they are teaching the subject? How does this view compare to what children believe is the purpose of their learning? Wider constituents, including headteachers, parents, the media, government and the subject community, will also have their views.

THOUGHT BOX

Reflect on what you believe the purpose of physical education to be. Are your reasons linked to sport, or education, or health? Could the purpose for physical education that you identified be delivered by other subjects or does physical education hold something unique?

In secondary education physical education 'takes on the identity of a specialised subject taught by specialist teachers in specialist settings. The bulk of what is known as physical education as an institution occurs in, or is significantly influenced by, secondary physical education' (Green, 2008: 3). It can be suggested that if this is an accepted position then it is not that primary physical education is of low status or that it is misunderstood,

Dominic Haydn-Davies

but that it has no status or inherent purpose other than to meet the needs of secondary physical education.

The history of practice in primary physical education can give useful insight into the challenges that are faced today (Kirk, 2011) with some of the same practices and even facilities being used. This will include the tracking of different aims and purposes and potentially the political reasons behind those (see Clay, 1999, for example). This said, 'the general aims of physical education do not change fundamentally over the years. The foremost aim is the education of the "whole" child … that due attention is being given to the maximum development of each individual child, physically, mentally, morally and socially, in the preparation for life and for living' (Bilbrough and Jones, 1968: 10). Even if this were agreed on as a core purpose, there is a difference between consistency in aims and in mechanisms for delivery.

When writing about the issues in primary physical education over twenty years ago Williams (1989) splits the 'subject' and the 'curriculum' into two separate areas to consider. This is a useful practice as the two are different and serve slightly different purposes. Physical education as a curriculum is changeable and open to interpretation. The curriculum does not always necessarily match the subject aims as they are debated at the time. As well as the purpose of the subject, its relationships with other fields also need to be considered. This is important because how the subject is positioned in relation to key discourses can and will alter and affect practices, funding and interested parties. In relation to physical education it is important to track policy with general education policy, those relating to childhood, health and sport.

Dependent on the aims and purpose of the subject there are a number of different directions that practice would need to work towards. For example, if primary physical education is a preparation for secondary physical education, and secondary physical education is about engaging young people in sporting activities and sporting excellence there would be a number of issues to consider. Which sports should be focused on? Would this link to early specialisation or a 'sampling' approach (Cote *et al.*, 2009). Alternatively, if primary physical education is about stopping children becoming obese and being physically active through exercise, should this be through an enforced exercise regime? Where do diet, nutrition and choice come into the equation? To extend this further it could be asserted that if primary physical education is about gaining knowledge about physical activities, this could be achieved without actually moving or participating in activity. Clearly these are not necessarily going to be achieved from the same approach, indeed some could even work against each other. The challenge is to justify which is the most important aim for the subject or can it just be one of these?

It is therefore suggested that unless there is some clarity or greater agreement as to what primary physical education is about and for, it is very difficult to truly identify the most effective solutions to those challenges. If a more holistic approach to the subject is advocated, in that it is different from what has been replicated over the past decades in practice, there will still be challenges. If an alternative approach was so clearly more effective or less challenging then surely it would have become common and established practice already? These challenges have not necessarily arisen in practice as yet,

27

but considering the 'hidden' challenge, that of purpose, must be given attention when attempting to move forwards in the 'right' direction. Challenges may be overcome not by a different approach but by a different direction.

How this vision and purpose are enacted – how subject and theory become curriculum and practice – are important considerations for those charged with developing outcomes for children within schools. It is still the responsibility of headteachers and governors of schools to ensure quality of provision. They may give responsibility either to class teachers or subject leaders and it is to challenges that may face these practitioners that attention is now turned. These challenges are characterised through two areas of focus: organisational challenges and practical challenges.

REVISITING THE ORGANISATIONAL CHALLENGES

Two main challenges face those who lead or coordinate the subject within a primary school:

- Planning the curriculum
- Ensuring continuity.

Planning the curriculum

Within primary schools annual (long-term) plans tend to be split into twelve 'modules' per year group, two each half term (medium-term plans) with one focus on activities that can take place in the hall and one outside. Indoor 'physical education' tends to focus on gymnastics and dance, although some indoor 'games activities' such as short tennis, badminton or 'bench-ball' may be included. Outdoor physical education or 'games' tends to spread across the year in a seasonal manner, with cricket and rounders in the summer. Athletic activities focus on the build-up to sports day, as would outdoor and adventurous activities in preparation for an offsite residential experience. Swimming, generally in later primary years, may occur throughout the year due to the logistics of transport and travel of attending an offsite pool. Some activities will be repeated in subsequent year groups.

This has been the traditional model of practice, at least for the past twenty years; physical education in primary schools has been planned around areas of activity. Initially this was to ensure 'breadth and balance' in the curriculum (Penney and Evans, 1999) to ensure that provision did not become too biased towards one particular activity. Although currently this may be seen as being towards a 'games-heavy' curriculum (Ofsted, 1999, 2005) this has not always been the case. Revisiting a much earlier textbook (Bilbrough and Jones, 1968) the authors readily acknowledge that 'although this book (*Physical Education in the Primary School*) has been chiefly concerned with the content and method of Gymnastics lessons, we are no less anxious to ensure that children … should enjoy opportunities to participate in effective games lessons. It is our opinion that the principles and methods of presentation suggested for the teaching of

Gymnastics apply equally to games lessons, where the aim should be to present a lesson full of potential for purposeful activity related to the age, ability and experience of the child, and one which offers the maximum opportunity for play and practice' (1968: 176).

Maintaining the provision of primary physical education based on an activity area-led curriculum is not supported by all. Kay (2003) fears that a move from child-centred rationale to activity-centred rationale may sound the death knell for the subject. Penney and Chandler (2000: 37) do not 'deny that activities should be a central focus in physical education … but that the issue is not the engagement in physical activities, so much as the focus of that engagement.' Primary physical education should be about learning in and through particular types of activities rather than just learning activities per se. It has been questioned for some time as to whether or not 'there is a core goal of the subject which is beyond, or fundamental to, specific proficiency in a number of different named activities' (Whitehead, 2001: 8). For others, the traditional or historical 'culture' of activity area-led practice is at odds with developments aimed at developing proficiency in movement (Morley, 2009).

This format leads to a number of challenges for those planning provision. How do I cover all areas or activities fairly? How do I create a balance between existing activities and new opportunities? How do I effectively link the planning to external sporting competitions or events? Although these are pertinent questions, they again are only relevant if it is accepted that an activity- or sports-led model is appropriate. Focusing on activities as discrete experiences does not necessarily ensure that children will make progress or achieve. Casbon suggests that 'with a fragmented curriculum, children and teachers, don't see the links and won't make the necessary links between the different areas of learning and activity' (Casbon, 2006: 7). Planning for areas of activity starts with, at best, curriculum guidance or outcomes following through areas of learning or activity but more than likely stem from an end point of a dance or a game – how do I get children to be able to play and compete in cricket or perform the 'Circassian Circle'. This type of planning can create problems in terms of pitch and expectation. It also fails to build on what is considered effective practice for younger children (Marsden and Weston, 2007). It can, however, help schools with the logistics of equipment and storage and appears to give children an exposure to a range of different activities from which they may be able to find out that they enjoy and want to pursue.

What this does not necessarily enable is for children to see learning across their experiences, to transfer knowledge. Planning for logistics does not necessarily enable efficient movement learning. Motor development literature (for example, Gallahue and Ozmun, 2006; Graham *et al.*, 2007) focuses on a need to progress movement skills and gain a level of mastery required to access more sophisticated activities and challenges. For this children need time and successful practice following feedback in order to gain mastery over physical skills. The planning of learning opportunities needs to meet curriculum guidance but must also meet the learning needs of the learners. Implementing curriculum guidance is a matter of professional interpretation of 'local' needs. The dominant language of the subject can influence teachers when they are planning. For example, teachers often refer to teaching 'physical education and games'. This may appear a minor point but it reinforces a separation between activities and a prioritising of games over other activities. There are also many misconceptions about how the subject can be taught. For example, games activities can be adapted to be taught inside and dance can be performed and learnt out of doors. Dance itself is a contestable area with recent curriculum reviews (Rose, 2009) considering its learning and participation more akin to creative 'arts' rather than physical education.

THOUGHT BOX

Reflect on the planning you implement for physical education. Push past answers such as 'it's always been this way' or 'someone else did it' and ask 'Could this be planned in a more thoughtful way?' Is it a balanced provision or do some areas dominate? Are there aspects of learning that are transferable or is everything considered separately?

Ensuring continuity

While learning could be progressed in discrete areas on a weekly basis, this may be compounded by a lack of consistency and continuity in how children experience that learning. This possible inconsistency may be caused by two main reasons: cancellation of sessions and workforce reform. Although reported time for physical education in primary schools has increased (Quick *et al.*, 2010) how often lessons actually take place is less certain. If lessons in particular activity areas take place only once a week there is a potential gap between sessions of seven days. In addition to this should be added potential absences from sessions caused by illness, absence, or participation in other activities and the cancellation of lessons due to the weather, alternative use of space or other curriculum commitments. Where teachers or schools do not value the subject it is very easy to 'miss' sessions on a regular basis. Although some continuity might be provided through planned activities at playtime or through cross-curricular links, this cannot be the whole solution. Children need time to make progress in physical education. They need time to practice, to explore, to develop and to apply. Principles of progression, of time and practice for mastery, do not fit with a potted, sporadic approach.

Further inconsistency in children's learning experiences can come through arrangements in response to workforce reform. It is becoming increasingly common practice (Blair and Capel, 2008) for outside agencies to be involved in the delivery of learning in primary physical education. Arguments for this focus on the 'specialist' sports knowledge that these coaches may have above that of a primary teacher. The potential benefits of having a 'specialist' in terms of sports coaching would need to be offset or balanced with the inconsistency of having more than one practitioner leading sessions (Griggs, 2008; Lavin *et al.*, 2008). Liaison between coach and teacher would need to be faultless to enable progression and consistency of expectations. This is further discussed within the next section where the focus shifts to the depth of a 'specialism' and a thought as to whether or not it is the right answer to the wrong question. Despite these challenges there are approaches to the organisation of learning and the curriculum that may overcome these potential barriers. It is not necessarily an upheaval or revolution but a change in perception. When viewed from a developmental perspective 'traditional content areas ... are a means to an end; namely learning to move and learning through movement with enjoyment and control' (Gallahue and Ozmun, 2006: 443). This would appear to be an answer to how activities can remain a central focus for physical education without overpowering the overarching aims.

REVISITING THE PRACTICAL CHALLENGES

Beyond these organisational challenges there lie a number of practical challenges that need to be overcome by those who work directly with the children, the learners:

- Teaching a class of children
- Staff expertise
- How do I make it active, fun, safe and inclusive?

The challenge of planning for a class of children

The majority of children in primary education are taught physical education in co-educational and age-grouped classes. The range of developmental difference within one class group can be significant. There may be up to a year difference in chronological terms but this may be wider in terms of physical growth, social, emotional or cognitive development. Rates of growth, development and learning are not consistent. Fisher (2010: 17) describes this process using words such as 'spurt' and 'plateau'. She also suggests that this creates a 'fusion' within each individual child, as well as within each group or class. Individualised learning is not practicable or necessarily desired. It is the interaction between children, others, tasks and their environment that makes learning and development rich and rewarding (Gallahue and Ozmun, 2006).

Even if teachers could draw on generalisations of ability or interests, these are not necessarily going to give a full picture and may even act against children's needs. While assumptions of children who are older or taller may have some use, those relating to gender or ability may be less useful. As primary education is taught in mixed-sex classes, this practice is generally continued within physical education. While this practice is less common in secondary schools it can be seen as a strength of provision for younger children. If planning and practice are based on assumptions about children's gender or educational ability they can miss important considerations. Contemporary research, in the field of gender studies, questions the view that what is appropriate for boys is appropriate for *all* boys (Francis and Skelton, 2005). Although there are some gender differences prior to puberty, these are minimal (Gallahue and Ozmun, 2006) other than if they are socially constructed to disadvantage particular groups. To group primary children based on a stereotypical assumption of what is socially acceptable for either boys or girls can reinforce dated perspectives. Similarly, the view is often held that children with physical disabilities will struggle most in physical education. Special educational needs across the breadth of learning needs can have equally profound effects on children's learning. Behavioural or social difficulties often cause more problems in primary physical education learning than a physical disability (Haydn-Davies and Coleman, 2010). Given the nature of the wide range of influencing factors in children's development and physical education it is almost a surprise that there are any similarities between children at all.

Staff expertise

The issue of staff competence and confidence is explored in greater depth within Chapter 11. However, the debate forms a key part of the discussion about the challenges of primary physical education and how the 'hidden' challenge of purpose is important. Time allocations within initial teacher training are considered a 'disgrace' (Talbot, 2007) and certainly not fit for purpose. Numerous studies have discussed and debated the issues and approaches (for example, Warburton, 2000; Caldecott et al., 2006; van Berlo, 2007; Haydn-Davies et al., 2010). Calls for specialist teaching in the primary age phase have grown (Carney and Howells, 2008) but this debate has been somewhat side-tracked by the use of sports coaches to answer workforce reform agendas. Sports coaches in primary physical education bring 'expertise' in sports activities. The 'hidden' challenge would question whether or not this is an answer to the right question. Carney and Howells (2008) acknowledge that this approach is 'not a quick fix solution … as outsourcing … serves to reduce physical education to bouts of activity specific exercise, jeopardising the development and holistic nature of the experience' (iv). Lavin et al. (2008) raise concerns about coaches' understanding of classroom management and control of the children. Griggs (2008: 36) suggests that 'whilst sports coaches do have something to offer … they lacked a significant amount of information and training … fundamental to effective teaching and learning'. Enhancing knowledge of sports activities does not necessarily overcome the challenges facing primary physical education if it has a more holistic focus.

Traditional arguments for sports coaches or specialist delivery stem from the generalist class teacher not having the ability or motivation to gain mastery over the wide range of sports and physical activities. Initial teacher education, with limited time allocation, cannot seek to provide any depth across the range of activities. Continuing professional development may help but is not compulsory. This also fails to acknowledge that if primary physical education is more than understanding a variety of physical activities then the core learning may be more accessible. Regardless of who is doing the teaching/ coaching there are fundamental challenges to overcome. Mike Jess (2011, and here in Chapter 4), argues that one of the main challenges that primary physical education faces is the view that it is an easy option for teachers; that letting the children have a run around or kick a ball around is easy and just a case of class management. His argument puts forward the notion that teaching primary physical education is a 'complex task' (Jess, 2011: 271). Although in agreement with this argument it is also important to see this complexity as not necessarily meaning difficult or impossible; something a class teacher cannot achieve. Just because something is complex and not easy does not mean it is difficult. It is more about primary physical education not being simplistic rather than not being easy. This perception of complexity is exacerbated when primary physical education is taught through discrete areas. Developing a pedagogical approach to stimulate and support learning in a more holistic model focuses professional learning needs differently. Acquiring expertise in different sporting areas may be beyond the scope of interest and capacity for many generalist class teachers. Developing pedagogical approaches used within the classroom and applying them within physical education can empower teachers. By drawing on an area of professional expertise and developing appropriate knowledge about movement and movement contexts in order to understand what needs to be observed and improved, offers an alternative.

How do I make it safe, fun, active, inclusive?

For those involved in the direct engagement with learners in primary physical education there are often many more pressing challenges. These can be summarised by the following type of questions: How do I keep them all safe? How do I make it fun? How do I include all of them? How do I make sure that they're active enough? These questions can all be linked back to values and clarity of purpose. Are the children active enough for what? To participate in sport? To counterbalance a poor diet? What kind of fun is being advocated?

If an example of behaviour management is considered within physical education: children misbehave which challenges teacher confidence. Children are placed in danger. Teacher needs to control this through tightening control and removing danger. Taking a step back from this – why are the children misbehaving? Are they being given appropriate challenge, are the expectations of effort high enough and consistent with those within the classroom? Could more appropriate teaching engage the children more effectively so that the initial misbehaviour will not manifest itself in the first place?

MOVING IN THE RIGHT DIRECTION?

Progress in terms of primary physical education and physical education as a whole is being made. Recent publications focusing on the relationship between physical education and health (AfPE, 2008), on standards in learning in physical education (Ofsted, 2009), for time allocations in schools (Quick et al., 2010) and sport in schools (Davis, 2005) all point towards progress. The importance of sustainability is significant (Ofsted, 2011), with particular focus on financial sustainability and whether or not it is moving in the right direction can also be questioned. If the subject is only justified in terms of how it supports other educational goals or potential outcomes for some children, rather than for its core purpose, it can lose its identity (McNamee, 2005). The benefits and outcomes of the subject are wide ranging but it cannot be assumed that this will be automatic (Bailey, 2005). Provision needs to be appropriate and of quality – benefits can be achieved, given the right approach (Bailey et al., 2008). The argument can also be put forward that until the 'hidden' challenge is addressed, all momentum and progress, in potentially disparate directions, could tear the subject apart.

CONCLUSION

Primary physical education needs a clearer purpose to work towards. Kirk (2010) sets out different 'futures' for physical education as a subject: 'more of the same', 'radical reform' or 'extinction'. Given the plethora of challenges outlined in this chapter, 'more of the same' would seem to be not a positive step. 'Extinction' is clearly not a desirable outcome but has been considered by others (Kay, 2003). It would seem then that some form of 'radical reform' may be most desirable. What this is or may be is the subject of later chapters but one thing is for certain. Given the 'socially constructed nature' (Green, 2008: 13) of physical education, whatever might be agreed in theory, would still need to be enacted in practice. 'If policy makers and those within the physical education profession are serious about effecting a real change, they must redirect their efforts and build upon the key principles which they already know, namely that primary physical education is of primary importance' (Griggs, 2007: 66) This cannot be achieved by one teacher or by one school. This is something that the profession needs to take 'collective responsibility' for (Carney and Winkler, 2008: 15). Teaching primary physical education is not easy and it is full of challenges but it is made more difficult if the professionals involved are not clear as to what they are trying to achieve. For professionals and practitioners to be able to work collectively towards overcoming the challenges within primary physical education they need to know precisely what they are working towards.

KEY READINGS

The various challenges and problems discussed in this chapter relate back to a series of articles published in 2007–08. To understand the wider context of this chapter such sources would be a useful place to start. See in particular, Haydn-Davies, D., Jess, M. and Pickup, I. (2007) The challenges and potential within primary physical education, *Physical Education Matters*, 2, 1, 12–15 and Carney, P. and Winkler, J. (2008) The problem with primary physical education, *Primary Physical Education Matters*, 3, 1, 13–15.

REFERENCES

AfPE (2008) AfPE Health Position Paper: Physical education's contribution to public health, *Physical Education Matters*, 3, 2, 8–12.

Bailey, R. (2005) Physical education and school sport: a review of the benefits and outcomes, in R. Bailey and D. Kirk (eds) *The Routledge Physical Education Reader*, London: Routledge, 29–37.

34

Bailey, R., Armour, K., Kirk, D., Jess, M., Pickup, I., Sandford, R. and BERA PESS SIG (2008) The educational benefits claimed for physical education and school sport: an academic review, *Research Papers in Education*, 1–26.

Bilbrough, A. and Jones, P. (1968) *Physical Education in the Primary School*, London: University of London Press.

Blair, R. and Capel, S. (2008) The use of coaches in primary physical education to cover planning, preparation and assessment time: some issues, *Primary Physical Education Matters*, 3, 2–3, ix–x and v–vii.

Caldecott, S., Warburton, P. and Waring, M. (2006) A survey of the time devoted to the preparation of primary and junior school trainee teachers to teach physical education in England, *British Journal of Teaching Physical Education* 37, 1, *Physical Education Matters* 1, 1, 45–8.

Carney, P. and Howells, K. (2008) The primary physical education specialist, *Primary Physical Education Matters*, 3, 3, iii–iv.

Carney, P. and Winkler, J. (2008) The problem with primary physical education, *Primary Physical Education Matters*, 3, 1, 13–15.

Casbon, C. (2006) The secret behind achievement and why core tasks may hold the key to higher attainment in physical education, *Physical Education Matters*, 1, 1, 15–17.

Clay, G. (1999) 'Movement' – backwards and forwards. The influence of Government on Physical Education: a HMI perspective, *British Journal of Teaching Physical Education*, 30, 4, 38–41.

Cote, J., Harton, S., MacDonald, D. and Wilkes, S. (2009) The benefits of sampling sports during early childhood, *Physical and Health Education*, 74–75, 6–11.

Davis, R. (2005) Competitive school sport receives a boost through PESSCL funding, *British Journal of Teaching Physical Education*, 36, 2, 40–42.

Doherty, J. and Brennan, P. (2008) *Physical education and development 3–11: A guide for teachers*, London: Routledge.

Fisher, J. (2010) *Moving onto Key Stage One: improving transition from the early years foundation stage*, Maidenhead: Open University Press.

Francis, B. and Skelton, C. (2005) *Reassessing gender and achievement*, London: Routledge.

Gallahue, D. and Ozmun, J. (2006) *Understanding motor development: infants, children and adolescents, adults* (6th ed) Boston: McGraw-Hill.

Graham, G., Holt/Hale, S. and Parker, M. (2007) *Children moving: a reflective approach to teaching physical education*, New York: McGraw-Hill.

Green, K. (2008) *Understanding Physical Education*, London: Sage.

Griggs, G. (2007) Physical education: primary matters, secondary importance, *Education 3–13*, 35, 1, 59–69.

Griggs, G. (2008) Outsiders inside: the use of sports coaches in primary schools, *Physical Education Matters*, 3, 1, 33–36.

Haydn-Davies, D. and Coleman, M. (2010) *First Steps to Inclusive Physical Education*, London: Roehampton University.

Haydn-Davies, D., Jess, M. and Pickup, I. (2007) The challenges and potential within primary physical education, *Physical Education Matters*, 2, 1, 12–15.

Haydn-Davies, D., Kaitell, E., Randall, V. and Spence, J. (2010) The importance of goats in primary initial teacher education: a case study in physical education, paper presented at British Educational Research Association, Warwick University, 2–5 September 2010.

Jess, M. (2011) Becoming an effective primary school physical education teacher, in K. Armour (ed.) *Sport Pedagogy*, Harlow: Pearson, 271–286.

Kay, W. (2003) Physical Education, RIP? *British Journal of Teaching Physical Education*, 34, 4, 6–10.

Kirk, D. (2010) *Physical Education Futures*, London: Routledge.

Kirk, D. (2011) Children learning in physical education: a historical overview, in K. Armour (ed.) *Sport Pedagogy*, Harlow: Pearson, 24–38.

Lavin, J., Swindlehurst, G. and Foster, V. (2008) The use of coaches, adults supporting learners and teaching assistants in the teaching of physical education in the primary school *Primary Physical Education Matters*, 3, 1, ix–xi.

McNamee, M. (2005) The Nature and Values of Physical Education, in K. Green and K. Hardman (eds) *Physical Education: Essential Issues*, London: Sage, 1–20.

Marsden, E. and Weston, C. (2007) Locating quality physical education in early years pedagogy, *Sport, Education and Society,* 12, 383–398.

Morgan, W. (2006) Philosophy and Physical Education, in D. Kirk, D. McDonald, and M. O'Sullivan (eds*)* *The Handbook of Physical Education*, London: Sage, 97–108.

Morley, D. (2009) Multi-skills: the 'culture' constraint, *Primary Physical Education Matters*, 4, 3, v.

Ofsted (1999) *Primary education: a review of primary schools in England, 1994–98*, London: HMSO.

Ofsted (2005) *Physical education in primary schools*, London: HMSO.

Ofsted (2009) *Physical Education in Schools 2005/08: Working Towards 2012 and Beyond*, London: HMSO.

Ofsted (2011) *Learning lessons from School Sport Partnerships*, Manchester: HMSO.

Penney, D. and Chandler, T. (2000) A Curriculum with Connections? *British Journal of Teaching Physical Education*, 31, 2, 37–40.

Penney, D. and Evans, J. (1999) *Politics, play and practice in physical education*, London: E and FN Spon.

Pickup, I., Price, L., Shaughnessy, J., Spence, J. and Trace, M. (2008) *Teaching Primary Physical Education – Achieving QTS*, Exeter: Learning Matters.

Quick, S., Simon A. and Thornton A. (2010) *Physical Education and Sport Survey 2009/10*, TNS-BMRB, London: Department for Education.

Rose, J. (2009) *Independent Review of the Primary Curriculum: Final Report*, London: DCSF.

Talbot, M. (2007) Quality, *Physical Education Matters*, 2, 2, 6–8.

Van Berlo, K. (2007) Primary Physical Education Initial Teacher Training, *Physical Education Matters*, 2, 3, 23–26.

Warburton, P. (2000) Initial teacher training: the preparation of primary teachers in Physical Education, *British Journal of Teaching Physical Education*, 31, 4, 6–8.

Whitehead, M. (2000) Aims as an issue in physical education, in S. Capel and S. Piotrowski (eds) *Issues in Physical Education*, London: Routledge-Falmer, 7–22.

Whitehead, M. (2001) The concept of physical literacy, *British Journal of Physical Education*, 32, 1, 6–8.

Williams, A. (1989) *Issues in physical education for the primary years*, London: Falmer Press.

Wright, L. (2002) Rescuing primary physical education and saving those values that matter most, *British Journal of Teaching Physical Education*, 33, 1, 37–38.

CHAPTER FOUR

THE FUTURE OF PRIMARY PHYSICAL EDUCATION

A 3–14 developmental and connected curriculum

Mike Jess

INTRODUCTION

Over the last thirty three years as a teacher and lecturer I have observed and experienced the marginal role that primary physical education has played in schools, within the physical education profession and in higher education. During this period the physical education literature has consistently emphasised the low status of primary physical education (Pollatschek, 1979; PEA, 1987; Williams, 1989; Shaughnessy and Price, 1995; Carney and Winkler, 2008; Griggs, 2010), especially in relation to the core subjects of English, mathematics and science (Pickup and Price, 2007). In recent years, however, there are signs that primary physical education is gradually beginning to receive more attention around the world (Xiang et al., 2002; Armour and Duncombe, 2004; Ha et al., 2004; Marsden and Weston, 2007; Morgan and Bourke, 2008; Quay and Peters, 2008; Petrie, 2010). This change in fortune is particularly noticeable in Scotland where, following the publication of a national Review of Physical Education (Scottish Executive, 2004), the number of primary school children receiving two hours of curriculum physical education increased from 5 per cent to 55 per cent in a four-year period (Scottish Executive, 2006; Scottish Government, 2010). In addition, the Scottish Government has supported a considerable increase in physical education CPD (continuing professional development) opportunities for generalist primary teachers by commissioning both the universities of Glasgow and Edinburgh to create and deliver postgraduate master's-level certificates in primary physical education to help class teachers develop a specialism in primary physical education. Available to all registered teachers in Scotland these programmes have attracted in excess of 1200 teachers from all 32 local authorities which, in a country with just over 2000 primary schools, is beginning to help primary physical education move from the margins of education.

Within this emerging context, the Developmental Physical Education Group (DPEG) at the University of Edinburgh has been involved in a longitudinal project to create a vision of primary physical education as the foundation for children's lifelong engagement in physical activity (Jess et al., 2011). While secondary physical education remains equally important, the DPEG believes that starting to take physical education seriously when children enter secondary school is far too late. However, the group also acknowledges that for this change to come about the physical education profession needs to have a much clearer *vision* of primary physical education: not an easy task given the traditional focus of physical education on the secondary school years. Therefore, building on its original Basic Moves efforts aimed at children between the ages of five and seven (Jess *et al.*, 2004), the DPEG has spent the last decade working to articulate a vision for a developmental physical education curriculum that covers the three to fourteen (3–14) age range (Jess, 2011). While this project remains a 'work-in-progress' this chapter presents an overview of the key principles underpinning these curriculum efforts before discussing how this developmental curriculum can be structured to act as the foundation for children's learning experiences in physical education.

A DEVELOPMENTAL VISION FOR 3–14 PHYSICAL EDUCATION

While the DPEG's curriculum efforts have concentrated on the childhood and early adolescent years, the project has been set within a broader lifelong vision of physical education: a view increasingly supported by physical education writers in recent years (e.g. Green, 2002; Corbin, 2002; Penney, 2006). Although a robust research base highlights the benefits of lifelong participation in physical activity (US Department of Health and Human Services, 1996), it is important to more clearly articulate this notion of lifelong physical education. Subsequently, the DPEG believes lifelong physical education has its basis in the different reasons why people take part in physical activity across the lifespan (Penney and Jess, 2004) and has categorised this process in five interrelated and ever-changing dimensions, four of which are 'activity' dimensions and one a 'supporting' dimension (see Table 4.1). Lifelong physical education is, therefore, presented as a multi-faceted concept based on a wide range of physical activities and is not concentrated on one or two specific physical activity categories e.g. sport or dance. At certain times across the lifespan, physical activity participation may only be for functional reasons like walking to work or school while at other times, a mix of health, recreational and performance reasons will be the drivers (e.g.

Table 4.1 The five dimensions of lifelong physical education

■ Functional Physical Activity (FPA)	In response to demands of everyday living, i.e. work and home life
■ Recreational Physical Activity (RPA)	Physical leisure pursuits, which, for many, are socially orientated
■ Health-related Physical Activity (HRPA)	Concerned with fitness, wellbeing and/or rehabilitation
■ Performance-related Physical Activity (PRPA)	Concerned with self-improvement and/or success in performance environments
■ Support Physical Activity (SPA)	The role we play to support others' pursuit of lifelong physical education

Adapted from Penney and Jess, 2004

football could be played for all these reasons at different times). In addition, from a social constructivist perspective, many children and adults regularly support others in their physical activity attempts.

From a school-age perspective, physical education curriculum time is the key to this lifelong process as it is the only context in which every child has the opportunity to access the learning experiences that help them develop a solid foundation for the ever-changing physical activity choices across the lifespan. This viewpoint, however, raises important questions about the restricted nature of the dominant physical education curriculum model which has traditionally focused on a 'physical education-as-sport-techniques' approach delivered through a short 'block' multi-activity model (Kirk, 2010). Furthermore, this lifelong perspective also highlights the importance of the preschool and primary years as it is during these years that most children receive the majority of their physical education curriculum experiences. Primary physical education, therefore, becomes a key component of a lifelong approach to physical education as it is the period when the foundation for future engagement needs to be developed.

THOUGHT BOX

Consider how the primary physical education experiences you offer contribute to the ever-changing physical activity choices across the lifespan. What will your pupils need now to help with their future health and wellbeing?

THE DEVELOPMENTAL PHYSICAL EDUCATION PRINCIPLES

Within this lifelong perspective, the DPEG has spent considerable time re-working the key principles to inform this curriculum vision (Jess and Collins, 2003; Jess et al., 2011). Currently, five principles inform the 3–14 developmental physical education curriculum effort (see Table 4.2).

Principle 1:	*Developmentally Appropriate*
Principle 2:	*Self-Organising and Emergent*
Principle 3:	*Inclusive*
Principle 4:	*Connected*
Principle 5:	*Lifewide*

Table 4.2 The developmental physical education principles

PRINCIPLE 1: PRIMARY PHYSICAL EDUCATION SHOULD BE DEVELOPMENTALLY APPROPRIATE

With physical education traditionally focused on the secondary years, primary physical education usually concentrates on a 'watered-down' version of a secondary physical education programme. For many children, however, these experiences are inappropriate as the activities are too complex in relation to their current developmental status. While occasional developmentally inappropriate experiences are a normal part of the learning process, undertaking tasks that are consistently inappropriate will often lead to children losing interest or believing they are unable to participate with any degree of success. Subsequently, to consistently offer children developmentally appropriate physical education learning experiences, teachers need to develop a knowledge base about the developing child in relation to physical education. While most class teachers have a good understanding of the developing child in relation to classroom learning, this is often not the case in the physical education context. In particular, many class teachers are unaware of the impact of children's psychomotor development on their physical education engagement. For example, how do children's changing body shapes impact on their movement and physical activity development? How do children's basic movements and more specialised skills develop over time? Teachers also need to understand the impact of children's cognitive, social and emotional development on their involvement in physical education. For example, what rules and tactics are eight-year-olds likely to understand and remember when playing a game? How many movements in a movement sequence will a five-year-old remember? What size of team is appropriate for children of different ages? What sort of competition is appropriate at different ages? To make a difference, teachers must be able use this information, and more, to positively influence children's physical education learning experiences. Without this understanding, learning experiences in physical education will often be 'pot luck' and significantly impact on the developmental appropriateness of the tasks. Understanding children's development in relation to physical education is key to the planning and delivery of learning experiences.

PRINCIPLE 2: PRIMARY PHYSICAL EDUCATION SHOULD BE SELF-ORGANISING AND EMERGENT

Primary physical education is often taught as a whole-class activity which usually means children are expected to learn the same content in the same way and at the same time. However, most physical education activities need not be performed in the same way by all children. Different and unexpected responses are key features of many games, dances and most other physical activities: a fact demonstrating the complex nature of physical education. In addition, children develop at different rates, learn in different ways and usually engage in different physical activity experiences outside school. As a result, some children are active, physically able and confident while others are inactive and lack the movement competence and confidence to engage successfully. In the same physical education activity these different children will produce different responses and,

40

Mike Jess

logically, will learn in different ways. As such, children's physical education learning evolves as part of a self-organising and often messy process that does not, and should not, result in all children learning 'set' movements that are expected to remain the same in every situation. While key features of movements may be consistent, children need to develop the ability to be adaptive and creative with their movements. Without this adaptability and creativity children will not be able to respond to the many different contexts they meet in physical education. Therefore, while children need to learn key movement features they must also be supported to develop the self-organising learning skills that will help them explore different movement contexts and become adaptable and creative movers.

PRINCIPLE 3: PRIMARY PHYSICAL EDUCATION SHOULD BE INCLUSIVE

Inclusive physical education is not just about children being in the gym and taking part. Linked with developmental appropriateness and self-organisation, inclusion is about all children receiving physical education experiences that seek to enhance their personal learning. In Scotland, moves towards two hours of primary physical education each week make personalised learning a more tenable proposition. However, teachers need to offer children the appropriate experiences that will help each child acquire the psychomotor, cognitive, social and emotional learning needed for a physically active life. This is not an easy task because each child's starting point is different and means physical education learning experiences need to be carefully differentiated over time. A teacher's ability to undertake an initial (or baseline) assessment of children's starting points in physical education and then set appropriate learning experiences to consolidate and move each child forward is at the very heart of inclusive physical education. Appropriate learning intentions, organisation and a host of delivery considerations including task setting, formative feedback and teaching styles all become much easier if teachers know each child's starting point (Gallahue and Cleland-Donnelly, 2003). Without this knowledge, children's physical education experiences, yet again, will often become 'pot luck.'

PRINCIPLE 4: PRIMARY PHYSICAL EDUCATION SHOULD BE CONNECTED

With primary physical education traditionally delivered through a short 'block' multi-activity curriculum, children's experiences often become fragmented. This disjointed approach highlights the need to develop curriculum experiences that are more *connected* and help children (and teachers) see physical education as a 'joined up' experience that plays a significant part in their whole education. As will be discussed in the next section, the DPEG believe there is an urgent need to identify those core learning elements that help children and teachers connect the different elements of the physical education experience.

41

PRINCIPLE 5: PRIMARY PHYSICAL EDUCATION SHOULD BE LIFEWIDE

The DPEG also acknowledge that children's physical education learning not only takes place in curriculum time but as a 'lifewide' endeavour taking place in school, community and at home (West, 2004). As such, a physical education curriculum focused on physical activities not available in the local community has the potential to have little relevance to children. It is therefore vital that children's physical education curriculum experiences connect with the authentic 'real life' experiences they will meet across and beyond the school.

Therefore, as the status of primary physical education in Scotland has grown, the DPEG has set out to develop a clear vision for a contemporary 3–14 developmental physical education curriculum. In particular, its aim has been to create a developmentally appropriate and inclusive curriculum to help all children develop the self-organising skills to take control of their own physical education learning experiences and to connect these experiences within, across and beyond the school (see Figure 4.1).

THOUGHT BOX

In light of the five principles named here, review the provision you offer. Which aspects do you deliver on and which ones need further consideration?

A WAY FORWARD FOR 3–14 DEVELOPMENTAL PHYSICAL EDUCATION

As this vision for developmental physical education has evolved the DPEG has made efforts to apply these five principles in practice. For generalist primary teachers these

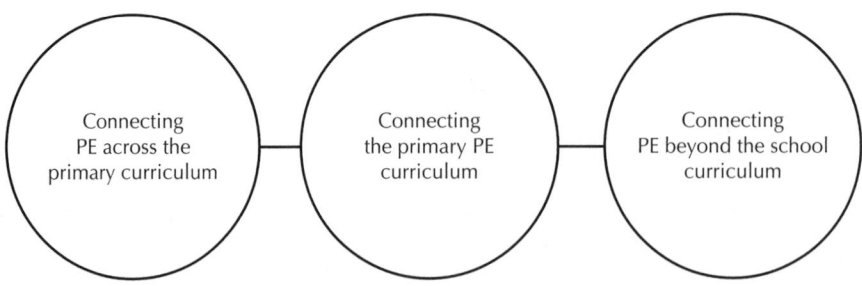

Figure 4.1 The connected lifewide nature of 3–14 physical education

42

efforts have concentrated on supporting their understanding of the complex relationship between the developing child, the physical education curriculum, the environment in which the curriculum is delivered and the pedagogical skills needed to successfully deliver the curriculum. However, although children may now be receiving more physical education, unless efforts are made to reorient the nature of the primary physical education curriculum these additional experiences are likely to be 'more of the same' and, for many, progress will continue the 'pot luck' scenario. Consequently, the main focus of the DPEG's work over the last decade has been to create a developmentally appropriate and connected curriculum structure that articulates with its vision of primary physical education. Therefore, the remainder of the chapter presents an overview of this innovative 3–14 developmental physical education curriculum by briefly describing the key elements that structure this curriculum. It is important to stress that each curriculum element will not be described in depth and that the intention is to offer a broad outline of the developmental and connected nature of the curriculum structure. For those interested in reading more about these curriculum elements please refer to the reference list at the end of the chapter.

AN OVERVIEW OF A DEVELOPMENTALLY APPROPRIATE AND CONNECTED 3–14 PHYSICAL EDUCATION CURRICULUM

Restructuring the primary physical education curriculum in line with this lifelong vision has been, and continues to be, a complex process, particularly as the DPEG's developmental principles have been concurrently evolving. For example, the original Basic Moves efforts in 2001 were targeted at five- to seven-year-olds, were focused on developmentally appropriate and inclusion principles and were a reaction to the perceived limitations of the multi-activity curriculum model (Jess and Collins, 2003). However, as the group sought to expand the curriculum to cover the 3–14 age range, engagement with dynamical systems (Thelen, 1995), ecological theory (Newell, 1986), situated perspectives (Lave and Wenger, 1991) and complexity theory (Light, 2008) extended the focus of the curriculum to include connectivity and lifewide principles (Jess *et al.*, 2007) and later self-organisation and emergence (Jess *et al.*, 2011). As a result of this reworking process, the structure of the 3–14 developmental physical education curriculum now includes two key interrelated elements whose integration acts as the foundation for engagement with the lifelong physical activity dimensions:

- Core learning: the learning experiences underpinning and connecting the range of physical education experiences across the 3–14 age range and beyond;
- Applications: the different contexts in which children apply core learning in order to enhance the development of their lifelong foundation.

These two elements have both been developed from an age phase perspective by focusing on the Early Years (3–8 years) and the Upper Primary and Early Secondary years (UPES) (8–14 years) (see Table 4.3).

Table 4.3 Core learning and applications in 3–14 developmental physical education

Age phase	Core learning	Applications
UPES	■ UPES Core Learning	■ UPES Developmental and Authentic Applications
Early Years	■ Basic Moves and Preschool Early Moves	■ Early Years Generic and Developmental Applications

EARLY YEARS AND UPES CORE LEARNING

Core learning is critical as it helps children develop the foundation underpinning their engagement in the physical activities they meet across the lifespan. While core physical learning is the main focus, children also need to develop the core knowledge and understanding (cognitive) and the social and emotional skills that support their physical activity participation. Given this perceived importance of core learning, the DPEG's original curriculum efforts were concentrated on core learning across the Early Years (ages 3–8) and primarily focused on the Preschool Early Moves and Basic Moves programmes that set out to develop children's basic movement foundation. In recent years, as the group has extended the range of its curriculum endeavours, closer scrutiny has been given to the more complex aspects of core learning for older UPES children e.g. perceived competence and decision making.

EARLY YEARS CORE LEARNING

Early Years core learning focuses on children's basic movement foundation: the ability to consistently perform basic movements in a technically efficient, adaptable and creative manner (Jess *et al.*, 2004). Although efficient movement is vital to successful participation, without movement adaptability and creativity children's capacity to respond effectively to the demands of different situations is limited. Therefore, Early Years core learning must prepare children for the varied responses needed in different games, sports, dance and other activity contexts.

Over the last decade, the DPEG has created the Early Years Movement Framework to specifically focus on Early Years core learning. The framework consists of three related components (see Figure 4.2): the Balance and Coordination Grid to help develop the movement foundation for preschool children; the Basic Movements that are the functional movements underpinning most physical activities and the Movement Concepts that are the cognitive, social and emotional aspects to support children's movement adaptability and creativity. These movement concepts were a key feature of the movement education approach from the 1960s and 70s (Laban and Lawrence, 1947). The next section will briefly consider the interrelated nature of these components.

44

Basic Movement Foundation			Movement Concepts
▪ The Balance and Coordination Grid	▪ Travelling ▪ Object Control ▪ Balance	*Made adaptable and creative by*	▪ Space ▪ Effort ▪ Relationships

Figure 4.2 The Early Years Movement Framework

THE BALANCE AND COORDINATION GRID

The Balance and Coordination Grid (Jess and MacIntyre, 2009) contains four underpinning movement elements: balance, coordination, postures and rotations (see Figure 4.3).

As young children learn to move, these elements come together in many different combinations to create an almost infinite number of movements. Most of these combinations produce generic, non-specific movements that do not resemble normal functional movements, e.g. moving across the floor (dynamic balance) in a low position (posture) with arms and legs working in opposition (coordination) with both legs twisting and turning (rotations). However, a small number of these combinations create the more functional basic movements that are key to successful participation in most physical activity contexts e.g. running, jumping or throwing. The grid was specifically created for preschool children because many basic movements are developmentally too advanced. As such, the grid helps the children develop a generic movement foundation through the regular exploration of the many balance and coordination possibilities of their bodies, including some basic movements. Although the grid was developed a number of years

Balance	Coordination
Two main types of balance ▪ Static balance/still body ▪ Dynamic balance/moving body	The relationship between body sectors and body parts ▪ All sectors doing same ▪ Sides or top/bottom only ▪ One or more sectors in opposition ▪ One or more sectors crossing the mid-line
Postures	**Rotations**
Main positions in which the body is being held ▪ Upright posture ▪ Mid posture ▪ Lying posture	Around different axes of the body ▪ Turn ▪ Twist ▪ Rock ▪ Roll ▪ Spin

Figure 4.3 The Balance and Coordination Grid

after the original Basic Moves programme, it now forms the basis of the Preschool Early Moves programme (McIntyre and Logg, 2011) and has become a key underpinning component of the 3–14 developmental Physical education curriculum. In addition, the grid also helps teachers break down many of the basic and more specialised movements used by older children.

THE BASIC MOVEMENTS

Basic Movements emerge from specific balance and coordination combinations and are the functional movements children need to take part in different physical activities. There are three main categories of basic movement (see Table 4.4). Travelling movements are those where the body, usually in an upright position, moves from one point on the ground to another. Examples include walking, running, jumping, and skipping. Object control movements involve working with an object and are the starting point for most of ball games. As such, objects are either *sent* e.g. throw, *received* e.g. catch, or *travelled with* e.g. football dribble. Some more complex object control movements involve receiving and sending an object e.g. striking a moving ball. Balance is the final basic movement category and focuses on static and dynamic body postures. Originally, these basic movements were the basis of the Basic Moves Programme but are now connected to the elements of the Balance and Coordination Grid to create the movement elements of children's basic movement foundation.

Table 4.4 The Basic Movements

Travelling movements	Object control movements	Balance movements
Basic	**Send**	**Static**
Walk	Throw	Upright posture
Run	Kick	Ready position
	Punt	Starting
	Ball roll	Stopping
Rhythmical	Static ball strike	Landing
Gallop		
Side slip		
Skip	**Receive**	**Dynamic**
	Catch	Stretch/curl
	Trap (feet)	Twist/turn
Jumps	Stop (stick)	Spin
1→1 (hop)		Sink/fall
1→1 (leap)	**Travel with**	Body roll
1→2	Dribble (hands)	Dodge
2→1	Dribble (feet)	
2→2 (high)	Dribble (stick)	
2→2 (long)		
	Receive and send	
Apparatus	Volley	
Climb	Strike (bat)	
Swing	Strike (stick)	

46

THE MOVEMENT CONCEPTS

Movement concepts are not movements but the cognitive, social and emotional factors that bring adaptability and creativity to movements. Although movement concepts are more apparent in the early years they are critical elements of movement competence across the lifespan. Specifically, movement concepts are split into three categories to help children know where *(space)*, how *(effort)* and who or what their body moves with *(relationships)* (see Table 4.5). As children develop their knowledge, understanding and use of movement concepts they become more comfortable at adapting their movements in different contexts e.g. moving quickly or slowly or changing from high to low when needed. In addition, children can also use the movement concepts to be creative by moving in ways that are unexpected or original. Without movement concepts, movements tend to be rigid and lack the capacity to respond to the demands of different contextual factors. Movement concepts are a particularly important feature of the Early Years movement vocabulary.

While much of the DPEG's original curriculum work focused on the core elements of the Early Years Movement Framework (Atencio *et al.*, 2011), it is only recently that national physical education curricula are beginning to adopt this more generic learning approach to young children's physical education curriculum and move beyond the constraints of the traditional short 'block' model.

Table 4.5 The Movement Concepts

Space (Where)	Effort (How)	Relationships (Who/what with)

Space
Self space
General space
	Speed
	Fast/slow
	Gradual/sudden
	Erratic/sustained
		Body parts
		Identify
		Body shape
		  Wide/narrow
		  Twisted
		  Symmetrical
		  Asymmetrical

Directions Forward Backward Sideways Diagonal	**Force** Heavy/strong Light/soft	**Objects** Over/under/through In/out Front/behind On/off

Pathways
Zigzag
Curved
Straight
	Flow
	Smooth/jerky
	Bound/free
		People
		Cooperative
		  Mirror
		  Shadow
		  Unison
		  Alternating
		Competitive
		  Chase/flee
		  Attack/defend

Levels High/medium/low		

UPES CORE LEARNING

As children grow older they become bigger and more complex in all aspects of their behaviour. Building on learning from the Early Years Movement Framework, UPES core learning focuses on the psychomotor, cognitive, social and emotional skills older children need to engage with the physical activities they meet. Table 4.6 highlights some, but not all, of the core UPES knowledge, understanding and skills that older children need as they continue to develop a foundation that connects across a range of more complex physical activity experiences.

While early years core learning may be developed through curriculum experiences specifically focused on core learning i.e. Early and Basic Moves, the DPEG continue to grapple with the most effective way to deliver core learning experiences in the UPES years. In particular, the group have found that de-contextualised core learning experiences are less interesting to older children which, as will now be discussed, has led to a close examination of the applied contexts in which this core learning is developed and employed.

EARLY YEARS AND UPES APPLICATIONS

Applications are central to the 3–14 developmental physical education curriculum because they act as the transitional mechanism between core learning and lifewide participation. On the one hand, applications help children progressively develop and apply core learning while, on the other hand, they also help create connections across and beyond the curriculum to lifewide contexts. As a consequence, the DPEG has been working to create a more flexible curriculum framework that offers children a wider range of early years and UPES applications (see Table 4.7).

Table 4.6 Examples of UPES core learning in physical education

Psychomotor (physical skills)	▪ Basic Movement combinations e.g. catching and throwing ▪ Health-related components: aerobic, strength, flexibility, etc ▪ Performance-related components: speed, strength, agility, etc ▪ Physical activity lifestyle: tracking
Cognitive (knowledge and understanding)	▪ Introduce lifelong physical activity dimensions ▪ Understanding adaptability and creativity ▪ Performance and practice principles ▪ Physical activity health issues ▪ Behavioural and decision-making skills
Affective (social and emotional)	▪ Individual and team behaviours: team affiliation ▪ Task and ego behaviours ▪ Self-determination ▪ Cooperation/competition: winning/losing ▪ Etiquette

48

Mike Jess

Table 4.7 Early Years and UPES applications

Early Years applications	Early Years generic applications
	Early Years developmental applications
UPES applications	UPES developmental applications
	UPES authentic applications

EARLY YEARS APPLICATIONS

Although the DPEG proposes early years physical education should focus on children's basic movement foundation, it also recognises children need opportunities to apply core learning in appropriate contexts. Subsequently, early years applications have been split into two categories.

▪ Early Years generic applications: similar to the non-specific balance and coordination movements discussed earlier, generic applications offer young children the opportunity to apply core learning in non-specific ways. This type of application is particularly important for younger children because the more specific constraints of games, gymnastics and dance activities are often developmentally too difficult for them. As such, generic opportunities to apply core elements from the Early Years Movement Framework are limitless and can include, for example, exploring different small and large apparatus lay-outs, responding to different music and percussion, playing with different objects, non-specific games involving basic movements e.g. tag/tig and many, many more. These generic applications are a critical part of children's physical education learning as they not only extend the range of their core learning but also enable the children to explore and take control of their own physical education applied experiences.
▪ Early Years developmental applications: similar in timescale to multi-activity 'blocks', developmental applications focus on applying children's core learning in more recognisable contexts. In the early years, these developmental applications include games and athletics, dance, gymnastics, outdoor learning and aquatic applications. These applications not only help children apply core learning they also act as the foundation for the UPES developmental applications that follow. Early Years applications are a central part of the developmental physical education curriculum and are included as part of Early Moves and Basic Moves core learning sessions but can also stand alone in sessions that specifically set out to help children apply their core learning.

UPES APPLICATIONS

UPES applications are a critical component of the 3–14 developmental physical education curriculum. As children get older, applications not only fulfil a key transitional role in consolidating, extending and applying core learning but also connecting with wider curriculum and lifewide contexts. As such, the DPEG has

49

taken the view that the focus and structure of UPES applications needs to move beyond the 'physical education-as-sport-techniques' approach discussed earlier (Kirk, 2010) and actively accommodate core learning and lifewide transitions. Two related application categories have subsequently been proposed: developmental and authentic applications.

- UPES developmental applications: build on Early Years developmental applications and focus on the development and application of children's core learning in different physical activity contexts e.g. games, dance, gymnastics, aquatics, athletics and outdoors. Developmental applications, however, have been created to involve more participative learning experiences than usually seen in the narrower and more behaviourist-inclined 'block' approach. As such, these applications seek to engage the children in a more self-organising and emergent process (Jess et al., 2011), much in line with the Teaching Games for Understanding (Bunker and Thorpe, 1982), Educational Gymnastics (Long, 1982) and Movement Education (Laban and Lawrence, 1947) approaches that have influenced physical education developments in the past. In addition, UPES developmental applications have a specific transitional role in preparing children for the more authentic applications now discussed.
- UPES authentic applications: extend children's core learning and developmental applications by setting out to offer more 'real life' learning experiences. As such, authentic applications not only seek to develop the children's specific physical education learning but also to connect this learning with the broader school curriculum and, critically, the 'real life' contexts in which they participate beyond school. From a curriculum structure perspective, authentic applications need much more time than traditional 'blocks' and can last for as long as a term or semester as different learning connections are explored and developed. Authentic applications are closely related to the characteristics of Sport Education (Siedentop, 1994), and have been extended by the DPEG to include Dance Education (Irvine, 2009), Outdoor Journeys (Beames and Atencio, 2008) and, tentatively, Physical Activity Education which sets out to connect with the lifelong physical activity dimensions (Penney and Jess, 2004).

By highlighting the need to apply core learning in authentic 'real life' contexts, the 3–14 developmental approach to physical education encourages teachers to shift from a narrow 'pedagogy of certainty' to a more open 'pedagogy of emergence' which recognises the importance of engaging pupils through the sharing of learning intentions, collaborative learning, problem solving, peer teaching and independent working (Jess et al., 2011). The self-organising and emergence principle become a key feature of the delivery of such a developmental curriculum. However, with the multi-activity model continuing to dominate physical education in Scotland (Thorburn et al., 2009) dissemination of the developmental approach has been slow in secondary schools as it challenges the short 'block' timetable structure and the more behaviourist teaching approaches focused on the perceived need to 'cover' specific skills. Consequently, while the proposed 3–14 developmental physical education approach is making significant inroads in primary schools (Jess et al., 2011), the DPEG has the future challenge of developing and presenting a more compelling case to secondary physical education colleagues.

Mike Jess

CONCLUSION

This chapter has presented the case that, because of its marginal status, curriculum innovation in primary physical education has been limited over many decades and has subsequently resulted in many children being offered a diet of 'watered-down' secondary physical education experiences. Within this context, the chapter reveals how a resurgence in the fortunes of primary physical education in Scotland has enabled the DPEG to explore the possibilities of a contemporary vision for a 3–14 developmental curriculum. By setting physical education within a lifelong perspective, the DPEG propose that preschool and primary school experiences are central to developing children's foundation for lifelong physical education. As such, this vision has evolved around five key principles: developmental appropriateness, self-organisation, inclusion, connectedness and lifewide endeavour. The chapter presents a broad structural overview of a 3–14 developmental physical education curriculum which articulates with these principles and highlights the complex developmental relationship between two key elements: core learning and applications. While this overview presents the broad framework for the curriculum, the DPEG are currently working with hundreds of teachers to disseminate this curriculum vision across and beyond Scotland.

KEY READINGS

The development of a clear vision of a connected curriculum which supports lifelong physical activity has evolved over time. Insights into this evolution can be seen by articles which have marked this journey. Good examples to begin a wider understanding of this topic are Jess, M., Dewar, K. and Fraser, G. (2004) Basic Moves: Developing a Foundation for Lifelong Physical Activity, *British Journal of Teaching in Physical Education*, 35, 2, 23–27, and then later Jess, M., Atencio, M. and Thorburn, M. (2011) Complexity Theory: Supporting Curriculum and Pedagogy Developments in Scottish Physical Education, *Sport Education and Society*, 16, 1, 179–199.

REFERENCES

Armour, K. M, and Duncombe, R. (2004) Teachers' continuing professional development in primary physical education: Lessons from present and past to inform the future, *Physical Education and Sport Pedagogy*, 9, 1, 3–22.

Atencio, M., Jess, M. and Dewar, K. (2011) It is a case of changing your thought processes, the way you actually teach: Implementing a complex professional learning agenda in Scottish physical education, *Physical Education and Sport Pedagogy*.

Beames, S. and Atencio, M. (2008) Building social capital through outdoor education, *Journal of Adventure Education and Outdoor Learning*, 8, 99–112.

Bunker, D. and Thorpe, R. (1982) A model for the teaching of games in secondary schools, *The Bulletin of Physical Education*, 18, 1, 5–8.

Carney, P. and Winkler, J. (2008) The Problem with Primary Physical Education, *Physical Education Matters*, 3, 1, 13–15.

Corbin, C. (2002) Physical Activity for Everyone: What Every Physical Educator Should Know about Promoting Lifelong Physical Activity, *Journal of Teaching Physical Education*, 21, 128–144.

Gallahue, D. and Cleland-Donnelly, F. (2003) *Developmental Physical Education for All Children*, Champaign, IL: Human Kinetics.

Green, K. (2002) Lifelong Participation, Physical Education and the Work of Ken Roberts, *Sport, Education and Society*, 7, 2, 167–182.

Griggs, G. (2010) For sale – primary physical education, £20 per hour or nearest offer, *Education 3–13*, 38, 1, 39–46.

Ha, A., Lee, J.C.K., Chan, W.K. and Sum, R.K.W. (2004) Teachers' Perceptions of In-service Teacher Training to Support Curriculum Change in Physical Education: The Hong Kong Experience, *Sport Education and Society*, 9, 3, 421–438.

Irvine, W. (2009) Dance Education, paper presented at the 3–14 Physical Education Tutor Training Course at the University of Edinburgh, June 2009.

Jess, M. (2011) From Basic Moves to Developmental Physical Education: A Curriculum Innovation Journey, *Physical Education Matters*, Summer.

Jess, M., and Collins, D. (2003) Primary physical education in Scotland: the future in the making, *European Journal of Physical Education*, 8, 103–118.

Jess, M., Atencio, M., and Thorburn, M. (2011) Complexity Theory: Supporting Curriculum and Pedagogy Developments in Scottish Physical Education, *Sport Education and Society*, 16, 1, 179–199.

Jess, M., Carse, N., Macmillan, P. and Atencio, M. (2011) Sport Education in Scottish Primary Schools: Emergence of an Authentic Application, in P. Hastie (ed.) *Sport Education: International Perspectives*, Routledge: London.

Jess, M., Dewar, K. and Fraser, G. (2004) Basic Moves: Developing a Foundation for Lifelong Physical Activity, *British Journal of Teaching in Physical Education*, 35, 2, 23–27.

Jess, M., Haydn-Davis, D. and Pickup, I. (2007) Physical Education in the Primary School: A Developmental, Inclusive and Connected Future, *Physical Education Matters*, 2, 1, 18–22.

Jess, M. and McIntye, J. (2009) Developmentally Appropriate Physical Education in the Early Years, *Nursery World*, 28 January.

Kirk, D. (2010) *Physical Education Futures*, Routledge: London.

Laban, R. and Lawrence, F. (1947) *Effort*, MacDonald and Evans: London.

Lave, J. and Wenger, E. (1991) *Situated learning: legitimate peripheral participation*, Cambridge University Press: London.

Light, R. (2008) Complex learning theory—its epistemology and its assumptions about learning: implications for physical education, *Journal of Teaching in Physical Education*, 27, 1, 21–37.

Long, J. (1982) *Educational Gymnastics*, London: Edward Arnold.

Macintyre, J. and Logg, L. (2011) *Early Moves*, City of Edinburgh/University of Edinburgh.

Marsden, E. and Weston, C. (2007) Locating quality physical education in early years pedagogy, *Sport, Education and Society*, 12, 4, 383–398.

Morgan, P. and Bourke, S. (2008) Non-specialist teachers' confidence to teach physical education: the nature and influence of personal school experiences in physical education, *Physical Education and Sport Pedagogy*, 13, 1, 1–29.

Newell, K. (1986) Constraints on the development of coordination, in M. Wade and H.T.A. Whiting (eds) *Motor development in children: aspects of coordination and control*, Elsevier Science: Amsterdam, 295–317.

PEA (1987) Physical Education in Schools, Report of a commission of enquiry, Ling House, PEA.

Penney, D. (2006) Curriculum construction and change, in D. Kirk, D. Macdonald, and M. O'Sullivan (eds) The *Handbook of Physical Education,* Sage: London, 565–579.

Penney, D. and Jess, M. (2004) Physical Education and Physically Active Lives: A Lifelong Approach to Curriculum Development, *Sport Education and Society,* 9, 269–287.

Petrie, K. (2010) Creating confident, motivated teachers of physical education in primary schools, European Physical Education Review, 16, 1, 47–64.

Pickup, I. and Price, L. (2007) *Teaching physical education in the primary school: A developmental approach,* Continuum: London.

Pollatschek, J.L. (1979) The ugly duckling of the primary school, *SPEA Sidelines,* 7, 3, 1.

Quay, J. and Peters, J. (2008) Skills, strategies, sport, and social responsibility: reconnecting physical education, *Journal of Curriculum Studies,* 40, 5, 601–626.

Scottish Executive (2004) *The report of the review group on physical education,* Edinburgh: HMSO.

Scottish Executive (2006) *Progress towards the recommendations of the Physical Education Review Group.* Available online at http://www.scotland.gov.uk/Resource/Doc/933/0019904.pdf (accessed 29 March 2008).

Scottish Government (2010) *Most primaries hitting Physical Education target.* Available online at www.scotland.gov.uk/News/Releases/2010/11/29084131 (accessed 1 June 2011).

Shaughnessy, J. and Price, L. (1995) Physical education in primary schools – a whole new ball game, *Bulletin of Physical Education,* 31, 1, 14–20.

Siedentop, D. (1994) *Sport education: Quality PE through positive sport experiences,* Champaign, IL: Human Kinetics.

Thelen, E. (1995) Motor development: A new synthesis, *American Psychologist,* 50, 2, 79–95.

Thorburn, M. Jess, M. and Atencio, M. (2009) Connecting policy aspirations with principled progress? An analysis of current physical education challenges in Scotland, *Irish Educational Studies,* 28, 2, 207–221.

US Department of Health and Human Services (1996) *Physical Activity and Health: A Report of the Surgeon General,* Atlanta, US Department of Health and Human Services.

West, L. (2004) The trouble with lifelong learning, in D. Hayes (ed.) *Key debates in education,* London: Routledge Falmer.

Williams, A. (1989) The place of physical education in primary education, in A. Williams (ed.) *Issues in Primary Physical Education,* London: Falmer Press, 1–16.

Xiang P., Lowy, S. and McBride, R. (2002) The impact of a field-based primary physical education methods course on preservice classroom teachers' beliefs, *Journal of Teaching in Physical Education,* 21, 2, 145–161.

Part 2
CURRICULUM

THE DEVELOPMENT OF THE PHYSICAL EDUCATION CURRICULUM IN PRIMARY SCHOOLS IN THE UNITED KINGDOM

Sue Chedzoy

INTRODUCTION

The relationship between a more widely focused primary education and a more narrowly focused physical education has changed over time. This journey has seen over a century of changes and includes numerous iterations of syllabi and curricula from competing agendas such as sport, health and education. The first part of this chapter charts this journey identifying significant milestones along the way. Second, this chapter will also explain how the commonalities found here conclude that ultimately children benefit from experiences which help them to master fundamental motor skills to develop dexterity and confidence in themselves. Importantly once these foundations have been laid curriculum programmes need to be developed to encourage children to integrate skills into simple phrases and more complex sequences of movement. This hereby sets a rationale for the different activities selected to be delivered which will denote the end of the journey.

EARLY CURRICULUM DEVELOPMENTS

The first official Syllabus of Physical Training for Schools was issued at the beginning of the century and was based on a series of Swedish exercises which had been used by the British Armed Forces (Board of Education, 1904). Children were not encouraged to think for themselves or expected to enjoy the drill in the programme. The value was thought to be in the formal nature of the work and beneficial effect on the physiological functioning of the body. At this time children were suffering the effects of poor nutrition, cramped conditions, disease and ignorance about hygiene. The new government of 1906 set out to address these problems and introduced a vigorous programme of social reform.

In 1908 physical education became the responsibility of the Medical Department of the Board of Education and part of the curriculum in all elementary schools. The Board was beginning to move away from the purely disciplinary approach favoured by the early military influence and recognised that physical training could contribute to the development of a healthy body and mind. However the health which was the aim of the early physical education programme was rather basic compared with the concept of health today (Start Active Stay Active, 2011). In the early part of the

57

century the subject was mainly referred to as 'physical training' but, as early as 1909, the term physical education began to be used within documents produced by the Board of Education.

The main focus was on short-term fitness and keeping the body free from disease. The 1909 syllabus was in essence therapeutic, general principles of physiology of exercise were outlined for teachers and some recreational exercises were included to encourage enjoyable pupil participation, for example simple dancing steps were introduced as part of the programme. The 1909 syllabus formed the foundations of physical education in the majority of elementary schools up to and throughout the Great War. It was revised in 1919, by which time the concept of physical education had broadened since it was recognised that healthy physique, keen intelligence and sound character were benefits of the subject. For the first time there appeared evidence of the Board not only being concerned with the growth and development of children but also with fostering the formation of habits of recreation for the future. Whereas the advice from the Board of Education in 1919 was sound, in reality the development of physical education varied since lack of funds during the inter-war years limited the provision of adequate facilities in the majority of schools. In 1925 the National Playing Fields Association was formally inaugurated and made great efforts to provide adequate facilities for games and recreation for every section of the community. It was recognised that if people were to enjoy physical activity in their leisure time then the facilities needed to be improved (Board of Education, 1926).

A MOVE TO A BROADER CURRICULUM

In the following decade one of the aims of the Syllabus of Physical Training for Schools (Board of Education, 1933) was to encourage safe and systematic teaching of all activities likely to promote a healthy way of living. It was devised for children up to the age of twelve years. It included gymnastics, games, swimming, dancing, sports, free play walking and school journeys, and also those pursuits which might create an appreciation of fresh air and a healthy way of living. It seems that some of the misconceptions of what might constitute a suitable games programme for children of primary school age have been around for a very long time. For example the follow extract from the syllabus could well have been written by educationists today:

> The interest aroused by competitive games and the publicity given to them might cause some misunderstanding of the type of game and methods of training suitable for ordinary school children. The organisation of games must be such to avoid the pitfalls of early specialisation, undue coaching of special teams, and the faults to which unrestricted competition can give rise. It is too commonly assumed that the games to be played should be football and cricket for boys, netball and tennis for girls, regardless of the fact that these games require a high degree of physical co-ordination as well as specially prepared pitches.
> (Board of Education (1933: 37) Syllabus of Physical Training for Schools)

58

Sue Chedzoy

In 1933 open air teaching was encouraged, not only to provide children with increased oxygen to supply their muscles during increased exertion but also to lay the foundation of the habit of seeking outdoor pursuits and enjoyment in taking part in physical activities after school. This recommendation may have been made in the light of lack of indoor facilities. Teachers were advised to encourage children to discard some of their outer garments to enjoy freedom of movement. Few could afford special clothing for these sessions and yet attention was drawn to the importance of suitable footwear and clothes for physical education.

The 1933 syllabus recommended a daily lesson of twenty minutes' activity, to include three periods of formal lessons and others to cover activities such as games and swimming. It is interesting to note that all those years ago it was believed that physical training was by now a sufficiently established part of the curriculum for the daily lesson to be accepted in all schools (Board of Education, 1933: 19). Even fifty years later when physical education was included in the National Curriculum for England and Wales (DES, 1989) in all state schools, there was no recommendation as to the amount of time that should be allocated to the subject. Looking back at the historical development of the subject the more recent five-hour offer to include two hours of physical education is hardly innovative. The challenge for the profession today is to ensure that children are provided with opportunities to benefit from a rich and varied physical education curriculum to enable them to develop and refine their physical skills, their confidence and a desire to engage in physically active lifestyles.

The Education Act (1944) established the right of children to receive a sound secondary school education and marked the end of elementary schools. Local Education Authorities (LEAs) were encouraged to improve the provision of facilities for physical training and recreation for older pupils and this probably had a positive effect on provision in primary schools as more funds became available. In 1945 the responsibility for physical education was transferred from the Chief Medical Officer to the Senior Chief Inspector of the Ministry of Education and this heralded a dramatic change of focus for physical education in schools. The emphasis moved away from the inclusion of the subject on remedial and therapeutic grounds and physical educationalists leant toward justification of their subject in the curriculum, a legacy some might argue educationists have struggled to justify ever since.

The influence of the military was again felt in schools after the war, but in a different way from that at the beginning of the century (Johnson, 1981). Primary schools took ideas for new equipment from apparatus used in commando and combat training by the forces. Children were encouraged to develop their strength by hanging, climbing and swinging on ropes, rope nets and logs appeared in many playgrounds. This was the beginning of equipment being introduced into schools for the prime purpose of promoting such activities. Later the apparatus became more purpose-built and sophisticated (Smith, 1974).

This period also saw a change of teaching method employed by many teachers (McIntosh et al., 1981). Teachers began to adopt a more child-centred approach since children were encouraged to interpret their own solutions in response to a given task.

This new approach encompassed the philosophies of Dewey and Piaget whose theories had a major impact on primary schools across the curriculum. Further to this, Rudolf von Laban and Lisa Ullman made a significant contribution to the teaching of dance in schools from 1944 and this influence spread more widely in the development of 'movement education' in the late 1940s and early 1950s. Wright (1977) suggested that extravagant claims were made that these principles of movement embraced all aspects of physical education. Men returning from their National Service favoured a direct approach to teaching skills and agilities which included exercises for their anatomical and physiological effects, and rejected the movement approach which they considered neglected these aspects of physical education.

MOVING AND GROWING

In 1952 the Ministry of Education published a guidance book for teaching primary school physical education. Called 'Moving and Growing' (Ministry of Education, 1952) it certainly reflected a different approach from that adopted in earlier government publications. It gave advice to primary school teachers on landmarks in children's growth and physical development and explained how these might affect the development of movement. The text was supported by a wealth of photographs showing children of all ages involved in a rich variety of physical activity. Even though two chapters were devoted to physical education as a general term the Ministry considered the physical education curriculum to be games, swimming, dance, dramatic movement and physical training (PT). In the section devoted to PT the Ministry compared gymnastics in the secondary school with PT in the primary school. This is illustrated by the published view that:

> Broadly speaking we may think of the 'PT' lesson as being concerned with the grammar of movement, this will include movements which have a compensatory or remedial purpose. It will include the practice of techniques such as throwing, hitting, dribbling, running and leaping, and it will include opportunities for agilities on all sorts of apparatus.
>
> (Ministry of Education, 1952: 72–73)

This was followed by a similar guidance book to support primary school teachers in the teaching of physical education, 'Planning the Programme' (Ministry of Education, 1953) in which teachers were offered a nucleus of material from which to plan their own programme of physical education. The activities were well illustrated and aims were clearly stated so that teachers were left in no doubt about the physical effects activities would have on the body. Guidance was given for lesson structure and progression. There was also an emphasis on claims for the subject on educational grounds, citing moral, social and psychological benefits alongside anatomical and physiological effects.

The influence of Laban's work (see Laban, 1963) was very evident in many primary schools and those teachers trained in his methods were able to adapt the principles of movement, not only to dance, but also in the teaching of gymnastics and games. Oslin and Mitchell (2006) reminded us that in the sixties Maulden and Redfern (1969) justified

the inclusion of games in the primary curriculum only if games could provide educational opportunities for all children. They were so innovative in their approach to games teaching and emphasised that in addition to the physical aspects of games playing, children could benefit from social, moral and intellectual aspects of involvement in a games programme. Hindsight is a wonderful thing, but anyone looking at the guidance on how to involve children in a programme of games that emphasised the developmental stages, problem-solving approaches, grouping skills, games strategies, and games invention in giving children choice and an appreciation for the value of rules could be wondering why this approach had not been taken on board more universally at that time. The next guidance in physical education from the government for primary school teachers did not appear until twenty years later. The publication *Movement – Physical Education in the Primary Years* (DES, 1972) focused attention on the application of general educational principles to the teaching of physical education and very little attention to either health or fitness. It was noted that gymnastics was often associated with physical development and fitness, but in the primary school gymnastics was to be regarded for its creative contribution to a child's development.

> Maximal physical effort should be encouraged, and it is almost unavoidable in games, athletics and swimming. But it is in the development of versatility and sensitivity, and in the ability to apply skill and control in purposeful creative and imaginative situations that the true values of physical education lie.
>
> (DES, 1972: 14)

In this guidance it was stressed that movement as a mode of expression gave physical education a more central place in the curriculum, offering children opportunities for individual exploration and creative learning. However, there was very little guidance on what and how the activities might be taught, unlike earlier documentation from the government.

About this time Her Majesty's Inspectors (HMI) (DES, 1978) found the extent and quality of work in physical education varied considerably and the balance of the programme depended on the types of facilities available and the interests and skills of the teachers. This survey highlighted the value of curriculum leadership within primary education. Often the role of curriculum leader for physical education was given to young energetic members of staff who showed an enthusiasm for the subject, but were not necessarily well enough trained in subject knowledge or leadership skills. The DES recognised this and at the time there was a national programme to address the training of curriculum leaders in physical education in primary schools. The issue of the length and depth of the initial training of teachers to fully equip them to teach high-quality physical education in the primary setting has been a debate that has rumbled on for decades. Ever since those earlier times professional associations have lobbied governments in an attempt to secure a substantial amount of time in primary initial training courses in physical education to train generalists and specialists to teach physical education to the highest of standards. The findings of Caldecott *et al.* (2006) revealed that in the 21st century this remains an issue to be addressed. Teachers need a sound initial training in physical education, but they also need and welcome curriculum material and support to aid them in their teaching. Most Local Education Authorities (LEAs) recognised this and during the 1970s and 1980s produced detailed written guidelines for use by primary school teachers in the teaching of physical education. A number of LEAs offered primary school teachers some support by employing advisory teachers to work in school alongside teachers and to advise and lead on matters relating to curriculum development. Gymnastics and dance tended to be the areas of activity in which primary school teachers sought most support as worries about progression and safety were paramount. LEAs also provided advice and schemes for games and athletic activities. Swimming was often given over to coaches in local swimming pools and advice for outdoor and adventurous activities was patchy.

Guidance was published by HMI (DES, 1989) setting out a framework within which schools might develop a programme for the teaching and learning of physical education. In this booklet precise objectives for seven- and eleven-year-old children were given and it was suggested that they be guided towards a variety of goals. They were encouraged to 'perform', 'copy', 'select', 'invent', 'participate', 'respond' and 'to share' but no mention was made of children beginning to understand the effects of exercise on their bodies. Cross-curricular possibilities were recognised but only links with language and mathematics were mentioned with reference to primary schools.

A NATIONAL CURRICULUM FOR PHYSICAL EDUCATION

For the first time in the history of physical education the 1988 Education Reform Act provided for the establishment of a National Curriculum for England and Wales and by Orders in Council, for Northern Ireland (Education Reform, Northern Ireland Order, 1990). In Northern Ireland the subjects were located within areas of study and in Scotland in the 5–14 curriculum there were five areas of the curriculum incorporating several subjects. In England and Wales core and foundation subjects were designated, physical education being a foundation subject for pupils from 5–16 years. In the primary years the areas of activity for physical education were athletic activities, dance, games, gymnastic activities, outdoor and adventurous activities and swimming. One of the most comprehensive documents (DES and the Welsh Office, 1991) illustrated the impact that high-quality physical education could have on our children and no aspects were left unturned. The guidance was very detailed and issues such as progression, balance and delivery of activities, special educational needs, assessment and cross-curricular matters were stated. Even today it's a 'good read' for anyone designing a curriculum for their school. It was suggested by the authors that athletic activities and outdoor activities could only be pursued in depth by pupils if the basic movements and actions had been laid through dance, games and gymnastics activities. These areas of activity have been at the heart of the primary physical education curriculum in the United Kingdom for years. Children were encouraged to be involved in the process of planning, performing and evaluating their ideas and their performances, changing the emphasis from a 'product' (activity) based curriculum to a process (learning) based curriculum (Murdoch, 2005) and yet the activity areas to be covered were deemed to be statutory. This model related well to other art forms in the primary curriculum

62

such as music, art and drama which involved the processes of composing, making and appreciating. The opportunities for developing and celebrating children's creativity through these processes have been suggested elsewhere. Chedzoy (2009) and Lavin (2008) expanded on approaches and ideas to help foster children's creativity through physical education.

THOUGHT BOX

Take time to find the documents indicated here concerning both the first official National Curriculum and its related guidance. Consider in what ways it may have changed and why. What lessons can be learned from these earlier documents?

The revised National Curriculum (DfEE/QCA, 1999) involved four strands which included: acquiring and developing skills; selecting and applying skills and compositional ideas; evaluating and improving performance; and knowledge and understanding of fitness and health. The level descriptors were central to planning in physical education and Gower (2005) reminded us that these can be broken down into four aspects: a gradual increase in the complexity of the sequence of movement; an improvement in the demonstrated performance qualities; greater independence in the learning context; and a gradual challenge to the level of cognitive skills required through the level descriptions.

Within the last decade with more devolution of power to each of the four countries in the United Kingdom there is more diversity than ever in developments in the National Curriculum which has impacted on the primary physical education curriculum. These authors drew our attention to the different and distinct models of curriculum development and questioned the notion of entitlement and parity in provision of physical education within the United Kingdom. They felt that there would be value in a more coordinated approach by the profession to enable young people throughout the United Kingdom to have an equal chance of high-quality physical education.

Bringing together the developments in the United Kingdom in recent years a brief overview is presented here. In England the National Curriculum for Key Stage 1 and 2 was revised in 2000 requiring teachers at Key Stage 1 to teach dance, games and gymnastics activities and at Key Stage 2 to also teach dance, games and gymnastics activities, plus two areas from swimming and water safety, athletics and outdoor and adventurous activities. The Early Years Foundation Stage (DCSF, 2008) was introduced and included six areas of learning from birth to five years with a focus on learning, playing and interacting. Various programmes have existed to help young children to develop physical literacy and basic movement and manipulative skills such as Leap into Life (Devon County Council, 2005) and in Scotland the Basic Moves programme (Jess, 1999) to enable early years practitioners to lay the foundation for children's later participation in more complex physical education programmes.

63

TOWARDS AN UNCERTAIN FUTURE

In 2009 the review of the primary curriculum by Sir Jim Rose explored a design for planning the primary curriculum. Physical education was located within one of the six areas of learning – Understanding Physical Health and Well-being. However, the new government in 2010 rejected the Rose Review and there will be no change to the English Primary National Curriculum at present, although at the beginning of 2011 the Government launched a consultation process for a review of the National Curriculum in England for 5–16-year-olds.

There are new developments in Wales with a holistic approach to the Foundation Stage for three- to seven-year-olds (Welsh Assembly Government, 2008a) where seven areas of learning are required within the Framework for Children's Learning for three- to seven-year-olds in Wales. This approach to learning emphasises the development key skills: thinking skills, communication, ICT and number to permeate all subjects and areas of learning. Whereas the revised guidance does not include subject areas the language used in the Foundation Phase outcomes for physical development and creative development imply that children will be expected to experience games and athletic activities, gymnastic activities and dance, as well as problem solving in indoor and outdoor spaces. The Key Stage 2 curriculum for physical education includes four strands: health fitness and wellbeing, creative activities, adventurous activities and competitive activities. The flexibility in the Physical Education Order gives schools more freedom to select the activities to suit learners' needs, interests and available resources. In this curriculum model activities may be located in any of the four strands according to their focus (Welsh Assembly Government, 2008b).

In Scotland the Curriculum for Excellence was implemented (Scottish Government, 2010) and, as is the case in Wales, schools have been given more freedom to develop their own curriculum within the framework to take into consideration their learners' needs. There are eight curriculum areas within health and wellbeing, with physical education, physical activity and sport (PEDPAS) being one of the six categories making up this curriculum area. Dance remains in the expressive arts domain. There are three courses of development in physical education which are: movement skills competencies and concepts which involve children 'learning to move' to developing towards 'moving to learn' cooperation and competition and evaluating and appreciating. The main change from previous curriculum guidance is that there is a move away from the emphasis being on the activity which traditionally has been games, gymnastics and dance (HMIE, 2001) towards the needs of the learner. There is also an expectation that children are given a voice and are consulted in terms of their needs and interests.

THOUGHT BOX

Gather together documents from across different countries and compare and contrast their content. What are the similarities and differences between them? What aspects are common to all and what can this tell us about primary physical education?

64

CONCLUSION

In conclusion, whichever curriculum model is adopted, young children need a rich variety of physical experiences and challenges as they grow and develop throughout their primary years. Children need experiences which help them to master fundamental motor skills such as locomotor and manipulative skills and to develop dexterity and confidence in themselves. Once these foundations have been laid through play and structured activities, programmes need to be developed to encourage children to integrate skills into simple phrases and more complex sequences of movement. It is at this stage that more recognisable forms of activity will be introduced so that children have opportunities to take part in activities which involve competing with and outwitting opponents in games activities, developing accurate replication of actions commonly found in gymnastics and dance, developing optimum performance in athletic activity and engaging in creative problem-solving activities. Children need to understand the changes that happen to their bodies and to recognise the value of making wise choices to adopt healthy lifestyles. Through a well structured programme children can learn to work independently and in groups and understand how to manage their responsibilities when working cooperatively or in competition with others. They also need to recognise and value difference and be sensitive to the needs of others. Even from an early age children can be encouraged to realise that learning takes place in physical education and if they listen, watch, think and practise, improvements can be achieved in their physical competence and performance. Their active involvement in planning, and evaluating their own work and that of others should underpin the curriculum. It is also important that cross-curricular links are made explicit by teachers and that children understand the contribution that physical activity can make to their health, fitness and wellbeing. They also need to understand that there is no such thing as being 'good or bad at physical education', and that physical education is a subject area designed to give them exciting and enjoyable experiences to aid them to become more skilful and confident in managing their bodies in a variety of situations. It is also a subject that can help them to know how to take a full and active part in activities that appeal to them outside school hours.

In the following chapters the authors have presented creative and imaginative perspectives on what continue to be common areas within primary physical education curricula, namely the teaching of games, gymnastics, dance, athletic and outdoor and adventurous activities. The contribution of these areas of activity towards promoting children's physical, social, cognitive and affective development is highlighted and innovative approaches to the curriculum are suggested.

REFERENCES

Board of Education (1904) *The Syllabus of Physical Exercises for Schools*, London: HMSO.

Board of Education, (1926) The Health of the School Child, *Annual Report of the Chief Medical Officer*, London: HMSO.

Board of Education (1933) *Syllabus of Physical Training for Schools*, London: HMSO.

Caldecott, S., Warburton, P. and Waring, M. (2006) A survey of time devoted to the preparation of primary and junior school trainee teachers to teach physical education in England, *The British Journal of Physical Education*, 37, 1, 45–48.

Chedzoy, S. (2009) Children, creativity and physical education, in A. Wilson (ed.) *Creativity in Primary Education* (2nd ed), Exeter: Learning Matters, 105–116.

Dent, H.J. (1947) *The Education Act 1944: provisions, possibilities and some problems* (3rd ed), London: University of London Press.

Department for Children, Schools and Families (DCSF) (2008) *Early Years Foundation Stage*, London: HMSO.

Department for Education and Employment/Qualifications and Curriculum Authority (DfEE/QCA), (1999) *Physical Education: the National Curriculum for England*, London: HMSO.

Department for Education (DES) (1978) *Primary education in England, a survey by H.M. Inspectors of Schools*, London: HMSO.

Department for Education (DES), (1989) *Physical Education from 5–16*, London: HMSO.

Department for Education (DES) and the Welsh Office (1991) *Physical education for ages 5–16*, London: HMSO.

Department for Education (DES), (1972) *Movement – Physical Education in the Primary Years*, London: HMSO.

Devon County Council (2005) *Leap into Life*, Exeter, Devon County Council.

Education Reform Order, Northern Ireland (1990) Curriculum and Assessment Department of Education, Northern Ireland.

Gower, K (2005) Planning in Physical Education in S. Capel (ed.) *Learning to teach physical education in the secondary school*, Abingdon: Routledge Falmer.

Her Majesty's Inspectorate of Education (HMIE), (2001) *Improving Physical Education in Primary Schools*.

Jess, M. (1999), *Basic Movements and Movement Concepts*, A Developmental Framework for a Lifetime of Physical Education, Sport and Exercise, Edinburgh, University of Edinburgh.

Johnson, J.C. (1981) Physical training in the army and its influence on British Schools, in D. McNair and N. Parry (eds) *Readings in the History of Physical Education*, Hamburg: Czwalina, pp 95–102.

Laban, R. (1963) *Modern Educational Dance* (2nd ed) London, Macdonald and Evans.

Lavin, J. (ed.) (2008) *Creative approaches to physical education: helping children to achieve their true potential*, Abingdon: Routledge.

Maulden and Redfern (1969) *Games teaching: a new approach for the primary school*, London: MacDonald and Evans Ltd.

McIntosh, P., Dixon, J.G., Munrow, A.D. and Willetts, R.F. (1981) *Landmarks in the History of Physical Education*, London: Routledge and Kegan Paul.

Ministry of Education, (1952) *Moving and Growing*, London: HMSO.

Ministry of Education (1953) *Planning the Programme*, London: HMSO.

Murdoch, E. (2005) NCPE 2000 – where are we so far?, in S. Capel (ed.) *Learning to teach physical education in the secondary school*, Abingdon: Routledge Falmer.

Oslin, J. and Mitchell, S. (2006) Game-centred approaches to teaching physical education, in D. Kirk, D. Macdonald and M. O'Sullivan (eds) *The Handbook of Physical Education*, London, Sage, 627–651.

Scottish Government (2010) *Curriculum for Excellence 3–18*, Edinburgh: Scottish Government.

Smith, D.W. (1974) *Stretching their Bodies – A History of Physical Education*, London: David and Charles, 106–162.

Start Active Stay Active (2011) *A report on physical activity from the four home counties' chief medical officers*, London: Crown Publishers.

Welsh Assembly Government (2008a) *Framework for Children's Learning for 3–7 year olds in Wales*, Cardiff: Department for Children, Education, Lifelong Learning and Skills.

Welsh Assembly Government (2008b) *Making the most of learning, implementing the revised curriculum*, Cardiff: Department for Children, Education, Lifelong Learning and Skills.

Wright (1977) Total health – a jubilee perspective, *British Journal of Physical Education*, 8, 80–81.

CHAPTER SIX

GAMES IN THE PRIMARY SCHOOL

They can't catch so what's the point in teaching them to play a game?

Gavin Ward

INTRODUCTION

Everyone has at some point been involved in playing games. Whether it is playing the full codified sporting version or more impromptu games played in the school play-ground, whatever the format and location, games form an integral part of our sporting culture (Jarvie, 2000). Games retain distinct identities, shaped not only by their rules, equipment and playing surfaces but also by distinctive terminology and metaphoric language (Blanchard, 1995). These game cultures can be mystifying, particularly for those who do not have an undying passion for them, or for those for whom games are a distant, but an all too often painful memory, of wet, cold, wintery days of obliga-tory participation at school. Games can pervade popular culture, with many people considering themselves unofficial experts. Even the most reluctant follower of team games can become an expert when our national sides are playing, particularly in World Cup competitions!

This powerful cultural positioning of games is reflected by their prominence within school curricula. Historically, public schools championed games for their character-building qualities and the adoption of games into the life of all schools, resulted in their own special place on the school timetable (McIntosh, 1980). The strong appeal of games has meant they have often been separated from physical education and taught by school staff and adults, other than those considered to be 'specialists' (Holt, 1989; Mangan, 1981). With the advent of the National Curriculum, games became located under the banner of physical education, however, their powerful allure has remained. Teachers' personal preferences and expertise have reinforced their dominant place on school curricula and have resulted in traditional sporting versions of games becoming a major part of our physical education landscape (Capel, 2007; Green, 2008).

Within the National Curriculum for primary physical education, games have continued to be presented as a medium through which knowledge, understanding and the appli-cation of skills can be learnt. Recent iterations have not demanded the teaching of specific sporting forms of games and this approach is underpinned by the accompanying Qualifications and Curriculum Authority (QCA) Units of Work, which were provided to support primary and secondary teachers in their delivery of the curriculum (QCA, 2000). This more generalist approach to teaching games, however, has been dominated

by a series of professional development programmes, particularly those promoted by National Governing Bodies of Sport, such as the Football Association.

These opportunities for professional development have been created to facilitate the strategic development of a particular sport, focused on the development of technical competence. This undermines the development of a broader understanding and competence of playing games such as that encapsulated by the National Curriculum for physical education (Armour and Evans, 2004; Armour and Yelling, 2004). When combined with the personal preferences and experiences teachers bring to their conception, planning and teaching of games, such professional development programmes serve to compound the dominance of specific games (Ward, 2011). School inspection reports have identified games teaching as a weakness in physical education particularly in respect of fostering an understanding of game play, encapsulated in the second strand of the National Curriculum for physical education; Selecting and Applying Skills, Tactics and Compositional Ideas (Ofsted, 2000; 2005; 2009). By overly focusing on the acquisition of sport-specific skills, rather than developing pupils' understanding of how these skills can be employed tactically, learning within this strand of the National Curriculum has been left to chance. Even when the current trend of employing so called external 'specialists', such as sports coaches, to deliver primary physical education lessons, the focus upon skill acquisition dominates pupils' learning experiences (Griggs, 2007; Griggs, 2010; Ofsted, 2009; Ward, 2011).

Playing games in physical education can be a very enjoyable and empowering experience, however, often game play is taught in ways that alienate and exclude, particularly those who struggle with mastering the various motor skills and tactics they demand (Hastie, 2010). For example, pupils may struggle with mastering sending and receiving, using a pass with their hands. Such difficulties are compounded when these pupils are not provided with sufficient time and space to decide when to use these skills and to execute them effectively. Very often game play in physical education develops into a place for those pupils who are exposed to particular games outside school, such as in specific sports clubs, to demonstrate their physical prowess and dominance over others. If this is allowed to occur, pupils who are not proficient players can cause play to slow and can be the reason why their team give away scoring opportunities. Such pupils can become the focus of blame for losing and this provides ample justification for others to choose not to involve them in the game. When teaching significant contrasts in knowledge, understanding and skills a class of primary school pupils may present, the importance of developing, progressing and differentiating learning experiences in games becomes very real.

When working with primary teachers, I have often found that many have been disillusioned, confused and frustrated with teaching games. Issues raised by staff have centred on how to make games fair and fun for everyone and how to avoid social conflict. The latter can present a very difficult hurdle when teaching activities that demand high levels of social cooperation. Many teachers are reluctant to teach certain games because they do not know all the 'official' rules. Furthermore, when they have taught particular games, teachers have also expressed difficulty in how to make the link teaching particular game skills with supporting and reinforcing their application in competitive game play (Ward, 2011).

In the case of games such as football, hockey and netball, I have lost count of the number of physical education specialists I have heard bemoan their pupils' performances. In such instances, staff have spent ages drilling pupils to pass and keep their distance from each other. Then, when it comes to applying this to a game, the pupils all crowd around the ball and a 'free for all' results and the teacher subsequently resorts to the age-old phrases of 'spread out!' and 'get into space!' This works for all of three seconds and then the game resorts to a smaller version, for example, of a historic game of village 'football'. A game which involves hundreds of people, many of whom never touch the ball and any tactical challenge is often indiscernible.

Issues involved in the teaching of games expose competing conceptualisations of 'sport' and 'physical education' and the very powerful relationships that exist between them (Capel, 2007). A helpful analogy of the sun and earth, used by Morley *et al.* (2007) can explain the symbiotic relationship which exists between these concepts. In their example, the sun is replaced with sport, providing the main source of subject content from which physical education, the earth, draws. This intense relationship is very evident in games teaching, creating and fuelling tension between our two solar concepts. At the extreme of one side of this debate there exists a belief that the aim of physical education should be to develop pupils who are competent at playing sporting versions of games, where afterschool clubs and competitions become a natural progression for this expertise. Such an approach is dominated by teachers' personal immersion in particular game cultures. Individual predispositions to particular sporting versions of games, underpinned by deep pools of specific terminology, frame personal understanding of these games and come to dominate pedagogical practice (Capel, 2007; Penney, 2000). Teachers who have excelled at playing football, for example, may choose to use this game as a curricular activity. They then attempt to reproduce versions of themselves within their class, using physical education lessons as a vehicle to develop the school football team. Such an approach becomes a significant issue when delivering the physical education curriculum, particularly for pupils who do not compare well to such narrow, performance-dominated success criteria (Capel, 2007).

THOUGHT BOX

When deciding which games to use with pupils, which ones do you choose? Is it the games you like or liked as a pupil or is it the games that might best help them to learn about games? How much fact finding have you done to find out about the different games that could be offered, or is it hockey again because 'we've got enough sticks' to do that?

In contrast to this view, there exists a belief that the pedagogical focus of games teaching should be the development of pupils' knowledge and understanding of the interrelationships between skills and tactics, within and across different types of

70

games (Kirk, 2005). Inherent features of such an approach include fostering pupils through the creation of their own games, providing opportunities to develop skills which are needed to play a variety of games and teaching the principles and practice of applying these skills tactically. This requires the radical adaptation of sporting versions of games to meet pupils' specific learning needs. Teaching games in this way has led to the emergence of a number of game-based pedagogic models, examples of these include Teaching Games for Understanding (TGfU) (Bunker and Thorpe, 1982), Tactical Games Model (Griffin and Sheehy, 2004) and the Play Practice Model (Launder, 2001), to name but a few. These approaches to learning provide a direct contrast with more traditional technically based instructional models. In these behaviourist approaches, learning is seen as a direct function of acquiring a particular behaviour, such as a skill or tactic, directly from the teacher. However, in game-based pedagogical models pupils are encouraged, for example, to explore and discuss with their peers which skills and tactics are key to their game play and should thus become a focus for their learning. In order for the teacher to develop a rationale for employing and developing a working command of these various game-based pedagogical models, their different approaches to learning and subject content require analysis.

Games can provide excellent opportunities for pupils to work cooperatively and competitively. They can also aid an understanding of the importance of fair play, decision making, planning and learning through reflection and feedback (Griffin et al., 2004, 2005; Light, 2005). Unfortunately, the terminology, numbers of players, numerous skills and complicated tactics can make games seem dauntingly complex and difficult to teach (Forrest et al., 2006). The aim of this chapter is to demystify games and provide a framework from which the primary school teacher can understand the underlying building blocks of games and how these can be taught progressively to enable all children to enjoy a fundamental part of their national culture.

LEARNING TO PLAY GAMES

Numerous resources exist in the form of lesson plans, 'skills and drills' type coaching books and task cards to support games teaching in physical education. These can be helpful to develop knowledge, such as how to help pupils to practise specific skills for particular games. However, they rarely offer a 'one stop shop' for developing sound pedagogical practice that will enable pupils to benefit from the educational opportunities games can offer. The use of these types of resources as substitutes for lesson plans narrows learning experiences to the acquisition of skills and omits the Selecting and Applying Skills, Tactics strand of the National Curriculum for physical education. Alongside this plethora of coaching resources, sits a similarly large amount of literature which supports the development and application of pedagogic models which can be used to create more holistic learning experiences in games. However, the existence of different pedagogical models of games teaching is an indicator of the debate which exists between supporters of these models as to what is learned and how something is learned in games.

One feature of this debate centres on the importance of a game-specific approach. In such pedagogical models playing specific sporting forms of games is deemed crucial because such an approach believes skills, decisions and tactics form a specific body of fundamental knowledge that is peculiar to that specific game (French and Thomas, 1987). Teaching pupils to play rounders is believed to be a vital part of their games education, for example, because the game demands specific skills, created by its rules and equipment, which are not found in other games. In contrast, the other side of the debate supports the proposition that there is a high level of transfer between some games due to common tactical components (Mitchell and Oslin, 1999; Mitchell et al., 2003). Proponents of this approach seek to make connections, for example, between what pupils learn by playing football and hockey, because these games present the learner with very similar tactical problems.

Pedagogical models also differ in their theoretical approach to learning. When it is believed actions in games are considered incidental, such as when to shoot or when to pass in netball, this is considered an *implicit* approach to learning i.e. there are no 'if-so-then' decisions to be made. In such an approach skills and decisions are learnt through generating experience of the game and result in 'non-verbaliseable' individual decisions (McPherson and Thomas, 1989; Rabb, 2007). However, if actions are taught by isolating a specific situation which demands the use of specific skills an *explicit* learning is adopted. For example, teaching pupils where to position themselves to support another player in order to provide a passing option and exploit the space available, such as standing square and wide in netball. A result of such an approach to teaching will be the ability of pupils to produce a 'verbaliseable' knowledge of specific actions to specific situations (Masters, 2000; Rabb, 2007).

In addition to this difference in how pedagogic models approach learning, they also differ in how the content to be taught is viewed. *Domain-specific* models apply to a specific sporting game form and *domain-general* approaches seek to make connections between different games and different situations. A domain-specific approach focuses on the specificity of an action to a particular situation, for example the use of a particular passing technique, such as the push pass in hockey. If this type of approach is adopted, actions are considered to be only tentatively related to situations in other games. However, in domain-general pedagogical approaches, transferability between skills and tactics is considered possible, despite varying specific situational conditions such as the equipment used or numbers of players involved (Rabb, 2007). For example, if a net game is being played where the aim is to hit an object into spaces left by an opponent, it is believed this tactical expertise can be applied to different games such as rounders and cricket.

Greater clarity can be achieved when these different approaches are viewed as continuums. This can be seen in Figure 6.1. Implicit learning and explicit learning form a line of intentionality of the decision to use particular actions, and domain-general and domain-specific form a line of transferability of actions and decisions reached in games (Rabb, 2007).

Gavin Ward

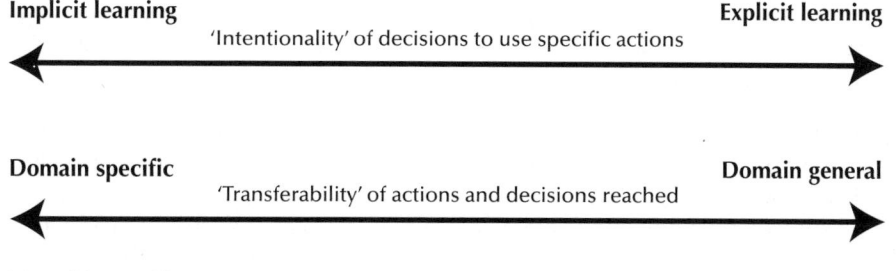

Implicit learning   Explicit learning

'Intentionality' of decisions to use specific actions

Domain specific   Domain general

'Transferability' of actions and decisions reached

Adapted from Rabb, 2007

Figure 6.1 Locating a pedagogical approach to games teaching using the continuums of 'Intentionality' and 'Transferability'

Analysing pedagogical approaches to games in this way enables the teacher to develop a clear rationale for their chosen approach (Rabb, 2007). The predominant pedagogical model for teaching games in the UK was developed by Bunker and Thorpe in 1982 and is called Teaching Games for Understanding (TGfU). Analysing their model using Figure 6.1 reveals that it is based on a *domain-general* and *explicit* approach to learning. The pedagogical premise of TGfU is the belief that there is a high degree of transfer of skills and decisions between games and that particular 'if–so–then' decisions can be taught and employed to aid pupils' application of skills to solve particular tactical problems which games can present. For example, when attempting to move the ball up the court in basketball, if a defender blocks your way and a supporting teammate is in a passable attacking position, then a pass is an appropriate response. In TGfU connections are sought between similar decisions that may have to be made in comparable situations in other games such as basketball, hockey and football.

Game-based pedagogical models such as TGfU are commonly associated with secondary-level physical education, primarily because they have developed predominantly from research based on their use with university and secondary aged pupils. Results of this research and theoretical debates have also been limited to specialist spheres of interest, and with little literature specifically aimed at primary school practitioners. However, by adopting their structure they can provide the primary practitioner with a pedagogical guide to creating learning experiences which include all strands of the National Curriculum for physical education.

DEVELOPING SKILLS AND LEARNING TO PLAY GAMES

It is commonly believed that in order to play games meaningfully pupils must be competent in a number of basic skills and firmly established rationales exist highlighting the importance for primary aged children to learn basic movement patterns. The latter are often referred to as fundamental movement skills (FMS) (Gallahue and Ozmun, 1995; Jess et al., 2004). FMS have been conceptualised and categorised by various authors and providers of professional development within the education and sporting worlds (STEPS Professional Development and Consultancy, 2004; Foreman and Bradshaw, 2009). This has served to cause some confusion over terminology, however, using Gallahue and Donnelly's (2003) definition, FMS broadly can be categorised into three groups: stability, locomotor and manipulation:

As with all concepts and definitions, some skills fit neatly into a category and can be easily recognisable, for example, a four point balance in gymnastics is quite clearly a stability skill. However, a significant number of skills require the mover to be competent in a combination of two or all three FMS. For example, hopping forwards is a locomotor skill as it is about transporting the body, however, it also requires stability because the base of support has been made smaller (one foot). By keeping the centre of gravity as close to this base of support as possible, stability is achieved by moving the body to the side over the hopping leg and by using the non-hopping leg to counterbalance the moving body weight.

It is argued that FMS are vital to becoming proficient in activities which require the application and execution of complex movements and skills, such as those demanded by games activities (Okley and Booth, 2004; van Beurden et al., 2002), hence the rise in professional development opportunities aimed at developing and understanding these categories of FMS. However, if FMS are developed in isolation, the ability to apply them to become proficient in games activities remains limited. This is because an understanding of how to apply these skills in an ever-changing perceptual and decision-making environment created by games, will not have been taught (Belka, 2004; Curtner-Smith, 1996; Capel, 2000). Later in the chapter I highlight some of the core skills required in games activities and link these to the FMS framework provided by Gallahue and Donnelly (2003). The aim of this is to help teachers understand the basic building blocks of these skills and where they may need to focus some specific work if pupils experience difficulty or are limited in their proficiency in some core game skills.

Pupils often long to play a game, however, they are regularly required to practise skills out of their game context, which is less meaningful and can be very uninspiring (Dyson, et al., 2004). In contrast, playing games can be highly motivating and is an important part of a physical education curriculum (Giménez et al., 2009; Griffin et al., 1997; Thorpe et al., 1984). I explain later in this chapter how, even with only basic skill proficiency, pupils can enjoy the pleasure of playing games purposefully. Playing

Table 6.1 Fundamental movement skills

FMS Category	Examples of other similar terminology	Definition
Stability	Balance, body management	Balancing the body in stillness and in motion
Locomotor	Agility	Transporting the body in any direction
Manipulation	Coordination, object control	Controlling implements or objects with the hands or feet e.g. bats, balls, hoops, etc.

Gallahue and Donnelly, 2003

74

games gives pupils significance to their development of skilfulness and this motivation can support continued effort to develop competence and may form the basis of a desire to play games in later life (Hopper et al., 2000). As we have seen, the National Curriculum for physical education at Key Stages 1 and 2 requires teachers to plan and deliver learning experiences where pupils not only have the opportunity to acquire and develop skills, but also the chance to select and apply these skills within the context of game play. Pedagogical approaches to provide such experiences will be examined in the next section.

TEACHING SKILLS AND THEIR APPLICATION TO GAME PLAY

Pedagogical models such as TGfU focus learning through a conceptual approach, underpinned by constructivist learning theories, in particular Situated Learning Theory (Lave and Wenger, 1991). Learning is viewed as a result of both teaching and the context and culture in which the learning activity takes place. Knowledge is considered to be socially constructed and a result of direct involvement in an activity. In the case of games education, the teacher facilitates a community of practice focused upon developing knowledge, understanding and skills as a 'beginner'. As the latter develop, pupils become a fully engaged member of the community of practice (Rovegno and Dolly, 2006).

The potential benefits of increased motivation, transfer of learning and improved decision making, which TGfU purports to develop, are located within a well defined landscape of psychological theories (Oslin and Mitchell, 2007). For example, the Schema Theory of motor learning and Action Systems Theory have been used to explain the conceptual transfer of principles underlying game play by learners, even when constraints such as those imposed by adapted games are imposed (Piggott, 1982; Hanford et al., 1997). Using these theoretical frameworks, the pedagogical effectiveness of game-based approaches in comparison to more traditional technical-based instructional models have been researched. However, evidence of the superiority of one approach over the other, in regard to improving game performance, has been inconclusive (Gréhaigne et al., 2005). These instructional models such as TGfU have attracted international attention and are presented as an innovation in games learning (Griffin et al., 2005; Light, 2005). Nevertheless, recent critical review has highlighted that, far from being a panacea for future games teaching, greater evidence-based research is required. This needs to be grounded in examining how and what students learn while engaged in game-based learning across the psychomotor, cognitive and affective domains (Dyson et al., 2004; Griffin et al., 2005; Pope, 2005; Wright et al., 2005). In an attempt to address this required analysis, Giménez et al. (2009) conclude that the overriding feature of pedagogical interventions such as TGfU are the positive influences they can have on the affective and social areas of learning, in addition to helping pupils to learn to make more effective decisions when playing. Despite the need for further evidence on their effectiveness, these pedagogical approaches place the student at the centre of the learning experience and help develop 'reflective' and 'self-directed' learners. By moving instruction beyond developing technical competence, emphasis is placed on development across psychomotor, cognitive and social learning domains. Their focus on the process of learning, reflecting and evaluating also means they provide excellent opportunities for authentic assessment (Kirk, 2005).

Specifically aimed at primary school teachers, Mauldon and Redfern (1981) proposed a model of teaching games that encourages the use of problem-solving approaches, which utilise game-like situations to emphasise tactical situations. In their approach, rather than presenting skills by their use in specific types of games, they are grouped by their common usage such as sending, receiving and travelling with objects. We see this approach in resources aimed at primary school teachers, such as those produced by the Youth Sport Trust in the 1990s in their 'TOP Play' and 'TOP Games' cards. Mauldon and Redfern (1981) encourage teachers to draw connections between skills and games, promoting awareness of similarities and differences between games by categorising them into groups based on similar rule types. For example, games in which the primary challenge is to hit a target in as few shots as possible, or as accurately as possible with singular attempts, are grouped into a Target Games category.

Using a similar basis of problem solving-based pedagogy, TGfU highlights the motivational aspect for learners of playing games rather than the traditional practising of skills. Bunker and Thorpe (1982) argue that games are the ideal context in which to develop skills and can be conditioned to highlight specific tactical situations. For example, playing a 3 versus 1 keep ball game, to develop an understanding of which skills and tactics are needed to maintain possession. They therefore argue that playing of games should become the main focus of learning. Their framework of games education includes developing an appreciation amongst learners of how rules shape games, for example, rules which demand players invade another team's space to score, as in football and rugby. The promotion of tactical awareness and decision making is encouraged by helping learners to recognise 'cues' to select appropriate responses and predict possible outcomes; for example, recognising key positions to support a fellow player in possession of the ball who is being pressured by an opponent. In direct contrast to technical models of games teaching, the TGfU model supports the view that this tactical application of skills precedes the acquisition and performance competence of specific game skills. This is not to say the model ignores the importance of developing specific technical skills. The significance of being able to perform technical skills proficiently is given meaning through the learner developing an understanding of their tactical importance (Ward and Griggs, 2011).

LIMITATIONS OF GAME-CENTRED INSTRUCTIONAL MODELS

Game-based instructional models such as TGfU demand considerable pedagogical skill and a significant breadth and depth of knowledge and understanding of games (Light and Georgakis, 2005). More specifically these game-based approaches demand the ability to: develop and ask appropriate questions at the appropriate learning moment; determine and select appropriate game forms to develop understanding of the game; and select or create modified games that truly parallel the actual game (Chandler, 1996; Light and Georgakis, 2005; Howarth, 2005; and Turner, 2005). Underlining this pedagogical expertise is the necessity to initiate and manage dialogue between pupils and the teacher and amongst pupils themselves. Advocates for game-centred approaches, argue this managed dialogue is their fundamental strength (Turner, 2005). However, these pedagogical skills and the demand for a broad and deep knowledge and understanding of games, pose particular issues for non-specialist and inexperienced teachers (Forrest *et al.*, 2006). Without such pedagogical knowledge and skills, learning activities and educational dialogue can become closed and shallow, reverting to teacher-centred, behaviourist approaches; thus the pedagogical strength of these instructional models is devalued (Forrest *et al.*, 2006; Gréhaigne *et al.*, 2005; Howarth, 2005; Piltz, 2004). For example, teachers can resort to asking closed questions in discussion because they are unsure of how to manage dialogue to link what the pupils may be doing and saying with what the teacher wants to teach or indeed with what needs to be taught.

However, more fundamentally challenging for the teacher is the ambiguity in the conceptual frameworks that form the basis of these game-centred instructional models. These frameworks form the core content and structure upon which understanding of the relationship between skills, tactics and principles of play is developed. Griffin and Sheehy (2004) present a conceptual framework for problem solving in games which attempts to layer tactical problems with levels of complexity. Rather than pursuing the relationships which can be drawn between the skills that need to be executed to exploit these tactics, the emphasis returns to an instructional focus.

Forrest *et al.* (2006) have created a framework of attacking and defensive principles which attempts to simplify the tactical solutions to games, however, these are not linked to skills. A framework which does attempt to provide a conceptual hierarchy of principles, skills and strategies has been constructed by Butler (1997) and situated within a TGfU conceptual framework by Mandigo *et al.* (2007). In a similar vein, Mitchell *et al.* (2006) present a series of frameworks based upon the tactical problems of scoring and preventing scoring, created by specific game-based sports. Within this structure connections are then made between the tactical problems and 'off-the-ball' movements and 'on-the-ball' skills. Using association football, Russell (1995) presents 'principles of play' in attacking, defending and the transition between these phases of play. O'Leary (2008) attempts to connect these principles of play with examples of appropriate individual skills in basketball.

These various frameworks do aid a conceptual understanding of games activities, tactics and skills. However, an absence of a coherent rationale and breadth across games activities is clearly evident. This is compounded by ambiguous terminology and indistinct relationships between principles, tactics and skills. For example, Mitchell *et al.* (2006) focus on 'tactical problems', while Forrest *et al.* (2006) propose attacking and defending 'principles'. O'Leary (2008) discusses 'principles of play', which is contrasted by Butler (1997), who conceptualises 'main intentions of a game' and 'Offensive and Defensive Strategies'. O' Leary (2008: 19) establishes 'passing ahead' as a principle of play, with the 'appropriate skills' of 'various passes and pivoting', however, a definition of a principle of play is not clearly established and 'passing ahead' could be considered both a tactic and a skill. In the next section of the chapter I will present a series of frameworks which serve to generate clarity out of confusing terminology and describe clear relationships between principles, skills and tactics. This is achieved by examining the specific tactical purpose of skills and their relationship with solving the tactical problems posed by the rules and equipment of games. The tactical solutions to these problems are linked with the overarching strategies that characterise the main purpose of these tactics. However, before we examine this further, it is important to begin to understand how games have been conceptualised by previous editions of the National Curriculum for physical education, as it is on this foundation that my frameworks are based.

UNDERSTANDING AND TEACHING GAMES AT KEY STAGES 1 AND 2

There are numerous ways of categorising games, ask any upper primary school children to create their own categories of games and they will propose all sorts of topologies in which to locate the myriad of games they have played or have seen being played. An agreed approach to classifying games is to look at the tactical problems created by their specific rules, equipment and playing areas (Bunker and Thorpe, 1982; Thorpe et al., 1986). This approach has also been adopted within different versions of the National Curriculum for physical education and provides an excellent basis to aid our understanding and in turn supports our teaching and learning.

The categorisation presented in Figure 6.2 illustrates how games develop in their complexity. Because of their rules, which stipulate a limited number of players and constrain the use of specific actions to achieve simple outcomes, target games demand less tactically sophisticated decisions to be reached. In contrast the rules of invasion games create a field of play which permits a number of players to perform a plethora of skills and as such a significant number of decisions to be reached. Obviously, there are many players of specific games who would argue against such a broad statement about target games, such as proponents of curling or crown green bowling. Despite being target games, these examples are tactically complex. However, such debate is distracting and ignores the broad understanding of games which the National Curriculum has aimed to develop.

The absence of identified specific sports in Figure 6.2, serves to illustrate the adaptability of the game form. This enables the teacher and pupils to create and adapt games, based upon chosen tactical problems, rather than being wedded to the specific sporting versions which are traditionally taught in primary schools. Planning the place of games in the curriculum in this way can serve to develop a greater understanding of the symbiotic relationship between rules, skills and tactics (Hastie, 2010). This is not to say that traditional sporting versions of games should not be included in the curriculum. However, in this pedagogical approach the sporting forms of games serve as a means for achieving specialised performance. For example, rather than attempting to play a 7 versus 7 game, employing all the rules stipulated by the International Rugby Board, smaller adapted games are created. In this instance, a 4 versus 2 tag rugby game can be devised, based upon simple rules, which supports consistent success in appropriate 'rugby' decision making and execution of 'rugby' skills. As pupils develop, the game can be continually modified into a more specialised sport-specific form. This pedagogical approach to teaching games is addressed later in the chapter.

78

Complexity	Game category	Tactical problems	
	Target games e.g. bowls, golf	Choosing a particular action to send an object accurately and consistently at a particular target.	
	Net and wall games e.g. tennis, badminton, squash	**Attacking/scoring**	**Defending**
		Setting up an attack by creating space on the opponent's side of the net Winning the point by sending into space or forcing an error	Limiting the space available by choosing a defensible position Making an opponent defend by setting up an attack by creating space on the opponent's side of the net (attack is a form of defence).
	Striking and fielding games e.g. rounders, cricket, softball	**Attacking/scoring**	**Preventing scoring**
		Sending an object to score as many points as possible	Limiting the points scored and getting batters out
	Invasion games e.g. netball, hockey, football, rugby, basketball	**Attacking/scoring**	**Defending**
		Transporting an object to scoring positions, in the opposition's area, and scoring	Limiting attacking options and regaining possession

Figure 6.2 A categorisation of games based upon their tactical problems

Conceptualising games on the basis of the tactical problems created by the interrelationship between their rules and equipment, enables further examination of each game category. From this analysis we can understand more about their structure and the interplay between skills and tactics. On the basis of the game categories presented in Figure 6.2 and by adapting current conceptual thinking, I have presented in Tables 6.2, 6.3 and 6.4 a set of conceptual frameworks for net and wall, striking and fielding and invasion games. These frameworks are constructed on five key concepts: 'principles of play', 'tactical problems', 'tactical solutions', 'on-the-ball skills' and 'off-the-ball skills'. 'Principles of play' form the overarching strategies which give meaning to the primary purposes of the 'tactical solutions' to the 'tactical problems' posed by a game, irrespective of the strengths and weaknesses of an opponent. 'Tactical problems' are created by the general rules and equipment which distinguish each games category. Rather than focusing on specialised skills relating to sporting versions of games, the 'on-the-ball skills' and 'off-the-ball skills' relate to the key purpose or outcome of the skill. These skills are applied under pressure exerted by opponents, to enact the 'tactical solutions' (den Duyn, 1997; Magill, 2004). 'Off-the-ball skills' are skills which players, not in possession of the ball, can employ such as supporting a teammate who is dribbling the ball in a game of football. 'On-the-ball skills' are techniques which players, in possession of the ball, employ, such as hitting the ball short to avoid a particular fielder in a game of rounders. In defensive phases of play in invasion games, 'on-the-ball skills' also relate to those applied when close to the ball, such as closing down a player and trying to regain possession through a tackle. These frameworks do not claim to be completely inclusive for all the distinct codified versions of invasion, net and wall or striking and fielding games. Instead, they attempt to provide the teacher with a clear and concise overview of the relationship between core skills and their tactical application across the main categories of games. This understanding can then be applied to curricular planning and the creation of learning experiences within games lessons, example of how this can be achieved are presented later in the chapter.

Target games have not been explored in this way because they do not present significant complexity in their overarching structure. It is the specific sporting versions of target games which present difficulty in the execution of the skills need to play them, rather than any major complexity in the relationship between these skills and their associated tactical problems and principles of play. For example in tri-golf, a game specifically devised by the Golf Foundation for primary pupils, the aim is to use one of two clubs to hit a ball as close to a target as possible, or in as few shots as possible. This does not present the teacher or pupil with any major decision making. The difficulty lies in the performance of the specific skills in using the two clubs i.e. putting or chipping.

DEVELOPING FMS THROUGH GAMES ACTIVITIES

The skills employed in playing games can be categorised in a similar manner to the classification of games based upon the tactical problems they present.

Skills can be seen as the tools to solve these tactical problems, and classifying them in this way enables the teacher to make a meaningful connection between skill development and the progressive learning of games; from simple tactical-focused games, to more complex sport-specific game forms. Table 6.2 establishes five core skill categories which can be applied to the tactical problems posed by different games. Each skill category provides examples of recognised game skills, how these relate to the categories of FMS outlined previously in the chapter. Examples are also provided to illustrate how simple forms of these skills can be applied to simple tactical problems. The figure also illustrates how these skills can be developed and refined into more specialised skills and applied to more complex sport-specific game forms.

THOUGHT BOX

Take time to reflect on the figures above and consider what problems you could set pupils in games lessons. If this process is difficult you may wish to think about a particular game to clarify how these problems might work in practice.

Gavin Ward

Table 6.2 Principles of play, tactical problems and skills in net games

Principles of play	Tactical problem / solutions	Off-the-ball/shuttle movements	On-the-ball/shuttle movements
Using depth and/or width to manoeuvre opponent(s)	**Tactical problem:** Scoring		
	Tactical solutions: Setting up an attack by creating space on the opponent's side of the net		Sending the ball/shuttle deep – using court depth Sending the ball/shuttle wide – using court width Sending the ball/shuttle deep and wide – using court depth and width Sending the ball/shuttle short and wide – using court depth and width
	Winning the point	Dominating space in own court by limiting the returning options of the opponent e.g. following deep shots in tennis with a move close to the net	Sending the ball/shuttle into the created space Attacking weakly returned shots e.g. using a smash or volley
	Tactical problem: Preventing scoring	**Off-the-ball/shuttle movements**	**On-the-ball/shuttle movements**
	Tactical solutions: Defending own side of net		Sending the ball/shuttle deep – using court depth Sending the ball/shuttle wide – using court width Sending the ball/shuttle deep and wide – using court depth and width
Using depth and/or width to manoeuvre opponent(s)	Defending against an attack	Recovery to the best position to defend the whole court	Returning the smash/drop shot – getting racket to the ball/shuttle Regaining the attack by: Sending the ball/shuttle deep – using court depth Sending the ball/shuttle wide – using court width Sending the ball/shuttle deep and wide – using court depth and width Sending the ball/shuttle short and wide– using court depth and width

Adapted from Butler, 1997, and Mitchell *et al.*, 2006

Table 6.3 Principles of play, tactical problems and skills in striking and fielding games

Principles of play	Tactical problem: Scoring as many points as possible	Off-the-ball movements Core examples:	On-the-ball skills Core examples:
	Core tactical solutions:		Sending/hitting skills with the intention for it to go in a specific; direction; distance, height/flight:
Sending into space	Sending/hitting an object into the field to make it as difficult as possible for the fielding team to retrieve	Running as quickly as possible to score	▪ throwing overarm/underarm, hitting a stationary object
Scoring	Once sent/hit, deciding whether to attempt to score and/or judging how much could be scored	Judging where the ball is in the field and how quickly it could be retrieved	▪ hitting a moving object
Staying in	Defending the target which the bowler is aiming at (e.g. wickets in cricket)	Keeping track of how quickly the ball is being retrieved	
	Tactical problem: Preventing scoring – Limiting points scored and getting batters out	**Off-the-ball movements** Core examples:	**On-the-ball skills** Core examples:
	Core tactical solutions:	Intercepting sent/hit objects Retrieving the sent/hit object as quickly as possible to limit the number of runs scored	Stopping or catching sent/hit objects which are travelling in the air, along the floor or bouncing; at different: speeds, flight paths and directions
Covering space	Marking the fielding space to limit the sending/hitting options of the batter by covering; width and depth		Sending objects – rolling, throwing; underarm, overarm as accurately and as quickly as possible
Limiting scoring	Choosing which fielding base/wicket/post to return objects to with the intention to: prevent further runs being scored and/or attempt to get the batter out whilst they are running	Backing up team members in case the sent object is sent too short or too far	Bowling with accuracy e.g. using line and length to force the batter to make mistakes or hit towards a particular part of the field
Getting the batter out	If the game involves bowling: delivering the ball to the batter to make it difficult for them to hit and/or to force them to make a mistake; miss the ball, miss-hit the ball, provide an easy catch, block their wickets (LBW cricket)	Covering the fielding base/ wickets/post/base when sent objects are being returned	

Adapted from Butler, 1997, and Mitchell *et al.*, 2006

Table 6.4 Principles of play, tactical problems and skills in invasion games

Principles of play		Tactical problems / Tactical solutions	Off-the-ball skills Core examples:	On-the-ball skills Core examples:
Attacking		**Tactical problems:** Scoring: Transporting the ball to scoring positions and scoring		On-the-ball control Passing
Supporting	Transition (moving from defence to attack)	**Tactical solutions:** Maintaining possession of the ball	Supporting the player in possession in positions which are: ■ passable (low risk of losing possession) ■ attacking (towards opposition's territory or goal)	■ Passing ahead of supporting players ■ Travelling with the ball ■ Drawing in defenders ■ Faking/dummying/turning ■ Sending the ball wide and/or deep to supporting players
Creating space		Moving the ball into attacking/scoring positions	Getting 'free and open' away from defenders: ■ faking ■ dummying ■ turning ■ cutting	■ Travelling with the ball ■ Crossing from wide ■ Passing/travelling between/behind defence ■ Shooting
Penetration and scoring		Attacking the goal and scoring	Moving into space between and behind defenders e.g. timed runs Acting as a target player(s) for player(s) on the ball	
Defending		**Tactical problems:** Preventing scoring: Limiting attacking options and regaining possession		
Denying space and applying pressure	Transition (moving from attack to defence)	**Tactical solutions:** Defending space	■ Covering space as a defensive unit ■ Covering undefended attacking space	■ Marking opponents entering your space ■ Intercepting
		Defending attacking players	■ Delaying/blocking ■ Positioning between the goal and attacker	■ Marking opponents ■ Closing down
		Regaining possession	■ Closing down	■ Intercepting ■ Tackling ■ Clearing the ball away from potential scoring areas
		Defending the goal	■ Positioning to stop a shot ■ Closing down	■ Shot stopping ■ Distributing

Adapted from Butler, 1997; Mitchell *et al.*, 2006; O'Leary, 2008; Russell, 1995

It is important to teach specific sport skills, however, consideration must be made to how pupils can apply these skills to solve tactical problems. Teaching complex skills and playing complex games too early can compound difficulties in performing the skill and applying the skill meaningfully i.e. with tactical significance. It is illogical to teach a complex and difficult skill such as passing and dribbling a hockey ball, if the pupils have yet to master the basics of sending and receiving with more simple equipment and have not grasped and developed consistent proficiency in solving the core tactical problems posed by a basic invasion game. Such problems can lead to significant issues with motivation and social cohesion because pupils can become disheartened with themselves and others when poor skills and decisions cause the game to break down. This highlights the importance of ensuring the correct level of challenge is reached for all pupils, so that games are created or adapted to meet their learning needs. In games teaching it is vital that pupils without certain proficiency in skills, or their tactical application, are not blamed for unsuccessful team play, or that highly competent pupils do not dominate game play or feel they are being held back.

In order to avoid such situations games can be created and adapted to accommodate pupil proficiencies in the execution and application of skills to game play. For example, even the most proficient bowlers, hitters, throwers and catchers can learn to refine, adapt and apply these skills in an increasingly tactical manner, without having to play an officially recognised game of cricket. In a similar vein, pupils who are not so proficient in sending and receiving skills can still learn to develop and apply these skills without having to spend every lesson practising the skills in isolated, drill-like practices. Differentiation of learning activities to accommodate different stages in pupil development can be achieved through the manipulation of the space, task, equipment and people (STEP) dimensions of a game and is commonly known as 'conditioning'. The STEP principle is a framework of differentiation which can be found on teaching resources such as those produced by the Youth Sport Trust in 'TOP Play' and 'TOP Games'. By adjusting the STEP dimensions of a game the complexity of the skills used and the conditions which require the application of these skills can be adjusted to match the level of challenge presented to the learning needs of all pupils (Lambert, 2010). However, it is important to adapt games not only to accommodate different pupil proficiencies in on-the-ball and off-the-ball skills but also to provide a conceptual scaffold which can support pupils in navigating the complex relationships between these skills and the tactical solutions which can be adopted to overcome the tactical problems that games present. The adaptation of the STEP dimensions of the game should thus provide regular and consistent opportunities for pupils to have the space and time to execute the skill, in addition to encouraging them to select appropriate skills to seek successful tactical solutions. How this can be achieved will now be explored.

TEACHING THE RELATIONSHIPS BETWEEN SKILLS AND TACTICAL SOLUTIONS THROUGH CONDITIONED GAMES

Figure 6.3 illustrates a conditioned game, adapted from a 'core task' which can be found in the QCA Unit of Work for striking and fielding games for Year 1 (QCA, 2000). Core tasks can be found on all QCA schemes and provide the teacher with a conditioned

84

Table 6.5 Core game skills

Core on-the-ball and off-the-ball skills	Fundamental Movement Skills and Tactical Significance	Specialisation and Progressive Complexity →
Travelling (off-the-ball) *e.g. running, jumping, turning, sidestepping*	**Locomotor Skills** Essential, but often ignored or untaught. Crucial in enabling pupils to move effectively on their own or as part of a team. Enables the player to move into valuable attacking and defending positions.	**Locomotor Skills** Running, sidestepping, running and jumping, running backwards, running and jumping, running and turning, dodging, running and feinting. *Complex application e.g. running to retrieve an object in a strike/field game, moving to support a player dribbling a ball, getting free from a defender.*
Sending (on-the-ball) *e.g. rolling, throwing, kicking, striking, shooting, passing*	**Combined Manipulative and Locomotor Skills** Key to all games involving the movement of objects. Takes various forms, their complexity depending on the equipment used. The further away from the body the object to be sent is, the more complex and difficult the skill e.g. sending a ball with the hands is less complex than hitting to send a ball in tennis, or shooting a ball with a hockey stick.	**Manipulation** From a stable position, throwing, rolling, striking with a hand, striking with feet, striking with equipment. *e.g. throwing a bean bag to score in a strike/field game, hitting a stationary ball in a strike/field game, hitting a bowled ball such as in rounders or cricket.* **Manipulation and Locomotor** Throwing, rolling, striking, shooting and passing on the move. *Complex application e.g. running and throwing to field a bean bag in a strike/field game, travelling with and shooting to score in an invasion game, dribbling and passing on the move in basketball, hitting a tennis ball into space into an opponent's court, dribbling and passing on the move in hockey.*
Travelling (on-the-ball) *e.g. dribbling with feet or equipment*	**Combined Locomotor and Manipulative Skills** Enable the player to manoeuvre with the object into attacking or away from defending positions.	**Locomotor and Manipulation Skills** Dribbling with hands, dribbling with a small-handled bat/racket, dribbling with feet, dribbling with a long-handled bat/stick. *e.g. dribbling with a basketball, dribbling a football, dribbling with hockey stick and ball.*
Receiving (on-the-ball) *e.g. stopping, blocking, trapping, controlling, catching*	**Combined Manipulative and Locomotor Skills** Enable the player to gain control of an object, from which they can then decide to travel, send or pass, depending on the rules of the game.	**Manipulation** From a stable position, receiving an object which has a consistent flight and speed. *e.g. trapping a ball rolled along the floor with different body parts.* **Manipulation and Locomotor** Moving to catch a ball with varying flight and speed. *Complex application e.g. moving to stop or catch a ball in cricket, moving to catch a ball in netball.*

continued overleaf

Core on-the-ball and off-the-ball skills	Fundamental Movement Skills and Tactical Significance	Specialisation and Progressive Complexity →
Passing (on-the-ball) *e.g. using a chest pass to give the ball to a supporting teammate*	**Combined Manipulative and Locomotor Skills** Often considered a sending skill or a tactical solution to invasion games. Owing to the significance of passing in the majority of games, it has been identified here as a separate core skill. Passing is complex, because it involves two people; one to send and one to receive. When a defender is involved this makes it far more complex and game forms need to be created to allow pupils the time to develop competence in executing the skill. Passing also involves a considerable amount of decision making and games forms need to be created to allow pupils the time to make successful choices and which can be positively and regularly reinforced.	**Manipulation and Locomotor Skills** Sender – sending from stationary or while on the move, accurately to a teammate. Receiver – moving into a position and signalling to indicate being ready to receive. e.g. *Complex application* **Sender** *Choosing to pass a ball which cannot be easily intercepted by a defender, just ahead of a supporting player to enable them to move on to the ball in the direction of the goal. This teammate should be away from any defenders likely to prevent their next attacking move and be positioned to attack the defenders' goal.* e.g. *Complex application* **Receiver** *Choosing to move to a position where the sender can move the ball accurately, without a defender moving between to intercept.*

game through which it is possible to teach both the game skills and their tactical application. Frapwell (2010) supports the use of core tasks within the teaching and learning process as they present the teacher with a valuable strategy to enable their pupils to learn and also engage in a meaningful performance context. This is not to say core tasks are the answer to effective games teaching, rather that they provide a useful illustration of how the STEP dimensions of a game can be manipulated to create sufficient time and space for pupils to select and apply specific skills when they are 'on' and 'off' the ball to achieve particular tactical solutions to the tactical problems the game presents. Conditioned games also demonstrate how altering the STEP dimensions can increase or decrease the level of challenge presented to the players. Examples of how the conditions can be changed to achieve the latter are presented in the bottom section of the game presented in Figure 6.3.

The conditioned game presented in Figure 6.3 involves four pupils; however, the task could be adapted to include more by adding them to the batting team. Teachers may use this game as a focus to develop specific 'on-the-ball' and 'off-the-ball' skills and the application of the skills to find solutions to a tactical problem and thus demonstrate the relevant principles of play. As with all games, it is the tension that is created between opponents which make them an enjoyable challenge. In the case of this

game the tension is between the batting team whose main tactical problem is scoring as many runs as possible. In contrast the main tactical problem for the fielders is to prevent this scoring (see Table 6.2). In this game the principles of play are the same whether throwing a bean bag or hitting a bowled ball. When striking, the aim is for the pupil is to send an object with a selected force and in a selected direction away from fielders (principle of play: sending into space), in order to score as many runs as possible (principle of play: scoring) and to avoid being caught out or stumped out (principle of play: staying in). The decisions made by players on how to achieve this are based upon the position of the fielders, the difficulty of the movement of the ball to hit and if relevant, the position of other batters in the field of play. Even pupils at the basic stage of throwing a bean bag can be introduced and guided through the tactical application of their sending skills.

In order to scaffold learning in this way it is necessary to focus periods of teaching on one particular tactical problem. In the case of the striking and fielding game in Figure 6.3, this will involve focused exploration of scoring or preventing scoring, rather than both at the same time. In a unit of work this might involve the progressive development of one or both, but this will depend on the learning needs of the pupils and the learning time available. This does not mean that the other skills involved in the game and their tactical application should be ignored. Indeed, in order to make the game purposeful, pupils will need to adopt roles in opposition and will be using similar or different skills or be involved in making different decisions. However, the main focus of periods of teaching and lesson design should concentrate on a particular tactical problem.

Designing games to focus learning in this way necessitates 'weighting' or 'conditioning' the game to highlight the chosen skills and tactics. This should provide opportunities, through either phases of play or changes in possession, to reinforce and enable reflection upon good decision making and effective use of these skills to enact appropriate tactical solutions. The latter will play a focal role in the content of the feedback and guidance offered to pupils. However, positive reinforcement of the correct execution of skills and good decisions made by pupils in opposition should still occur, but should not detract from the purpose of the learning activities. It is the aim of the conceptual frameworks presented in Tables 6.2, 6.3 and 6.4 to provide a secure platform from which decisions can be made on how to plan periods of teaching to facilitate this progressive development of FMS and their application within games activities.

In the conditioned game presented in Figure 6.3 the pupils who are striking are required to use their 'on-the-ball' skills of sending and 'off-the-ball' skills of running and judging to solve the tactical problem of scoring as many runs as possible. The fielding team, on the other hand, are required to use their 'off-the-ball' skills of intercepting, retrieving, backing-up and covering and 'on-the-ball' skills of stopping, catching and sending to limit this scoring and get the striking players out. If, for example, we focus on the striking aspect of the game, the variety of sending skills, presented in Table 6.5, can be applied in this game. Taking the most simple to the more complex, specialised skills, pupils could throw a bean bag, kick a stationary ball, hit a stationary ball with their hand, kick a bowled ball, hit a stationary ball with a bat or hit a fed ball (consistent flight and direction) or hit a bowled ball (with the intention of being difficult to hit) with a bat.

Play a cricket-type game of 3 versus 3

- 3 are batters (throwing or striking) and 3 are fielders
- Batters take it in turns – they can be caught or 'stumped' if the fielders return the ball to the fielding base while they are running to score. If this happens the batter takes 1 run off their score, they continue to bat until their 3 scoring chances have been used.
- Aim of the game to score as many runs as possible on your turn and as a team of batters (ball/bean bag must go forward)
- Fielders are to limit the runs by returning the ball/bean bag back to a given point e.g. a hoop where the batter has started
- To encourage fielders to use throwing and catching skills introduce the rule – fielders are not allowed to run with the ball/bean bag

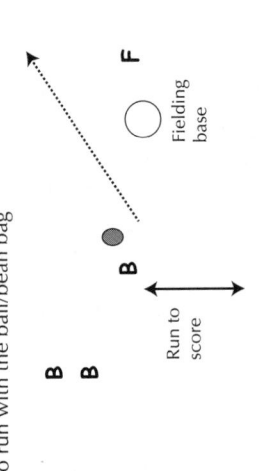

Strike/Field
Core task
to encourage
achievement of
a standard
equivalent to a
LEVEL 1

Level 1 Attainment Target
Acquiring and developing skills

- I can roll a ball underarm
- I can track an object and move inline to collect
- I can throw a ball in a variety of ways depending on the game
- I can throw at an object and hit a target (e.g. a person or hoop) most of the time
- I can catch a bean bag most of the time
- I can catch a medium-sized ball most of the time
- I can stand in a place which makes it difficult for my opposition to score

Selecting and applying skills, tactics, and compositional ideas

- I can choose an appropriate skill within the game I am playing

Evaluating and improving performance

- I can tell you what skill I am using
- I can tell you what somebody else is doing

Knowledge and understanding of health and fitness

- I can tell you what my body feels like when I have been active

---

For children working towards this level use these ideas to simplify the core task to help them progress to Level 1

Easier – Batters
S – Space – provide a bigger space for batter to throw into
T – Task – batters throw rather than strike a ball
E – Equipment – use big soft balls or bean bags
P – People – reduce the game to 1 batter v 2 fielders or even 1 v 1

Easier – Fielders
S – Space – provide a narrower space for batter to throw into
T – Task – batters can only throw using a particular technique e.g. underarm
E – Equipment – use big soft ball or bean bag rather than a tennis ball-sized ball
P – People – increase the fielding team to 4

For children working beyond this level use these ideas to develop the core task to help them progress to Level 2

Harder – batters
S – Space – batters have to throw into a wedge/'v' shape/vector-shaped area
T – Task – batters have to e.g. hit ball out of hand, kick or hit a stationary ball on the floor with a hand or bat
E – Equipment – batters to use smaller ball and batting surface
P – People – increase the game to 4 v 4, put in one of the fielders to feed/bowl batter catches/stops then throws or hits or strikes the feed/bowl directly

Harder – Fielders
S – Space – batters have to throw into a wedge/'v' shape/vector-shaped area
T – Task – fielders cannot run with the ball (have to work together to send the ball to the fielding base)
E – Equipment – use of a smaller lighter ball such as a sponge tennis ball – harder to throw and catch than a bigger-sized ball
P – People – limit the fielders to 2 people

Figure 6.3 Striking and fielding game core task – Level 1

It is important to point out here the significant role the different physical qualities that the surface, playing space and equipment can have on the level of challenge which the game presents to learners. For example, in the case of the game presented in Figure 6.3, if pupils are playing on a surface upon which a ball will roll very quickly, a significant demand is placed upon the fielding team because stopping or moving to limit the distance moved by the ball is more challenging than if a more resistant surface is being used. It is important that these factors are taken into consideration when deciding on how to adjust the 'space, tasks, equipment and people' (STEP) dimensions of the game.

FACILITATING LEARNING THROUGH PRINCIPLES OF PLAY, TACTICAL PROBLEMS AND SOLUTIONS

If we examine our game in Figure 6.3, the teacher could focus upon the principles of play of sending into space and scoring as a central sphere of learning for their unit of work. In this game pupils could be required to use a self-fed bounce and strike of a ball and run between two cones to score. The teacher may support the pupils' learning by offering skill practices which develop: a consistent and reliable self-feed using a bounce, striking the ball from this bounce and striking the ball with the aim of hitting into pre-selected zones to encourage hitting consistently in particular directions and with particular forces. This may then be transferred into the conditioned game presented in Figure 6.3. With the principles of play of sending into space and scoring in mind the teacher could then alter the STEP dimension of the game to adjust the technical and/or tactical challenge. For example, the teacher could ensure the technical execution of sending into space is less technically difficult by allowing pupils to use a large ball or large bat. The tactical ease of sending into space could, for example, be supported by limiting the number of fielders to ensure space clearly exists and it is easy to score by limiting the distance batters are required to run to score. Learning could then be progressed by developing the complexity of the technical requirements to hit the ball into space, such as using a small ball and bat or hitting a bowled ball. In a tactical sense, learning can be progressed by limiting the space batters can hit into by giving them a set zone, increasing the number of fielders and increasing the distance required to score and thus increasing the possibility of being 'stumped out'. This should encourage the batter to judge whether they have hit in sufficient space to ensure they are able to make a run or not. When running to score, learning can also be directed to their decisions on how many runs or points can be scored by correlating their hit with the time it takes to score a run. Learning can also be progressed to focus on the importance of keeping track of the ball being fielded in case fewer or more runs can be scored.

The teacher can also take the game presented in Figure 6.3 to focus learning upon the tactical problem presented to the pupils who are fielding, namely to limit the points scored and try to get the batter out. This is achieved through the tactical solutions of marking the fielding area, choosing the best place to return the ball to and, if the game involves bowling, sending the ball to make it hard to score from and/or attempting to get the batter out (see Table 6.4). The complexity of the skills they use will vary according to the equipment employed, for example if a bean bag is used then the pupils will focus on moving to stop or retrieve the object or catching and throwing the object. If a ball and stumps are being used then they may need to use a specific bowling action, stopping skills and more refined and accurate throwing skills. The tactical application of the skills remains the same, despite the complex demands of the equipment. As with a game focused upon the striking aspect, the STEP dimensions of the game can be similarly altered to ensure learning remains focused upon the fielding aspect of the game. Examples of these adaptations can be seen in Figure 6.3 in the section below the main description of the game. The relevant principles of play, tactical problems and solutions for this game, and possible strategies to develop the game are also presented in Figure 6.3, in addition, questions the teacher might pose to facilitate discussion are presented in Table 6.6.

It is important to point out here that in order to facilitate learning, the side the game is 'weighted' towards (and is the focus of the learning) must be put under appropriate levels of pressure to ensure particular skills and decisions are emphasised. For example, in the case of 'conditioning' the game in Figure 6.6 to teach the fielding aspects of the game, the teacher will need to adjust the sending task of the striker to ensure they challenge the skills and tactical solutions sought by the fielders, if the striker's score is being kept in check through his/or her own mistakes. This can be achieved by increasing the frequency of the striker successfully sending their ball into spaces in the field. If the issue centres on poor judgement by the batter not keeping track of the ball in the field, reducing the distance they have to run can serve to alleviate this problem. If on the other hand, the fielders are not having any success in limiting runs scored or in getting the batter out, the teacher will need to make adjustments to the STEP dimensions to weight the game even more in their favour, such as for example, reducing the space there is available for the batter to send their object into.

It is important, however, that the game remains focused upon the challenge presented to the fielders, which is created by the striker sending into space and running to score. The importance of adjusting the STEP dimensions of the game to accommodate different levels of pupil attainment and ensure learning is being facilitated, demonstrates the need for teachers to take a step back, observe and analyse games whilst the pupils play.

UTILISING THE NATIONAL ATTAINMENT TARGET FOR PHYSICAL EDUCATION TO SUPPORT ASSESSMENT FOR LEARNING

Described by the National Curriculum for physical education, and divided into nine levels, this requires that primary pupils work within Levels 1–3 at Key Stage 1, achieving Level 2 by Year 2 and working within Levels 2–5 at Key Stage 2, achieving Level 4 by Year 6. In order to provide the teacher with how this attainment target may look in games, I have presented within Figure 6.3 'I can' statements for each strand of content identified by the National Curriculum: Acquiring and Developing, Selecting and Applying, Evaluating and Improving and Knowledge of Health and Fitness. These have been created by integrating the Attainment Target Level and the suggested content of the QCA Unit of Work. When combined together they can be used by the teacher

Table 6.6 Core concepts involved in teaching the strike and field game core task for Level 1

Key ingredients to achieve success in this core task	Key teaching points to develop assessment for learning
Principles of play ■ Scoring ■ Sending into space ■ Covering space ■ Limiting scoring **Tactical problem** Scoring as many runs as possible **Solutions** ■ Sending an object and running to score, while the other team retrieves the object. ■ Throwing into space. ■ Throwing far and throwing near – away from the fielders. **Develop the game by asking the pupils to review** ■ Looking for places where the fielders are not standing. ■ Throwing using an underarm or overarm throw – depending on how far they want it to go and how accurate they need to be. ■ Standing sideways when they throw. ■ Running quickly between markers to score runs. ■ Stop running when the ball is returned to the fielding base. **Tactical problem** Preventing scoring: limiting runs scored **Solutions** ■ Retrieving an object quickly to limit the number of runs scored by a batter. ■ Positioning yourself as a member of a team to cover the width of the playing area. ■ Working as a team to retrieve the object. **Progressions to achieve fielding as a team** ■ Initially all the fielders will run to retrieve the ball and this can be a good strategy as throwing and catching can be less efficient! ■ Introduce the rule that no one can run with the object if they have it in their hand. ■ Develop the teamwork approach – one collects, one stands by the fielding base, one stands in between to help get the object to the fielding base. ■ Rotate fielding positions after each batter (especially the middle fielder close to the fielding base). ■ Ask pupils to review how they field the object – accuracy of throw, could they roll it if they are not such a good catcher?	**Questions to develop good batting** ■ 'Where do you want to throw the ball to score as many runs as possible?' ■ 'How are you throwing the ball?' ■ 'Why did you choose to throw the ball that way?' ■ 'Can you point to the best places to throw the ball?' ■ 'How do you know how many runs you have scored?' **Questions to develop good fielding** ■ 'Where do you think are the best places to stand to stop the batter scoring many runs?' ■ 'Are fielders doing a good job, if the batter has scored lots of runs?' ■ 'If someone cannot catch the ball all the time, what can you do to help make sure the ball goes in the fielding base?'

in formative assessment to provide detailed feedback to pupils. However, it is important that these 'I can' statements do not become a tool to merely label pupils with a National Curriculum Level in isolation from the learning experience. The intention of the 'I can' statements is to aid the recognition of pupil progress as it happens (Frapwell, 2010) and should help the teacher to formulate open-ended questions to stimulate pupil discussion, and which should serve to inform continuous and progressive teaching and learning. In order to exemplify how core tasks can be applied to other National Curriculum Attainment Levels, Figure 6.4 and Table 6.7 demonstrate how Level 3 may be connected with a net and wall game and Figure 6.5 and Table 6.8, complete the same process for an invasion game at Level 4. These figures and tables also provide examples of how conditioned games may be adapted to facilitate learning of principles of play drawn from the conceptual frameworks in Tables 6.2, 6.3 and 6.4 for net/wall and invasion games.

BALANCING FAIRNESS, DIFFERENCES IN PUPIL ATTAINMENT AND CREATIVE GAME DESIGN

It is evident that the process of designing a game which creates the conditions that help learners to focus on particular skills, tactical solutions and principles of play is a complex pedagogical challenge. The issue of weighting games in favour of one side through rules or more obviously by having more players on one side can create difficulties in the perceived 'fairness' of such games by pupils. This requires the teacher to balance the maturity and cognitive understanding of pupils with the form of the weighted conditions of their game. In the case of the game in Figure 6.3 which focuses on fielding, 'fairness' is created by ensuring the striking pupil is convinced that they have enough space into which to send their object and that the distance required to run to score is deemed achievable. This issue of weighting games in favour of one side can be a particular focus of debate when designing conditioned invasion games. Many pupils can find it difficult to see the fairness and relevance, for example, of a 3 v 1 invasion game. Possible solutions to these problems can be achieved by making it easier for the sole player to score, such as simply regaining possession.

However, it is also important that the outcomes of attacking or defending tactical solutions in invasion games are discussed with pupils, in particular, the creation of situations on the field where one side is outnumbered by the other. Any search on YouTube of successful attacking play or good defending in invasion games can generate material which demonstrates this aspect of invasion games. Showing such footage to pupils may serve to counter these issues and has the potential to help facilitate an understanding of what the outcomes of tactical solutions can look like in game play. They can also draw attention to the relevance of playing games which focus on particular phases of play.

It is an inherent feature of competitive games that players compete to dominate their opposition by outwitting them. Conditioned games should not attempt to avoid this tension, otherwise their authenticity is lost. Managing fairness and being 'outplayed' are very important pedagogical considerations and through careful manipulation of the

Gavin Ward

To play a 1 v 1 game over a net or cones

- Aim is to score points by hitting a ball over a net or barrier so it passes the opposition
- Use a soft sponge ball – to provide time for the players to catch and hit the ball
- Players catch the ball with hand and racket after on bounce, then self-feed (drop to bounce) and hit over the barrier/net – into space
- Players cannot walk with the ball and must hit from where they catch it
- Ball must bounce in the court to count – ball can only bounce once
- If the ball passes your opponent or your opponent hits the ball out of the court or ball bounces twice before opponent catches it – you score 1 point
- Court area needs to be about 3m x 6m
- Players have to let the ball bounce to catch, except when standing/attacking from the net

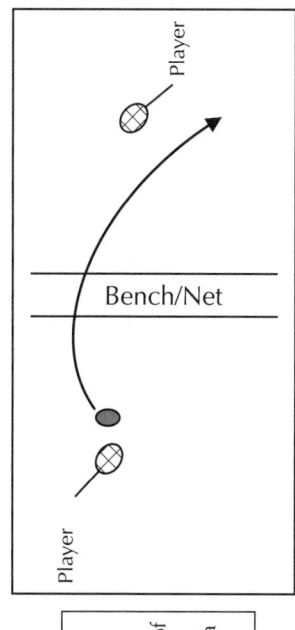

Player

Bench/Net

Player

Net and wall core task to encourage achievement of a standard equivalent to a **LEVEL 3**

Level 3 Attainment Target
Acquiring and developing skills
- I can show control and coordination when I perform skills
- I can hit a ball with a racket
- I can vary the speed and direction of a ball
- I can begin to have a rally with a partner

Selecting and applying skills, tactics, and compositional ideas
- I can choose actions and skills which help me and my team to attack and defend
- I can use my teammates to beat opponents

Evaluating and improving performance
- I can compare what I have done with somebody else's performance and use this understanding to improve my performance

Knowledge and understanding of health and fitness
- I can tell you why warming up is important and why physical activity is good for my health

---

For children working towards this level use these ideas to simplify the core task to help them progress to Level 3

Easier to score and defend
S – Space – make the court wider and or deeper
T – Task – striker can only throw one- or two-handed
E – Equipment – use big soft balls, bean bags, etc.
P – People – reduce the game to 1 v 1 targets to throw/hit into to score

---

For children working beyond this level use these ideas to develop the core task to help them progress to Level 4

Harder to score and defend
S – Space – make the area smaller
T – Task – on receiving the ball the player pats the ball down, lets the ball bounce up then uses their racket to hit the ball straight up, lets the ball bounce again and then hits it into their opponents court – demands timing and control of hitting
E – Equipment – use mini red or green tennis balls (slower bounce than regular tennis balls)
P – People – play 2 v 2 on a bigger court

Figure 6.4 Net and wall game core task – Level 3

Table 6.7 Core concepts involved in teaching the net and wall game core task – Level 3

Key ingredients to achieve success in this core task	Key teaching points to develop assessment for learning

Principle of play
- Using depth and width to manoeuvre opponents.

Tactical solutions
Setting up an attack by creating space on the opponent's side of the net.
Winning the point.
- Looking where your opponent is standing.
- Choosing a space in which to hit the ball.
- Bouncing a ball and hitting with accuracy over a net/central barrier – into space.

Hitting either:
- at the front of the court.
- at the back of the court.

More advanced tactics
- Hitting into the two front corners of the court.
- Hitting into the rear corners of the court.

Recognising when you have:
- hit a good long shot.
- pushed your opponent back.
- done these together – moved closer to the net to catch the ball without it bouncing and returning it quickly into the corners.

Tactical solutions
Defending own side of net.
Defending against an attack.
- Returning to the middle and rear of the court after returning the ball.
- Being ready – feet in line, heels off the floor, shoulder-width apart, hand and racket in front.
- Receiving a ball by letting it bounce – once – catching it using a hand and the racket head.
- Hitting good attacking shots.

Progressions to develop the game
Progress to hitting the ball straight off the bounce, rather than catching it, when the player thinks they can, so long as they maintain their accuracy and hitting for space.

Questions to develop good attacking
- 'How do you score a point?'
- 'What do you look at before you hit the ball?'
- 'Where do you want to hit the ball?'
- 'How do you swing the racket to make sure the ball goes where you want it to?'
- 'How hard do you have to hit the ball?'
- 'How do you know when you have hit a good shot?'
- 'When is it a good time to move towards the net to catch without a bounce?'

Questions to develop good defending
- 'What do you look at when you want to catch the ball?'
- 'How do you stand to be ready to catch the ball?'
- 'Where is the best place to stand on the court to be ready?

End of Key Stage Core Task for Level 4 (Year 6)

- Aim of the game – to invade the opposing team's half and score as many goals as possible
- The game can be based on any invasion game – basketball, netball, football, hockey, rugby – just use the equipment needed for these sports
- Wingers are placed on both sides of the pitch – off the pitch
- Wingers can move up and down the sides of the pitch with or without the ball – they must not go onto the pitch – other players cannot come off the pitch to tackle them
- If a winger is passed to by one team – the winger becomes one of their team and must help attack – they must eventually pass to someone on the team that passed them the ball in the first place – the winger then becomes free again and can be used by any team – the winger is in effect on both teams
- When a player is in possession of the ball they should have a 5 v 3 game on their hands (2 wingers at their disposal)
- The goal can either be marked out – or players can be tasked with catching or stopping the ball over or on the whole back line to score

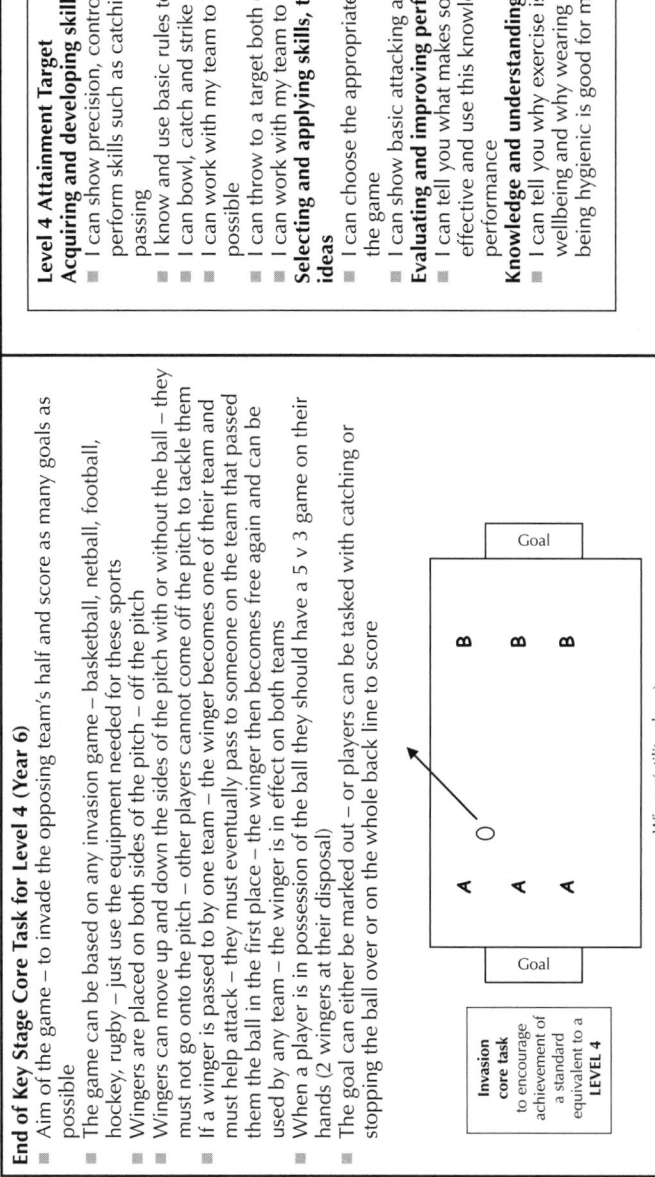

Goal

A   B

A O   B

A   B

Goal

Winger (utility player)

Invasion core task to encourage achievement of a standard equivalent to a **LEVEL 4**

Level 4 Attainment Target

Acquiring and developing skills

- I can show precision, control and fluency when I perform skills such as catching, hitting, throwing and passing
- I know and use basic rules to keep games going
- I can bowl, catch and strike consistently well
- I can work with my team to score as many goals as possible
- I can throw to a target both close and a distance away
- I can work with my team to minimise goals scored

Selecting and applying skills, tactics, and compositional ideas

- I can choose the appropriate skill for different parts of the game
- I can show basic attacking and defending tactics

Evaluating and improving performance

- I can tell you what makes someone's performance effective and use this knowledge to improve my performance

Knowledge and understanding of health and fitness

- I can tell you why exercise is good for my health and wellbeing and why wearing appropriate clothing and being hygienic is good for my health and safety

---

For children working towards this level use these ideas to simplify the core task to help them progress to Level 4

Easier – Attacking

S – Space – increase the size of the pitch – especially the width

T –Task – add in more than 2 goals – or make them wider – or use the whole back line

E – Equipment – base the game on a catch and throw game (netball like)

P – People – reduce the number players in the middle to 4 rather than 6 (2 v 2 + wingers)

For children working beyond this level use these ideas to develop the core task to help them progress to Level 5

Harder – Attacking

S – Space – reduce the size of the pitch

T –Task – allow the winger to be tackled, make a 'two touch rule' – one to control, one to pass

E – Equipment – make the goal smaller – do not allow dribbling

P – People – remove a winger or both wingers

Figure 6.5 Invasion game core task – Level 4

Table 6.8 Core concepts involved in teaching the invasion game core task – Level 4

Key ingredients to achieve success in this core task	*Key teaching points to develop assessment for learning*
The primary focus of this game is attacking **Principles of play** ■ Supporting ■ Creating space **Tactical solutions** Maintaining possession of the ball Moving the ball into attacking/scoring positions Attacking the goal and scoring ■ Consistent and accurate passing ■ Passing to a free player ■ Passing and moving forward ■ Using wingers to help attack – i.e. use of width – by passing to winger – moving forward – receiving back ■ Wingers – moving sideways in line with the ball as a constant passing option	**Questions to develop good attacking** ■ 'What are you looking for when you have the ball?' ■ 'What do you do when you have not got the ball?' ■ 'How can you make sure it is easy for the ball carrier to pass to you?' ■ 'What do you think are attacking positions?' ■ 'When attacking, how can you make it easy for the ball to get to you?' ■ 'If the goal is being marked by a defender, what can you do to try to create an opportunity to score?' Praise good choices made by the **passer** and the **supporting players** (positioning) – both are key to developing good attacking play Encourage thinking of corridors – both supporters and ball carrier: ■ not too long ■ not too short ■ no defender near to block the corridor. If pupils are using long passes to score i.e. looped and high – bring in the rule that the ball must not touch the floor – if so, the pupils have to start the game again.

STEP dimensions of the game this can be achieved. It is important, however, that any changes to the game do not detract from progressing towards and exploring the authenticity of outwitting opponents. Forcing all players to touch the ball during game play in an attempt to include all players, for example, does not constitute authentic game play. It creates an unnecessary layer of decision making, requiring pupils to concentrate on how to ensure all players are involved, rather than seeking a quick and effective tactical solution. Such rules can have the reverse effect to their intended aim, by making pupils with weaker skills the focus of play, rather than full attention being given to the enactment of the tactical solution. For example, if a player with weak skills is unnecessarily thrown a ball because they have to falsely touch it, they are placed under double pressure: from both the opposition and their own team. Any mistake then causes a false delay in play and it is the pupil who makes this mistake that then becomes the weak link in reaching the tactical solution, not the initial play of the opposition. In order to ensure all players progress in their ability to contribute to the tactical solutions it is important that they also have regular opportunities to perform their on-the-ball and off-the-ball skills. This is best achieved by avoiding 'all players must touch the ball' rules and providing a balance of opportunities for progressive technical practices and enabling these skills to be performed in context. Such spaces for technical work might be created in initial lesson stages or as an activity once pupils have played their conditioned game and reflected on their performances.

In the case of designing a fielding game based on the game in Figure 6.3, a solution to ensuring all the fielders have an opportunity to apply their skills and to work together to field the ball is to have a rule that no fielder can run with the ball when it is in their hands. The application of this rule helps minimise the dominant or busy player because one player has to intercept or retrieve the ball, one player needs to cover the fielding base and the other player can either backup the fielding base in the case of an over-throw; alternatively, the player may choose to place themselves in between the fielding base and the retrieving player if the throw is unlikely to reach the fielding base. Such a decision will demand that fielders get to know their strengths and weaknesses and work together to support potential weaknesses through their choice of tactical solutions. Rules such as this also enable the teacher to draw attention to the efficiency of an accu-rate throw rather than running with the ball to the fielding base. It also helps emphasise backing up and covering as tactical solutions, because they need to occur in order to limit scoring and get the batter out.

Adapting the conditions of games can facilitate other pedagogical solutions to teaching groups of pupils with different abilities. When there is a gulf in pupils' devel-opment, grouping pupils to play games with those who have similar ability levels enables the teacher to make efficient and focused adjustments to the STEP dimen-sions of the game. It also enables the teacher to progress learning when groups of pupils are achieving success by increasing the whole challenge of the game, rather than trying to increase the challenge for particular pupils, as would be the case in a mixed-ability game. It might be that in a lesson there are seven or eight games being played, all with slightly different STEP dimensions which meet the learning needs of each group of pupils. However, this does not mean that pupils are learning vastly different skills and tactical solutions. The structure of a conditioned game played in primary school can be exactly the same as one played with a group of Year 11 pupils learning a specialised sporting form of a game. The only difference will be the equipment, specialised techniques and STEP dimensions. The tactical solutions and problems should be exactly the same.

Designing conditioned games which enable the teacher to scaffold the learning in this way requires clear learning objectives and outcomes before the design process commences. This will facilitate easier decisions on an appropriate instructional style. The exploration of relationships between principles of play, tactical problems, tactical solutions and skills presented by the frameworks in Tables 6.2, 6.3 and 6.4 requires a convergent approach. To prevent confusion of the learner, games which demand too many decisions from the learner should be avoided. The creative nature of the game design should focus upon on careful consideration of the STEP dimen-sions of the game in order to create consistent and regular opportunities for learners to have the time and space to select and apply the skills and tactical solutions being explored.

PUPIL-DESIGNED GAMES

Asking pupils to design their own games is a strategy which can engage pupils in creative processes and, in turn, increase pupils' interest and ownership over their own learning (Rovegno and Bandhauer, 1994; Lavin, 2007). This strategy can also help pupils to understand the close relationship between rules, the tactical problems they create and the skills which need to be used to overcome them (Lambert, 2010). Inherent within the process of asking pupils to engage in 'game making' are the requirements for groups of pupils to think critically about their game playing experiences and to work cooperatively to problem solve. However, as Hastie (2010) emphasises, there is a great danger in simply providing equipment for pupils and asking them to create a game. Without careful structuring of the game creation process, extremely valuable learning experiences can be lost (Rovegno and Bandhauer, 1994). Almond (1986) believes that the teacher's role is vital in creating and guiding pupils through the creative process. He argues this requires the teacher to learn to tread the line between 'observing', to allow pupils time to create and trial, and 'intervening', to assist pupils in finding workable solutions to their 'games making' problems. In fulfilling this delicate role the teacher becomes a facilitator, consultant, mentor and learning resource.

According to Hastie (2010), effective 'games making' should be based on the progressive process of: designing, trialling, refining, presenting and allowing others to play and evaluate the created game. This process requires the teacher to highlight the two fundamental ingredients to enjoyable games; first, the game must present opportunities for players to develop their 'skilfulness' to overcome the tactical problems imposed by the rules and second, that scoring should be directly related to skilfulness and not luck. He argues in order for the pupils to design games which will support these qualities, pupils need to be given the following framework to support their game design. The game must:

- Contribute to skill development
- Be safe
- Include, not eliminate players
- Require high participation
- Be structured so all players are challenged and have consistent opportunities to be successful.

(Hastie, 2010: 6)

Lavin (2007) suggests the use of cards which establish the initial problem of creating a game, however, also provide children with a structure within which they can work, such as the identification of particular equipment, skills or tactics which have to be employed within the game. Engaging in such a pedagogical approach to games teaching is challenging and requires the teacher to be knowledgeable about different categories of games. In recognition of this, Hastie (2010) advises teachers to start with simple 'running and tagging' games or target games, and as confidence and experience grows the teacher can venture with encouraging pupils to create more complex games (for a very useful and comprehensive guide to 'game making' see Hastie, 2010).

Gavin Ward

PLANNING THE TEACHING OF GAMES ACROSS KEY STAGES 1 AND 2

Knowledgeable and skilful game play stems not only from careful game design but also considered curricular design. Primary school physical education curricula should aim to spiral skill learning so that pupils regularly revisit the technical aspects of fundamental movement skills. This entails designing routes of learning which allow pupils to regularly review and develop their technical execution of skills alongside opportunities to explore their decisions to select and apply these skills. This aspect of learning should fall at the centre of the provision of a variety of different movement contexts, which demand particular kinds of decisions and skilled movement.

We have seen in Figure 6.6 that games vary in their complexity and this is predominately determined by their rules which create particular tactical problems. Some games demand the simple application of skills to overcome these problems, whereas other games demand more complex decision making. Target games present a very simple tactical problem to the player, which, depending on the rules of the game, can demand the performance of very easy or very difficult skills. For example, throwing the ball into a hoop from a cone two metres away, presents much less difficulty in skill performance than playing a hole in tri-golf. However, when the complexity of net and wall, striking and fielding, and invasion games are examined, a different level of difficulty arises, which focuses around their respective principles of play.

A comparison of the frameworks presented in Tables 6.2, 6.3 and 6.4 demonstrates that there is a distinct difference between the number and complexity of principles of play, tactical problems and the respective on-the-ball and off-the-ball skills. Net and wall games require players to understand and enact a simple and small number of principles of play, while invasion games demand players to apply more complex combinations of skills to solve more difficult tactical problems and thus enact more involved principles of play. Striking and fielding games occupy the middle ground of complexity between invasion and net and wall games. It is very important to emphasise here, that any game can be made complex by creating rules which demand players to use sophisticated skills. This can be misleading for both the learner and teacher.

As we have seen from the analysis of game-based pedagogical models, the planning of learning experiences in games requires a balance to be reached between developing the technical competence of pupils to perform a range of complex skills and developing the ability of pupils to develop a holistic and coherent understanding of games. Overtly focusing on the expert performance of particular skills in order to play certain games prevents those learners unable to perform these skills from learning about the relationship between principles, tactics and skills, within and between categories of games. Therefore, by employing principles of play as a conceptual approach to planning learning, a progressive and holistic understanding of these aspects of games education can be achieved. Using hierarchical levels of complexity for the different categories of games presented in Figure 6.2, I have constructed a suggested overview of how to plan for learning across Key Stages 1 and 2 in Figure 6.6. This identifies when particular categories of games may be introduced and developed. It does not represent a definitive guide to curricular time phasing and apportioning of lesson time for each category of game. It merely serves as an illustration of how careful planning is required to take into consideration game complexities and thus, achieve a balanced games curriculum. Obviously, local school-based operational logistics, such as time, equipment and available work spaces need to be considered. However, decisions about learning in games must be based upon the learning needs of the pupils and a thorough rationale, such as the conceptual approach discussed, rather than learning being determined by individual teacher preferences towards particular sporting versions of games.

As can be seen in Figure 6.6, the simplicity of target games lends them to the first game category to be studied. Net and wall games are introduced slightly later at Year 1. Both remain a consistent feature of the curriculum overview, allowing time for 'revisiting' with the progressive development of more complex hitting skills and the introduction of more demanding playing areas. Striking and fielding games appear towards the end of Key Stage 1 and occupy a prominent role at the beginning of Key Stage 2, this presents the opportunity for pupils to apply their accurate sending skills and become familiar with key principles of play and tactics. This also provides further curriculum space for pupils to continue to develop their understanding, gradual application of more difficult skills and the inclusion of more players.

Owing to their complexity, the time allotted to invasion games grows more significant as Key Stage 2 progresses, occupying a key role in Years 5 and 6. This also allows pupils to develop their ability to cope with working cooperatively and competitively within small teams. Games making is a consistent feature across the curriculum and can be integrated into games learning, providing the opportunity to reinforce particular relationships between rules, tactical problems and skills.

Game category	Foundation Stage	Key Stage 1		Key Stage 2			
	Reception	Year 1	Year 2	Year 3	Year 4	Year 5	Year 6
Games making				────	────	━━━━	────
Target games	━━━━	━━━━	━━━━				
Striking and fielding games		━━━━	━━━━	━━━━	━━━━	━━━━	━━━━
Net/wall games		━━━━	────	────	────	────	────
Invasion games				━━━━	━━━━	━━━━	━━━━

Line thickness corresponds to amount of time dedicated to each game category; the thicker the line the more time is allocated.

Adapted from Doherty and Brennan, 2007

Figure 6.6 Suggested phased introduction of games in Key Stages 1 and 2

Gavin Ward

CONCLUSION

This chapter has introduced the following concepts which aim to provide a helpful rationale for the teaching of games in the primary school:

1   Tactical game-based pedagogical models which can be employed to teach games.
2   A categorisation of games based upon the tactical problems created by their specific rules, equipment and playing areas: target, net/wall, strike/field, invasion games (Figure 6.2).
3   On the basis of this categorisation of games, conceptual frameworks have been presented which utilise consistent terminology and core concepts to provide the teacher with an overview of the core principle(s) of play, tactical problems and solutions, on-the-ball and off-the-ball skills, demanded by each game category (Tables 6.2, 6.3 and 6.4).
4   Five core skill categories which can be applied to the tactical problems posed by different games (Table 6.5). For each category examples have been presented of recognised game skills and how these relate to the categories of fundamental movement skills, which in turn underpin all movement in physical education. Examples are also presented which illustrate how simple forms of these skills can be applied to simple tactical problems. In addition further examples of how these skills can be developed and refined into more specialised skills and applied to more complex sport-specific game forms are provided (Table 6.5).
5   Conditioned games based upon the adaptation of the STEP dimensions to create opportunities to scaffold learning about the relationships between principles of play, tactical problems, tactical solutions and on-the-ball and off-the-ball skills. Examples of basic forms of conditioned games which can be adapted for use across Key Stages 1, 2 and 3 are presented (Figures 6.3, 6.4, 6.5 and Tables 6.6, 6.7 and 6.8). These identify:
    ■ How the game is played – key rules and processes.
    ■ How the game can be adapted to increase or decrease the level of challenge.
    ■ 'I can' statements which map with the National Attainment Target for physical education and the QCA units of work for games at Key Stages 1 and 2, and describe how each level relates to learning in games.
    ■ Core concepts involved in playing the game, including examples of open-ended questions to help promote reflection and evaluation through pupil-focused discussion.
6   Weighting games in favour of one side of the conditioned game to focus learning and provide opportunities through either phases of play or changes in possession, to reinforce and facilitate reflection upon good decision making and effective use of skills to enact appropriate tactical solutions.
7   Planning a games curriculum across Key Stages 1 and 2 based upon a conceptual model of complexity comprised of: principles of play, tactical problems, on-the-ball and off-the-ball skills (Figure 6.6).

The challenge now remains to demonstrate how these concepts and content knowledge may be linked to provide progressive and differentiated learning experiences.

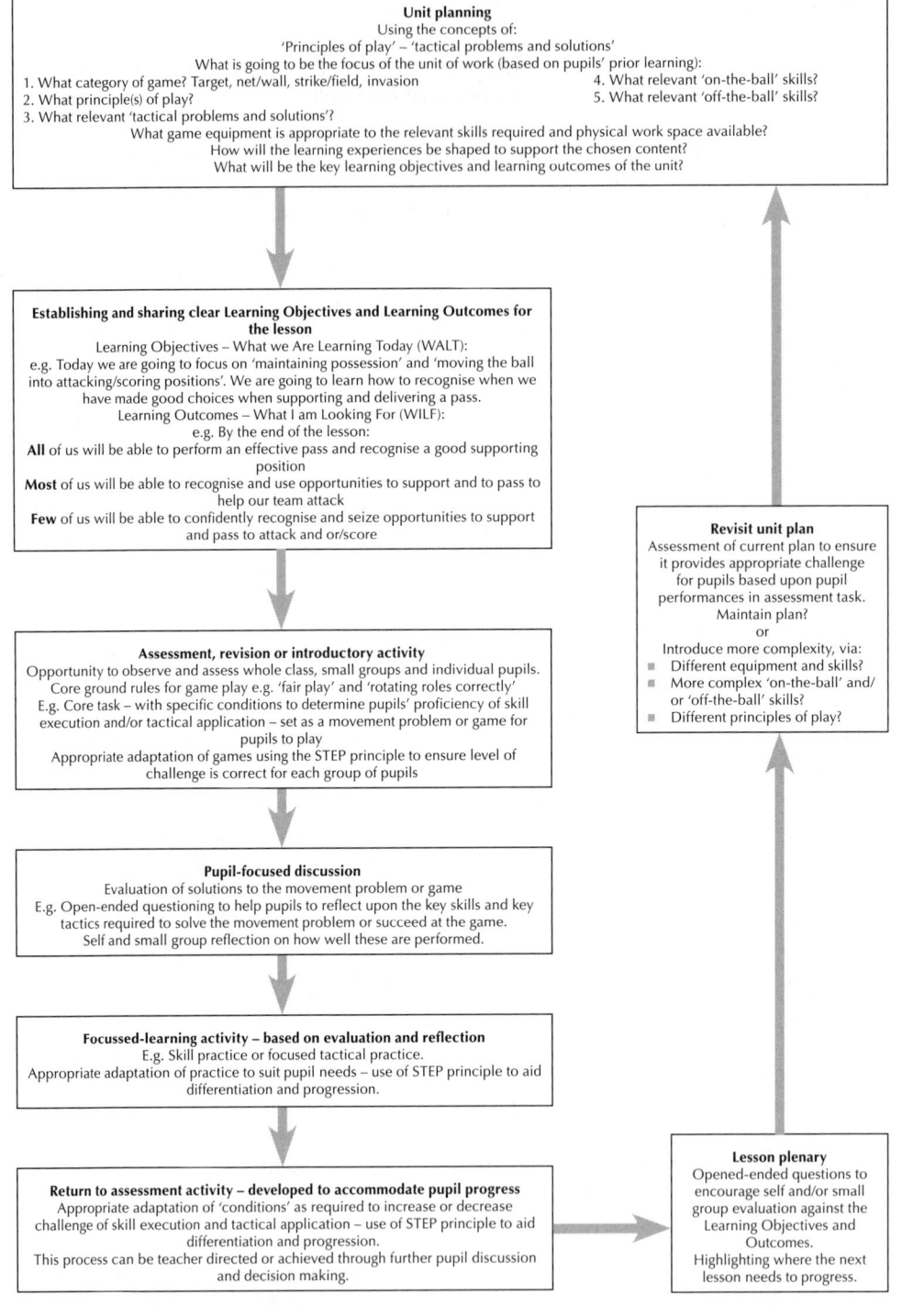

Unit planning
Using the concepts of:
'Principles of play' – 'tactical problems and solutions'
What is going to be the focus of the unit of work (based on pupils' prior learning):
1. What category of game? Target, net/wall, strike/field, invasion   4. What relevant 'on-the-ball' skills?
2. What principle(s) of play?   5. What relevant 'off-the-ball' skills?
3. What relevant 'tactical problems and solutions'?
What game equipment is appropriate to the relevant skills required and physical work space available?
How will the learning experiences be shaped to support the chosen content?
What will be the key learning objectives and learning outcomes of the unit?

Establishing and sharing clear Learning Objectives and Learning Outcomes for the lesson
Learning Objectives – What we Are Learning Today (WALT):
e.g. Today we are going to focus on 'maintaining possession' and 'moving the ball into attacking/scoring positions'. We are going to learn how to recognise when we have made good choices when supporting and delivering a pass.
Learning Outcomes – What I am Looking For (WILF):
e.g. By the end of the lesson:
All of us will be able to perform an effective pass and recognise a good supporting position
Most of us will be able to recognise and use opportunities to support and to pass to help our team attack
Few of us will be able to confidently recognise and seize opportunities to support and pass to attack and or/score

Assessment, revision or introductory activity
Opportunity to observe and assess whole class, small groups and individual pupils.
Core ground rules for game play e.g. 'fair play' and 'rotating roles correctly'
E.g. Core task – with specific conditions to determine pupils' proficiency of skill execution and/or tactical application – set as a movement problem or game for pupils to play
Appropriate adaptation of games using the STEP principle to ensure level of challenge is correct for each group of pupils

Pupil-focused discussion
Evaluation of solutions to the movement problem or game
E.g. Open-ended questioning to help pupils to reflect upon the key skills and key tactics required to solve the movement problem or succeed at the game.
Self and small group reflection on how well these are performed.

Focussed-learning activity – based on evaluation and reflection
E.g. Skill practice or focused tactical practice.
Appropriate adaptation of practice to suit pupil needs – use of STEP principle to aid differentiation and progression.

Return to assessment activity – developed to accommodate pupil progress
Appropriate adaptation of 'conditions' as required to increase or decrease challenge of skill execution and tactical application – use of STEP principle to aid differentiation and progression.
This process can be teacher directed or achieved through further pupil discussion and decision making.

Revisit unit plan
Assessment of current plan to ensure it provides appropriate challenge for pupils based upon pupil performances in assessment task.
Maintain plan?
or
Introduce more complexity, via:
■ Different equipment and skills?
■ More complex 'on-the-ball' and/ or 'off-the-ball' skills?
■ Different principles of play?

Lesson plenary
Opened-ended questions to encourage self and/or small group evaluation against the Learning Objectives and Outcomes.
Highlighting where the next lesson needs to progress.

Figure 6.7 A suggested pedagogical model for teaching games at Key Stages 1 and 2

Gavin Ward

Figure 6.7 presents how this can be achieved through: initial unit planning, presentation and sharing of learning objectives and learning outcomes, assessment and revision of prior learning, pupil reflection and evaluation, focused skill and/or tactical practice, revisiting of the initial learning activity, lesson plenary and finally a re-evaluation of the unit planning. This model follows a similar format to the game-question-reflect-practice-game process proposed by Pill (2007). Such an approach encourages teachers to move their thinking from a technical-based model of teaching games to one which allies itself closer to pedagogical models such as TGfU. Teaching games in this way requires the teacher to create learning experiences that enable pupils to understand and enact the relationships between skills, tactics and overarching principles of play. This is dependent upon the teacher having a clear understanding of what is to be taught in the form of learning objectives and allowing pupils to know what achieving these objectives will look like, in the form of success criteria or learning outcomes. These learning objectives and outcomes determine the choice and sequencing of learning activities. They will also drive the shaping of pupils' discussion through the effective use of open-ended questioning that enables pupils to reflect upon their execution and application of skills in game contexts. As Giménez et al. (2010) have discovered, pedagogic approaches such as the model presented are very influential in helping pupils to learn to make effective decisions and develop a greater understanding of game play. More fundamentally, allowing pupils to play games, if taught successfully, is both motivating and socially stimulating. It is has been the aim of this chapter to enable the teacher to create such learning experiences.

KEY READINGS

What this chapter reveals is the highly complex nature of the games environment. Ward, G. and Griggs, G. (2011) Principles of play: a proposed framework towards a holistic overview of games in primary physical education, *Education 3–13*, 39, 5, 499–516 http://dx.doi.org/10.1080/03004279.2010.480945 will provide a clear overview of this landscape. Furthermore, to understand how games might be developed in practice at this level, see Mitchell, S., Oslin, J. and Griffin, L. (2003) *Sport foundations for elementary physical education: A tactical games approach.* Champaign, Il: Human Kinetics.

REFERENCES

Almond, L. (1986) Primary and secondary rules in games, in R. Thorpe, D. Bunker and L. Almond (eds) *Rethinking games teaching*, 73–74, Loughborough: University of Technology.

Armour, K.M. and Evans, J. (2004) *Continuing professional development: provision for physical education teachers*, London: Economic and Social Research Council.

Armour, K. and Yelling, M. (2004) Continuing professional development for experienced physical education teachers: towards effective provision, *Sport Education and Society*, 9, 1, 95–114.

Belka, D. (2004) Substituting developmental for traditional games in elementary physical education, *Teaching Elementary Physical Education*, 15, 4, 21–24.

Blanchard, K. (1995) *The anthropology of sport: An introduction*, New York: Bergin Garvey.

Bunker, D. and Thorpe, R. (1982) A model for the teaching of games in the secondary school, *Bulletin of Physical Education*, 18, 1, 5–8.

Butler, J. (1997) How would Socrates teach games? A constructivist approach, *Journal of Physical Education, Recreation and Dance*, 68, 9, 42–47.

Capel, S. (2000) Approaches to teaching games, in S. Capel and S. Piotrowski (eds) *Issues in Physical Education*, London: RoutledgeFalmer.

Capel, S. (2007) Moving beyond physical education subject knowledge to develop knowledgeable teachers of the subject, *Curriculum Journal*, 18, 4, 493–507.

Chandler, T. (1996) Reflections and further questions (teaching games for understanding method), *The Journal of Physical Education, Recreation and Dance*, 67, 4, 49–53.

Curtner-Smith, M. (1996) Teaching for understanding: Using games invention with elementary children, *The Journal of Physical Education, Recreation and Dance*, 67, 24–28.

den Duyn, N. (1997) *Game sense: Developing thinking players*, Canberra: Australian Sports Commission.

Dyson, B., Griffin, L. and Hastie, P. (2004) Sport education, tactical games, and cooperative learning: theoretical and pedagogical considerations, *Quest*, 56, 226–240.

Frapwell, A. (2010) Assessment in physical education: Fit for purpose? We've got an APP for that! *Physical Education Matters*, 5, 3, 13–18.

Foreman, G. and Bradshaw, A. (2009) *An introduction to the FUNdamentals of movement*, Leeds: SportsCoach UK.

Forrest, G., Webb, P. and Pearson, P. (2006) Games for understanding in pre service teacher education: A 'Game for Outcome' approach for enhanced understanding of games, Conference proceedings for the Asia Pacific Conference on Teaching Sport and Physical Education for Understanding, University of Sydney 14–15 December.

French, K. and Thomas, J. (1987) The relationship of knowledge development to children's basketball performance, *Journal of Sport Psychology*, 9, 15–32.

Gallahue, D. and Donnelly, F. (2003) *Developmental physical education for all children* (4th ed), Champaign: Human Kinetics.

Gallahue, D. and Ozmun, J. (1995) *Understanding motor development: Infants, children, adolescents, adults* (6th ed), Madison, WI: Brown and Benchmark.

Giménez, A.M., Valenzuela, A.V. and Casey, A. (2009) What are we being told about how to teach games? A three-dimensional analysis of comparative research into different instructional studies in physical education and school sports, Revista Internacional de Ciencias del Deporte, 6, 18, 37–56.

Green, K. (2008) *Understanding Physical Education,* London: Sage Publications.

Gréhaigne, J., Richard, J. and Griffin, L. (2005) *Teaching and learning team sports and games,* New York: RoutledgeFalmer.

Griffin, L., Mitchell, S. and Oslin, J. (1997) *Teaching sports concepts and skills: A tactical games approach*, Illinois: Human Kinetics.

Griffin, L. and Sheehy, D. (2004) Using the tactical games model to develop problem-solvers in physical education, in J. Wright, D. Macdonald and Burrows, L. (eds) *Critical inquiry and problem-solving in physical education*, London: Routledge, 33–48.

Griffin, L., Brooker, R. and Patton, K. (2005) Working towards legitimacy: two decades of teaching games for understanding, *Physical Education and Sport Pedagogy,* 10, 3, 213–223.

Griggs, G. (2007) Physical education: primary matters, secondary importance, *Education 3–13*, 35, 1, 59–69.

104

Griggs, G. (2010) For sale – primary physical education, £20 per hour or nearest offer, *Education 3–13*, 38, 1, 39–46.

Hanford, C., Davids, K., Bennet, S. and Button, C. (1997) Skill acquisition in sport: Some applications of an evolving practice ecology, *Journal of Teaching in Physical Education*, 20, 55–77.

Hastie, P. (2010) *Student-designed games: Strategies for promoting creativity, co-operation and skill development*, Champaign: Human Kinetics.

Holt, R. (1989) *Sport and the British – A modern history*, Oxford: Oxford University Press.

Hopper, B. Grey, J. and Maude, P. (2000) *Teaching physical education in the primary school*, London: RoutledgeFalmer.

Howarth, K. (2005) Introducing the teaching games for understanding model in teacher education programmes, in L. Griffin, and J. Butler (eds) *Teaching Games for Understanding. Theory, Research and Practice*, 91–105, Illinois: Human Kinetics.

Jarvie, G. (2000) *Sport, culture and society: An introduction*, Abingdon: Routledge.

Jess, M., Dewar, K., and G. Fraser (2004) Basic moves: Developing a foundation for lifelong physical activity, *The British Journal of Teaching Physical Education*, 35, 2, 23–27.

Kirk, D. (2005) Model based teaching and assessment in physical education: The Tactical Games Model, in Green, K. and Hardman, K. (eds) *Physical Education: Essential Issues*, London: Sage.

Lambert, J. (2010) Learning and teaching through games activities, in G. Stidder and S. Hayes (eds) *The really useful physical education book: Learning and teaching across the 7–14 age range*, London: Routledge.

Launder, A.G. (2001) *Play practice. The games approach to teaching and coaching sports*, Champaign, IL: Human Kinetics.

Lave, J. and Wenger, E. (1991) *Situated learning: Legitimate peripheral participation,* Cambridge: Cambridge University Press.

Lavin, J. (2007) The creative approach to teaching games in key stage three and four: the forgotten aspect of physical education, *Physical Education Matters*, 2, 4, 20–23.

Light, R. (2005) An international perspective on teaching games for understanding, *Physical Education and Sport Pedagogy*, 10, 3, 211–212.

Light, R. and Georgakis, S. (2005) Integrating theory and practice in teacher education: The impact of a game sense unit on female pre-service primary teachers' attitudes towards teaching physical education, *Journal of Physical Education New Zealand*, 38, 1, 67–80.

Magill, R. (2004) *Motor learning and control: Concepts and applications* (7th ed), Boston: McGraw-Hill.

McIntosh, P. (1980) The curriculum of physical education: an historical perspective, in J. Kane, (ed.) *Curriculum development in physical education*, London: Crosby Lockwood Staples.

Mandigo, J., Butler, J. and Hopper, T. (2007) What is teaching games for understanding? A Canadian perspective, *Physical Education and Health Journal*, 73, 2, 14–20.

Mangan, J. (1981) *Athleticism in the Victorian and Edwardian public school*, Cambridge: Cambridge University Press.

Mauldon, E. and Redfern, H. (1981) *Games teaching: An approach for the primary school*, Plymouth: Macdonald and Evans.

Masters, R. (2000) Theoretical aspects of implicit learning in sports, *International Journal of Sport Psychology*, 31, 530–541.

McPherson, S. and Thomas, J. (1989) Relation of knowledge and performance in boys' tennis: age and expertise, *Journal of Experimental Child Psychology*, 48, 190–211.

Mitchell, S. and Oslin, J. (1999) An investigation of tactical transfer in net games, *European Journal of Physical Education*, 11, 3, 8–11.

Mitchell, S., Oslin, J. and Griffin, L. (2006) *Teaching sport concepts and skills: a tactical games approach*, Leeds: Human Kinetics.

Mitchell, S., Oslin, J. and Griffin, L. (2003) *Sport foundations for elementary physical education: A tactical games approach*. Champaign, Il: Human Kinetics.

Morley, D., Tremere, R. and Fitzsimmons, T. (2007) *Talent development in physical education and sport CPD 2007 module*, Loughborough: Youth Sport Trust

Okley, A. and Booth, M. (2004) Mastery of fundamental movement skills among children in New South Wales: Prevalence and sociodemographic distribution, *Journal of Science and Medicine in Sport*, 7, 3, 358–72.

Office for Standards in Education (Ofsted) (2000) *Teaching of physical education in primary schools*, London: HMSO.

Office for Standards in Education (Ofsted) (2005) *Physical education in primary schools*, London: HMSO.

Office for Standards in Education (Ofsted) (2009) *Physical education in schools: 2005/2008 working towards 2012 and beyond*, London: HMSO.

O'Leary, N. (2008) Teaching games for understanding in learning to outwit opponents, *Physical Education Matters*, 3, 4, 18–20.

Oslin, J. and Mitchell, S. (2007) Game-centred approaches to teaching physical education, in D. Kirk, D. Macdonald and M. O'Sullivan (eds) *The handbook of physical education*, London: Sage Publications, 627–651.

Penney, D. (2000) Physical Education, Sporting Excellence and Educational Excellence, *European Physical Education Review*, 6, 2, 135–150.

Piggott, B. (1982) A psychological basis for new trends in games teaching, *Bulletin of Physical Education*, 18, 1, 17–22.

Pill, S. (2007) Teaching games for understanding, *Sports Coach*, 29, 2, 27–29.

Piltz, W. (2004) *Reading the game—A key component of effective instruction in teaching and coaching*. Paper presented at the 2nd International Conference: Teaching Sport and Physical Education for Understanding, Melbourne, 11–14 December.

Pope, C. (2005) Once more with feeling: affect and playing the TGfU model, *Physical Education and Sport Pedagogy*, 10, 3, 271–286.

QCA (2000) *A scheme of work for Key Stages 1 and 2*, London: Department for Education and Skills.

Rabb, M. (2007) Think SMART, not hard – a review of teaching decision making in sport from an ecological rationality perspective, *Physical Education and Sport Pedagogy*, 12, 1, 1–22.

Rovegno, I. and Bandhauer, D. (1994) Child-designed games: experience changes teachers' conceptions, *Journal of Physical Education, Recreation and Dance*, 65, 6, 60–63.

Rovegno, I. and Dolly, J. (2006) Situated learning perspectives, in D. Kirk, D. Macdonald and M. O'Sullivan (eds) *The handbook of physical education*, London Sage, 262–274.

Russell, R. (1995) (ed.) *The FA Football Development Programme: Football Curriculum Guide*, London: The Football Association.

STEPS Professional Development and Consultancy (2004) Learning, teaching and assessment: preparing children for an active healthy lifestyle, Watchfield: STEPS Professional Development and Consultancy.

Thorpe, R., Bunker, D. and Almond, L. (1984) A change in the focus of games teaching, in Pieron, M. and Graham, G. (eds) *Sport pedagogy: Olympic scientific congress proceedings*, Illinois: Human Kinetics.

Turner, A. (2005) Teaching games for understanding at the secondary level, in Griffin, L. and Butler, J. (eds) *Teaching Games for Understanding: Theory, Research and Practice*, Illinois: Human Kinetics, 71–89.

van Beurden, E., Zask, A. and Barnett, U. (2002) Fundamental movement skills? How do primary school children perform? The 'Move It Groove It?' program in rural Australia, *Journal of Science and Medicine in Sport*, 5, 3, 244–252.

Ward, G. (in press) Examining Primary School Physical Education Coordinators' Pedagogical Content Knowledge of Games: Are we just playing at this? *Education 3–13*.

Ward, G. and Griggs, G. (2011) Principles of play: a proposed framework towards a holistic overview of games in primary physical education, *Education 3–13*, 39, 5, 499–516 http://dx.doi.org/10.1080/03004279.2010.480945

Wright, S., McNeill, M., Fry, J. and Wang, J. (2005) Teaching teachers to play and teach games, *Physical Education and Sport Pedagogy,* 10, 1, 61–82.

CHAPTER SEVEN

GYMNASTICS IN THE PRIMARY YEARS

The foundation of learning to move with enhanced confidence, competence and imagination

Lawry Price

INTRODUCTION

When primary teachers are confronted with the prospect of teaching gymnastic activities to their class their starting point is often to think about activities that focus on particular skills such as travelling, rolling, jumping and balances. They are aware that these are developed firstly on the floor, then onto single pieces of equipment of various types and conclude with the challenge of combining these actions into phases, patterns or sequences of variable length and complexity dependent on the outcomes of the learning that has accrued across the period of delivery.

Do they consider their own rationale for why they are teaching such material? How do they ensure they are both consolidating yet also extending the gymnastic repertoire of their pupils? Do they consider working within themes that promote and therefore ensure progression in the work? Do they engage their learners in the planning, teaching and evaluation process to make sure every child is benefiting from their work in the area? Above all else do teachers recognise the significance and importance of gymnastic activity in the all round development of physical development of children?

This chapter advocates the importance of gymnastic activity to support children's growth and all round development during the primary years of learning. It outlines the skills to be addressed, the planning required within a gymnastic themes approach to ensure learning in the area is effective and transferable to other elements of physical education, and an approach that is developmental through a range of suggested themes to ensure continuity and progression across the period. It provides a rationale and philosophy that is underpinned by experience and practice to ensure that children attain an ultimate outcome of skilled, controlled movement competence to take into their physical education beyond the age of eleven. It is a central tenet of the chapter that the role of gymnastic activity within all of this is crucial in providing relevant and meaningful learning experiences and opportunities for all children during this vital period of growth and development.

Providing children throughout the primary age range with opportunities to improve and enhance their body management skills is therefore the overall thrust of this chapter.

By stating firstly a rationale and baseline philosophy for the inclusion of this activity area in children's physical development, the chapter will highlight a proposed thematic approach to teaching the skills to be included in giving a worthwhile, meaningful and relevant gymnastic learning experience to all children in primary school settings.

The chapter includes an identification of fundamental skills that can be learnt in and through gymnastic activities; the knowledge, skill and understanding accrued from learning in this area of the physical education curriculum; the planning, organisation and basic assessment of primary gymnastic activities; advocated teaching styles that promote learning in the area; and the relevance and importance of equipment and resources that support gymnastics learning. In essence, then, the chapter makes a case for gymnastic activities' unique contribution in helping children become more skilful and more controlled within their physical abilities. It also promotes and highlights the significant contribution such activity provides in contributing to raised personal confidence and self-esteem that accrues from those experiences through the sheer sense of enjoyment of movement.

WHY GYMNASTICS?

The legacy and the influence of two Swedish nationals (Per Ling and Martina Bergman-Österberg) have had an enduring impact on why gymnastics continues to be a feature of the physical education curriculum in British schools as well as schools around the world. Their teaching of the importance and significance of an emphasis on equipping children with basic and core body movement skills stems from the principles of ensuring healthy bodies as well as 'sound minds' set against a practical need for exercise to support natural growth and development. A recognition amongst teacher practitioners of the value and purpose of such an important part of children's education is a starting point from which to approach the practicalities of teaching gymnastic activities to primary aged children.

How this translates into the weekly gymnastic activities sessions conducted in our primary schools is the essence of this chapter. An understanding of why we should teach gymnastics, what such activity includes, how to teach it effectively, and where and when are fundamental to the way an individual teacher conceptualises and puts into practice such material. If the word 'gymnastics' conjures a range of thoughts, emotions and feelings particularly when applied specifically to primary school settings, then it is equally important to stress that responses that can provide a more informed stance and perspective are to be lauded. When teachers are knowledgeable, have an understanding of the subject material and can practically apply this to the teaching context, they are well placed to teach with confidence any area of the curriculum and this clearly applies to gymnastics teaching as much as any other area of the primary child's learning experience.

One other set of pointers worthy of acknowledgement that also services teachers confidence to teach effectively in this area is the knowledge about individual children primary teachers and those who work with young children already hold. This derives from daily interaction with their charges, an ever-developing knowledge base about what children can do and when they are ready to move onto the next stage of their learning. The strategies adopted to monitor children's learning during these crucial periods range from close observation, teacher and peer modelling, to peer assessment, to the use of formative and summative commentaries. Each of these also has valid application when confronted with delivering gymnastics lessons. *Knowing the child* is an additional tool in the armoury of teachers, and primary practitioners are particularly well equipped in this area of practice.

Perhaps the strongest claim for gymnastic activity to be included as part of children's learning experience is that it can be regarded as the core of all movement experience and thereby stands as an absolute must for all children but specifically within the years of maximum growth and development. As a recognised core component of acquiring motor competence is the provision of opportunities and activities that contribute to gross motor development, gymnastic activities are well placed to stake a major claim as key within this aim. Gross motor development in growing children is hallmarked by the need for improved coordination, balance, flexibility, strength and stamina. Out of this comes greater overall physical competence, greater body control and efficiency and quality of movement as well as improvements in cardiovascular efficiency. Additionally, social skills are developed within this learning experience aiding speaking and listening, aesthetic development, problem solving, interpersonal and observational skills. Gymnastic activities also provide unique opportunities for handling (and naming) different types of apparatus, for exploring, discovering and experimenting with what the body can do in space and on different surfaces provided by a variety of apparatus.

The rationale therefore for the need for gymnastic activities in the learning experience for young children is a well founded and sound one. Providing opportunities that contribute to core skill competence alongside the basics of body management needs makes this area of learning crucial to growth and development. A child who has experienced a comprehensive, continuous and progressive exposure to gymnastic activity throughout their formative primary years will be increasingly receptive and capable of meeting the increasing demands of more technical skill performance required of other motor skill challenges that come their way as they mature and develop physically and cognitively.

WHAT DO WE WANT CHILDREN TO LEARN THOUGH THEIR GYMNASTIC ACTIVITIES?

Within the Physical Development Practice Guidance for the Early Years Foundation Stage there is a profound emphasis placed on the need to encourage plenty of provision of opportunities for children to be active and thereby improve their skills of coordination, control, manipulation and movement. Alongside this 'developing an understanding of the importance of physical activity' is likewise stressed and a recognition that:

- Babies and children learn by being active and Physical Development takes place across all areas of Learning and Development.
- Physical Development helps children gain confidence in what they can do.

110

- Physical Development enables children to feel the benefits of being healthy and active.
- Physical Development helps children to develop a positive sense of well-being.
- Good health in the early years helps to safeguard health and well-being throughout life. It is important that children develop healthy habits when they first learn about food and activity. Growing with appropriate weight gain in the first years of life helps to guard against obesity in later life.

(The Early Years Foundation Stage – Practice Guidance (DCSF, 2008))

Furthermore, early learning goals specify that the period should provide opportunities for children to:

> move with confidence, imagination and in safety ... to move with control and coordination ... travel around, under, over and through balancing and climbing equipment ... show awareness of space, of themselves and of others ... recognise the importance of keeping healthy, and those things which contribute to this ... recognise the changes that happen to their bodies when they are active ... use a range of small and large equipment.

Participation therefore in a range of activity that promotes physical development in these ways is to be encouraged. The provision therefore of movement programmes that give children the opportunity to explore what their bodies are capable of, which service their need to explore their immediate surroundings and to explore the properties of apparatus of various shapes and forms, are clearly pertinent to promote such learning, aiding as they do physical growth and the all round development of young children.

A gymnastics learning programme based therefore on providing opportunities and activities that continue to promote this fundamental skill development, improved efficiency of movement and the development of an understanding and awareness of what bodies are capable of is of the essence here. Having established that the main objective of gymnastics teaching and learning is to support a notion of children becoming increasingly *skilful* then highlighting the characteristics of what that looks like will help articulate and identify what it is that children gain from participating in gymnastic activities.

So what will children learn in and through a gymnastic learning experience across these key formative years? In general terms generic and fundamental movement skills learning is what is being aimed at here but specifically:

- Essential body actions like rolling and rocking actions (forwards, backwards, sideways), manipulation of the body around its axis, on combinations of large and smaller body parts, on and around a range of surfaces (floor, mats, apparatus).
- Travelling actions like running, hopping, galloping, skipping, walking, stepping, on tip-toes, crawling, and sliding.
- Jumping and landing skills – to include take-offs from two feet, one foot, landings on two feet and one foot, into/out of, and onto, across and over obstacles and platforms.
- Starting and stopping and stillness skills.

- An ability to work at a range of speeds – slow, fast, acceleration, deceleration.
- Work at different levels – high, low, intermediate, face up, face down.
- Observation and listening skills.
- Ability to join/link/sequence actions and movements.
- Directions – forwards, backwards, sideways, diagonally, up, down.
- Pathways to follow including away from/return to starting position, to finish a series of movements at a different point, to follow straight, zig-zag, circular, routes.
- Balancing skills on different body parts, large and small, and combinations.
- Collecting, lifting, carrying and positioning of gymnastic equipment.
- Swinging, climbing, hanging skills.
- Spatial awareness skills including the ability to work in one's own space, and to work alongside others sharing similar space.
- Shape – stretching, curling, twisting, turning, wide, long, etc.
- Taking weight on hands for initially minimal moments but increasingly longer ones too.
- Cooperative work with partners, in groups, as a class.
- Supporting the development of upper body strength.

Imagine as a teacher practitioner, as a parent, as an observer of child development the benefits of a full encompassing experience of the above set of skills practice. The benefits of providing such a range of exploration of what the body can do in relation to a provided environment that nurtures such possibilities is patently obvious in the pursuit of servicing fully individual child development during this period.

THOUGHT BOX

Consider your existing provision for gymnastics and consider how well you are delivering on the generic and fundamental movement skills indicated above. Where are your strengths and weaknesses? Are there any barriers to be overcome in order to deliver on these? What changes could you make to ensure greater coverage of these fundamental movement skills?

ENSURING CONTINUITY AND PROGRESSION ACROSS THE AGE PERIOD

Teachers fully appreciate and apply the key principle of continuity and progressive learning. This is embedded in their medium- and short-term planning as well as an informed understanding of where this needs to be developed across the primary age range (or longer-term planning). Acknowledging where the children to whom they are teaching gymnastic content have come from, and where they need to get to, is fundamental to providing consolidation, refinement, and progression in the learning opportunities provided.

To inform these needs within the Foundation Stage and Key Stage 1 the importance and significance of being aware of children's background of play and movement experience cannot be overstated. Some children will have attended playgroup settings, tumble tots or kindergarten classes (as well as possibly nursery provision) which may well have provided a variety of physical and movement experiences. However, others may not have benefited from such experiences and may exhibit a marked lack of physical competence and confidence.

The basic gymnastic activity work at this stage therefore needs to facilitate opportunities for children to explore, experiment and practise the simple actions of jumping, rolling, balancing, climbing and swinging. This will enable them to find out which particular body parts are needed to support their activity when it is moving or at points of relative stillness – hands, feet, shoulders, knees, seat and so on. The teacher's role within this period of exploration is to support the child's growing awareness of where the body in action is in relation to space and others sharing that space, an identification of what body parts are being used to support the movement, whether it is moving on the spot, in limited or greater space. The introduction of varied and suitable apparatus (which provides a variety of surfaces, heights and arrangements) that affords further opportunities and challenges of a different kind further facilitates the learning at this stage.

As the individual child becomes more skilful he or she should be encouraged to join actions together to form a simple movement phrase or pattern. Initially the children should be restricted to linking two actions that lead smoothly from the first to the second before additional actions are added. A simple example would be to jump and land with control, followed by a roll of choice (and then finished off potentially with a point of stillness).

The teacher's choice of words, which promote movement responses from the children and need to be understood by them, is of great importance at this stage. The personal vocabularies of children can be increased by their greater appreciation and understanding of the meaning of words that have been used to stimulate, extend and enhance body actions for example moving along, through, up, down, across, underneath, stepping, sliding. Other words may be used that increase children's awareness of space and help them to grasp concepts, for example backwards, sideways, behind, forward, in front of, behind, left, right.

By the end of this crucial stage of development, given that they have accessed the opportunities a well planned programme of gymnastic work has provided, most children are adventurous enough to be able to move confidently, freely and safely on the floor, and on a variety of apparatus moving at the same time as others. The role of the teacher within this has been crucial in providing a safe learning environment, one that is conducive to promoting movement learning, and been the facilitator in providing the early steps in ensuring a movement repertoire has been established conducive to the stage of growth and development of children for the age range.

In the early part of Key Stage 2 (that is Years 3 and 4) the emphasis needs to move towards reinforcing and extending the basic work covered previously. The material to be covered during this period requires teachers to set tasks around specific action words and vocabulary, with clear reference to the body parts that are used to turn these words into movement action and thereby achieve a response from the learner. Greater control and appreciation of quality performance should be an expectation at this stage, together with an increased awareness of other children in close proximity, especially when working on apparatus.

It will be necessary to continue to encourage children to link their movements together in simple, yet increasingly developing, sequences of actions. A combination of more than three or four actions is likely to be within the capabilities of most children of this age, although there will be marked differences in terms of the continuity and flow of action achieved, the skill levels achieved and the range of actions performed.

When setting tasks on the floor and on apparatus the teacher's choice of language continues to be very important. A great deal of the work continues to be exploratory, and quick responses to tasks set for this age group are to be emphasised and encouraged, since too detailed analysis or description of actions can lead to a lack of spontaneity and (potentially) to subsequent repetition and possible boredom. The keynotes for this particular age group are clearly action, participation and maximised involvement in the learning.

Early work with a partner should be carefully considered at this stage of learning and development. Many children do not find it easy to match the movement of others, or to adapt their own ideas to working with someone else. However, working at simple tasks with a partner can be both challenging and enjoyable, and may help some children to clarify their movements and ideas.

This is a period when children should be increasingly encouraged to observe the movement of others as well as appreciate their own performance. By careful and informed observation they can learn a great deal that will improve or add variety to their own work. The ability to observe and extract from what they have seen, what is significant in the movements and actions observed, should be developed by asking children to look for particular features of the work, for example what parts of the body are being used to support the weight, at what speed is the body working, does the body movement change direction during the sequence, what pathway does the body follow during the actions performed.

Demonstrations by the teacher or children should be short and used sparingly. The point of any demonstration should be clearly established and positive teaching points made as a result. One word of caution here – ensure that any demonstrations are within the attainment of the children being taught. Nothing detracts more from potential performance than to see action demonstrated beyond the scope of the majority of children.

Within Years 5 and 6 of Key Stage 2 children will be working towards and achieving a higher level of skilful response to tasks set by the teacher (and possibly setting tasks themselves) provided that the lead-up work to develop strength, endurance, suppleness and an appreciation of quality of movement has been successfully carried out and followed through. The children by this stage should be able to respond to

the demands of thoughtful, sustained and concentrated work. Their own choice of actions can be refined to produce movement sequences appropriate to the problems and tasks set by the teacher. Their awareness of body movement should equip them to select actions that flow naturally from one movement to another. An example would be the choice of an appropriate movement to follow an inverted action/movement using the momentum created by (deliberately) overbalancing and controlling and adapting it to produce the next phase of the sequence, as in handstand into controlled forward roll.

The ability to observe the work of others should be further developed so that constructive, positive criticism is expected and encouraged in the pursuit of quality work. The exploration of tasks with a partner or in small groups is an important aspect of the work at this stage and may lead to a greater variety of response and a greater appreciation of the needs, strengths and limitations of others. It may also help the less skilful child to work with more confidence.

THOUGHT BOX

Consider what the benefits are of enabling children to watch each other perform their gymnastic work on a regular basis. Take time to think about what kind of environment this will need to be and what plan you will need to maximise these experiences.

Table 7.1 illustrates the continuity and progression to be worked on across the primary age phases with a model based on both teachers' and children's involvement in the ongoing process of planning, performance and evaluation. Table 7.2 illustrates the related vocabulary and themes.

PLANNING TO TEACH – SUGGESTED THEMES

What follows is an advocated approach that is both developmental in its approach and makes allowance for the variables of prior experience of both teachers and learners. A structure specific to the different stages of primary development is provided that is progressive but also flexible with the potential to drop in to particular themes. To support planning each theme description has an emphasis on what the body is doing, the dynamics of movement being developed, and the relationships encountered through such potential activity. As a suggested framework or set of guidelines the advocated approach is one that promotes the essentials for successful practice in supporting gymnastic teaching in our primary schools. These include:

- The need to plan units of work and the lessons that follow thoroughly using a thematic approach;

115

Table 7.1 Planning for continuity and progression in gymnastics

Children need to be given opportunities to Plan, Perform and Evaluate their work	Plan	Perform	Evaluate
Early Years – Nursery and Reception	▪ provide a range of opportunities for children to explore what their bodies can do in restricted and open floor space, and on selected individual pieces of apparatus ▪ with adult support (including use of relevant and simple vocabulary) set basic tasks to promote movement in, around and on the surfaces provided	▪ explore a variety of ways to travel on feet, hands and feet, turn, roll, jump and land safely ▪ focus on safe use of space and awareness of others' work, on travelling and stopping, changing direction, following different pathways ▪ explore a variety of apparatus – travel on and around, swing, climb, and balance	▪ begin to prompt spoken responses to movement and actions performed ▪ seek repetition of movement in preferred and different places working on greater control and quality of performance
Years 1 and 2	▪ explore and select responses to simple movement tasks solve simple problems (can you travel on two hands and one foot with tummy facing the floor?) ▪ plan simple sequences individually and in pairs in response to tasks ▪ help to arrange apparatus with guidance from the teacher	▪ explore a variety of ways to travel on feet, hands and feet, turn, roll, jump and land safely with increasing control ▪ balance on wide and narrow bases ▪ transfer some of the basic actions performed on the floor to low surfaces (travel on and around large apparatus, swing, climb and balance) ▪ link actions together to form short sequences individually and when ready in pairs ▪ practise, repeat and refine performance ▪ vary the speed and direction and use of space and the levels worked at in performance	▪ talk about their work and the gymnastic actions of others ▪ talk about what they and others have done, identifying key features through guidance by the teacher ▪ make simple judgements about content and quality of performance, and the cooperative work when working together in pairs

Children need to be given opportunities to *Plan*, *Perform* and *Evaluate* their work	Plan	Perform	Evaluate
Years 3 and 4	▦ describe and reflect on solutions to tasks ▦ discuss decisions made when working in pairs and groups ▦ comment on the quality of work observed in relation to content, performance, compositional design	▦ practise and further refine the basic actions of travelling, turning, rolling, jumping, climbing and balancing ▦ remember and perform more complex sequences of movements on the floor and on an increased amount and variety of apparatus ▦ add variety to performance through change of shape, speed and direction (and levels)	▦ describe their own and others' performance and make comments on use of space, clarity of body shape in stillness and in action ▦ talk about the composition of the sequence (the fluency of the movement, the use of floor and aerial pathways and changes in level) ▦ make comment on changes of speed and dynamics in the work observed
Years 5 and 6	▦ solve simple problems individually, in pairs, in small groups ▦ plan and compose more complex sequences of movement ▦ design apparatus layouts appropriate to the task	▦ longer and more complex sequences of movement ▦ practise and refine performance, demonstrating clarity in body shape in stillness and in action, smooth transitions between elements of the sequences ▦ imaginative use of space, floor and apparatus ▦ changes of dynamics in movement, including changes in speed and tension ▦ alone, with a partner and in groups	▦ describe and reflect on solutions to tasks ▦ discuss decisions made when working in pairs and groups ▦ comment on the quality of work observed in relation to content, performance, and compositional design

Table 7.2 Gymnastic activity in the primary years – movement vocabulary

Gymnastic themes

Reception, Years 1 & 2
- Space
- Use of apparatus
- Movement tasks
- Supporting body weight
- Transference of weight
- Travelling
- Feet together and apart
- Curling and stretching

Years 3 & 4
- Use of space
- Transferring weight
- Joining movements
- Directions
- Parts together and apart
- Lifting and lowering
- Shape
- Speed
- Twisting and turning

Years 5 & 6
- Sequences
- Levels
- Partner work
- Flight
- Pathways
- Symmetry and asymmetry
- Balance and continuity
- Flow
- Strength and lightness

Possible additional themes:
- Locomotion
- Balance
- Simple linking
- Body awareness
- Acceleration and deceleration
- Rhythm and timing
- Relation to floor and apparatus
- Matching actions
- Making and negotiating obstacles
- Lifting, carrying and lowering

Skills

Stability (Balance)
Static
Stillness
Dynamic
Posture
Upright/horizontal
Inverted
On different parts
Ready position
Stopping
Landing
Coordination
Cross laterality
Spinning
Body rolling
Dodging
Floating
Gliding

Locomotion (travelling)
Crawling
Stepping
Walking
Jogging
Skipping
Hopping
Galloping
Running
Striding
Sprinting
Jumping
Leaping
Rolling
Rocking
On different parts
Continuous
Paused

Manipulative
Grasp
Grip
Hook
Hang
Swing
Spring
Push
Pull
Slide

Body

Whole body
Large parts
Small parts
Fixed
Free
Near
Far
Leading
Following
Isolated

Body Parts
Hands
Feet
Fingers
Toes
Arms
Legs
Head
Forehead
Face
Eyes
Nose
Ears
Cheeks
Chin
Mouth
Neck
Shoulders
Chest
Knees
Elbows
Ankles
Balls of feet
Heels
Thighs
Hips
Stomach
Back
Bottom

Surface
Front
Back
Side
Top
Bottom

Shape
Arrow
Wall
Ball
Twist
Spiky
Gesture

Size
Big
Small
Medium

Spatial

Personal
Near
Next to
Far away
In front
Behind
At the side
Following
Leading

General Directions
Forwards
Backwards
Sideways
Diagonal
Up/down

Levels
High
Low
Medium
Near floor
Away from the floor
Near the surface

Pathways
Straight
Circular
Square
Curved
Spiral
Rectangular
Angular
Zig-zag
Direct
Indirect

Dynamics

Speed
Go and stop
Fast
Slow
Quicker
Accelerate
Decelerate
Slower
Short time
Long time
Sudden
Stillness

Weight
Strong
Powerful
Firm
Light
Soft
Tension

Time
At same time
Within a set time
After another
Before another
Use same space

Apparatus

Portable
Mini apparatus
Hoops
Cones
Skipping ropes
Bean bags
Skittles
Canes
Quoits
Discs

Mats
Benches
Linking planks
Perches
Nesting tables
'A' frames
Ladders
Movement tables
Boxes
Stools
Foam modules

Fixed
Climbing frames
Ropes
Beams
Bars
Poles

Relationships

Individual
Partner
Groups
Class
Work alone
Work with others
Copy
Contrast
Mirror/match
Support actions
Talk and discuss movement
Observe
Describe
Evaluate
Notice
Watch

Movement skill vocabulary

On to
Off
Across
Around
Between
Beside
Up
Down
On top
Over
Under
Around
Next to
Near to
Towards
To the side of
Far away from
Close to
Through
Underneath
Into
Out of
Near to
Towards
Away from
Height
Length
Width
Obstacle
Inside
Outside

- The expectation that children will be enthusiastic and receptive to their gymnastic activities and therefore teachers need to have high expectations of what their charges can achieve;
- The acceptance that teachers need to be prepared to revisit, repeat and therefore consolidate previous work;
- The importance of setting different or alternative tasks for floorwork and when the work moves on to apparatus;
- To ensure learning opportunities are characterised by plenty of active work, are fully participatory, and include minimal instruction;
- Detailed planning of sessions creates positive learning environments by adopting and implementing good working routines, which need to be taught, learnt and applied (they don't just happen!);
- Sessions are continuously assessed to help inform ongoing planning.

It should be added as a postscript here that it is only through practice and accrued experience over time that one's own teaching improves and becomes increasingly effective. A committed investment in planning well in this area will reap its rewards and ultimately ensure that children are provided with ample opportunity to consistently improve their movement repertoire and at the same time increase their physical confidence, skill, control and precision.

Gymnastic activity – teaching material

Reception, Year 1 and Year 2

Themes:
1. Space
2. Using apparatus
3. Movement tasks
4. Supporting body weight
5. Transference of weight
6. Travelling
7. Lifting body parts high
8. Feet together and apart
9. Curling and stretching

Theme 1: Space – a theme that emphasises 'spatial' aspects of movement

One of the essential and key aims of work with a very young class will be to see that the children allow themselves sufficient space in which to work. This concerns the space they work in as an individual and how that impacts on the space that they share with others. This is crucial learning that will impact on all later work. The teacher will also be concerned with safety and general response, but without lessening the children's sense of exploration, adventure and sense of pleasure from movement opportunity. Children's ability to be creative, individual and naturally responsive to particular tasks set will be a focus of this work.

Theme 2: Using apparatus – a theme that emphasises 'body, spatial and relationships' aspects of movement

In the early stages it is crucial to allow time for children to become familiar with the range of apparatus they will confront through their gymnastics work. There is no need to introduce all of this at once – better to do this over time, with new apparatus being introduced at irregular intervals to inject more excitement and interest, and therefore more possible applications to their movement. They will need to become aware of the variety of apparatus available, their different textures and surfaces, the way in which they can be gripped, how to get on and off, and how they need to be shared with others in the class. The early experience of handling the different apparatus as well as using it for their gymnastics is all part of the learning to be derived here. Helping children to explore the possibilities presented by a range of different and varied apparatus including lightweight equipment like skittles, cones, hoops and ropes is an important stage to experience before adding in mats, benches, linking equipment, platforms, nesting and agility tables, and climbing frames.

Theme 3: Movement tasks – a theme that emphasises 'body, spatial and relationships' aspects of movement

Here the work is concerned with movements and actions that children perform naturally in their everyday lives and therefore bring to their learning in physical education generally. Therefore activities that involve travelling in different ways, using different parts of their bodies to move from place to place, momentary and more prolonged stillness, jumping and landing skills, and their application to work on apparatus, is the focus of this particular theme of work.

Theme 4: Supporting body weight – a theme that emphasises 'body' aspects of movement

It is important from an early stage of work in this area to provide children with many opportunities to experience taking their weight safely on different parts of the body and of controlling movement and their momentum (and balance) as they do so. This theme accounts for the changing growth patterns prevalent in young children and builds on previous work that will have provided the basic increased competence and confidence in their abilities. They will be ready for this work if this has been established.

Theme 5: Transference of weight – a theme that emphasises 'body' aspects of movement

As a progression from the previous theme, this particular one takes account of the fact that any movement involves a transference of body weight. Children are used to doing this quite naturally in their everyday movement, but experience and skill need to be

developed for the more challenging and difficult situations presented by particularly apparatus of different types and surfaces. The emphasis on *how* the body moves between different points of support, aiming therefore to identify and clarify different ways of transferring weight, and thus to improve skill by practising the movement involved, is the key to what is involved in this theme. This theme also involves locomotion, but while locomotion emphasises travel between two points, weight transference emphasises the bodily movements between two weight-bearing positions.

Theme 6: Travelling – a theme that emphasises 'spatial' aspects of movement

Once children are able to transfer their body weight increasingly competently and confidently, they should be encouraged to explore the multitude of ways of travelling and moving their body weight to expand their individual repetoire of different physical movements and actions. This theme may be conveniently introduced with small or mini-apparatus or with just benches and mats and other similar low-level apparatus, with a view to progressing the work to larger apparatus eventually to test similar or different tasks and skills.

Theme 7: Lifting parts high – a theme that emphasises 'body' aspects of movement

The ability to extend and stretch the body or particular parts of the body is an important feature in gymnastics and has a natural link to work in other areas of the physical education curriculum. This theme stimulates the children to think of parts of the body that can be elevated and stretched in different directions while using a variety of points of support (body and that afforded by apparatus). It also encourages them to invert (or reverse the position of) the body while using apparatus and to become more adventurous as skill thresholds rise.

Theme 8: Feet together and apart – a theme that emphasises 'body' aspects of movement

If previous themes have been covered in depth then this theme will have been reached with the children very much more aware of individual parts of the body, how they can move them in different ways and in different combinations, and where all of this can take place. This theme helps them to increase control of their legs particularly and is a beginning for children to start thinking about clarity and types of body shapes that they can achieve.

Theme 9: Curling and stretching – a theme that emphasises 'body' aspects of movement

Children who have had plenty of experience of taking and transferring weight should be ready to explore the use of the body as it moves between the two extremes of flexion and extension. The ability to extend and flex fully is associated particularly with the spine, and it is from here that movements should begin. Curling can take place by curving the spine forwards, backwards or sideways, while stretching may be achieved by elongating the body or by making it wide. This theme is a very good one in concluding work covered during the Foundation/Key Stage 1 period and also as a lead-in to that to be provided at the beginning of Key Stage 2.

Gymnastic activity – teaching material

Years 3 and 4

Themes:
1. Use of space
2. Transferring weight
3. Joining movements
4. Directions
5. Parts together and apart
6. Lifting and lowering
7. Shape
8. Speed
9. Twisting and turning

Theme 1: Use of space – a theme that emphasises 'spatial' aspects of movement

One of the key early themes at the earlier stage was concerned with the need for spacing (and the sharing of space) between individuals working on the floor and on apparatus. This theme now develops a greater awareness of the working space and of where the body can move in relation to the apparatus as well as the children moving in relation to each other. Later themes are concerned in more detail with space by considering directions, levels and pathways, and the body shape when moving or still in space.

Theme 2: Transferring weight – a theme that emphasises 'body' aspects of movement

A central component of gymnastics is the acquisition of fundamental locomotor skills, as learning about control and management of the body when moving is an absolute 'must' for young children. The body moves by transferring the weight from one part of the body to another or from one part to the same part. Children need lots of opportunities to discover the very great variety of ways in which this can be done with safety and increased competence.

Theme 3: Joining movements – a theme that emphasises 'body' aspects of movement

Working progressively towards ever-increasing smooth and fluent linking of movements is an important feature of gymnastic work. During the earliest stages of work in Key Stage 2 the children should be encouraged to think in terms of continuous movement rather than isolated movements interspersed with periods of rest, wandering and waiting for turns. In order to move continuously, the children must be trained to use the floor as well as the apparatus, to work at a variety of levels and speeds, and in varied directions, working at the same time as their peers. Practice should be given in the selection of appropriate ways of linking movements. It must be stressed that thought and planning should precede movement, and that during movement the performer must be alert to the way one action can lead naturally into the next. By being required to repeat linked movements, children increase their ability to remember movements and improve the quality and continuity of their work. This is where the beginnings of establishing the notion of the importance of a clear start and a defined finish to movement patterns emerges. The opportunity also exists here to build in the evaluative element to children's work to inform future (improved) performance.

Theme 4: Directions – a theme that emphasises 'spatial' aspects of movement

The body has enormous potential for moving in different directions – it can move forwards, backwards, sideways, up or down. Children need to acquire this knowledge and be increasingly aware of the range of possibilities, how a change in direction can be achieved, and how apparatus can contribute considerably to building this repertoire of skill. This is a further element to quality aspects of the work and a significant feature of all gymnastic performance.

Theme 5: Parts together and apart – a theme that emphasises 'body' aspects of movement

This theme consolidates and extends some of the work which needs to have gone before on awareness of parts of the body, what can be achieved in a movement sense, and is used here to bring enhanced control and greater variety to the work.

Theme 6: Lifting and lowering – a theme that emphasises 'body' aspects of movement

This theme seeks to emphasise more fully the control with which parts of the body are moved, either against or with gravity. The movements may require strength or demand a quality of lightness, qualities that are increasingly coming into play in the age band. This theme gives important practice in the effective use and feeling of 'muscle tension' in movement.

Theme 7: Shape – a theme that emphasises 'body' aspects of movement

An important element of efficient motor function is body image and to help develop this children need to be encouraged to develop an awareness of the outline of the body, both when holding a still position and when they are moving. The four basic shapes are wide, long, curled and twisted, but these will be modified considerably by the way in which the body is supported or suspended, and the need to adapt the shape to the spaces and different surfaces presented by a range of apparatus. When working on this theme, clarity of body shape in still positions should be explored before shape in movement can be appreciated. There is a danger, therefore, that the work will become static, and this needs to be guarded against by encouraging linking movements and actions of a dynamic nature. In the appreciation of body shape, observation of others is an important feature and needs to be integrated into the learning experience. The theme also makes an important contribution to adopting good body posture, a vital cog in fluent and efficient motor performance.

Theme 8: Speed – a theme that emphasises 'spatial' aspects of movement

The theme of 'speed' is another, like 'directions' and 'shape', that adds qualitative elements to gymnastics work. In all aspects of movement an element of time is involved. Some actions require a quick, explosive speed for their efficient performance, while others can best be carried out in a slow, deliberate manner. Children can best learn the effect of varied speeds on movements by exploring at first the extremes of quick and slow. Later they may experience the sensation of accelerating and decelerating as they perform gymnastic movements.

*Theme 9: Twisting and turning – a theme that emphasises 'body and spatial'
aspects of movement*

Twisting and turning are body actions which require some definition and clarity of explanation. A twist occurs when one part of the body is fixed and the rest of the body is rotated to produce torsion (twisting). In a turn, the whole body rotates about an axis, as in jumping to face a new direction, forward or backward rolling, or cartwheeling. Twisting and turning are both important body actions in gymnastics in that both can be used to link movements and to establish new directions in which to continue travelling during sequences. Twisting and turning also represent additional qualitative elements to overall gymnastic performance.

124

Gymnastic activity – teaching material

Years 5 and 6
Themes:
1. Sequences
2. Levels
3. Partner work
4. Flight
5. Pathways

6. Symmetry and asymmetry
7. Balance and continuity
8. Flow
9. Strength and lightness

Theme 1: Sequences – a theme that emphasises the 'body' aspects of movement

An earlier visited theme was concerned with the joining of movements. This ability, to show continuity and flow to movement in transferring weight, is a vitally important feature of gymnastic work. Earlier the children will have been encouraged to think about their movements in readiness to experiment and practise their responses to tasks set. Now, as children become increasingly versatile, thought and action need to be more intrinsically linked to produce more harmonious movement sequences. Sequences will often be demanded which are appropriate to particular tasks set by the teacher. These sequences should have a definite starting position, illustrate the theme in continuous action, show varied and original work, and have a clear and controlled finishing position – elements of gymnastic work expected of children as they near the end of the primary age phase.

Theme 2: Levels – a theme that emphasises the 'spatial' aspects of movement

When using the floor space the body may move at a low level or with parts reaching to a high level. A jump is a good example of an action that may be used to take the body higher still in relation to the floor. This use of levels brings interest and variety to floor work. Similarly, on the apparatus the body may work at varied levels. This may be either near the point of support or stretching away both above and below it, and also possibly away from the point of support. Apparatus will also provide opportunity to move from one level to another, from floor to apparatus and vice versa.

Theme 3: Partner work – a theme that emphasises the 'relationships' aspect of movement

The 'educational' approach to teaching primary school gymnastics promoted throughout these suggested themes does not require children to assist and support each other to perform vaults or agilities. However, to work with a partner in order to create move-ment sequences on both floor and apparatus can be a rewarding experience for all concerned, and that includes the teacher! The children are challenged both physically and socially to cooperate in answering a movement task set by the teacher.

It is unwise to start on partner work with a class that has not already achieved a good standard of individual work. The children should be fully experienced at managing their bodies on apparatus, working to interpret themes in a creative and imaginative way, and fully able to work sensibly as individuals in a group situation. With a new class, or one that has not yet reached a stage of responsible self-discipline, it is better not to try partner work until the children have shown that they are ready to accept the difficult challenge of adapting their movements to another person. A sensible and skilful class can go on to do work in which three or four cooperate to produce patterns of movement, but the more children there are in a group the more the quality of the finished sequence will be affected by individual variations in performance.

In introducing partner work, the following points should be considered by the teacher:

1   A good standard of individual work should already have been achieved.
2   Children are best left to choose their own partners, except when it may be necessary to match up particular body types, or for reasons of 'desirable or less desirable' pairings.
3   The tasks set and the arrangement of apparatus used should not be over-complicated initially.
4   Time needs to be allowed for discussion, observation and experimentation and practice. It often appears that a class working on partner work is noisy and unproductive. This is a natural stage as ideas are being worked out, decisions made, which in turn may need modification and further practice. This process all takes time if the ultimate aim is to produce quality work that has been planned through a shared experience.
5   Children should be encouraged to select and clarify their movements. A short sequence of controlled movement which answers the task set is always preferable to a long series of movements which peter out in exhaustion or ove-repetition.
6   Partner or group sequences should eventually be able to be performed with little significant change or difference when required to repeat the actions and movements.
7   Once a class is skilled in partner work, it can become a feature of subsequent lessons. In addition to the tasks suggested in this section, most other themes can be interpreted by children cooperating in twos, threes or fours. Beyond this, potentially bigger groupings are possible when the experience is well established as a part of gymnastics provision.

Theme 4: Flight – a theme that emphasises 'body and spatial' aspects of movement

This theme is concerned with the movement of the body through the air, how this is achieved, and how to establish a sense of control throughout, including, crucially, landings. The teacher will be particularly concerned with ways of propelling the body into the air, control and movements of the body during flight, and the achievement of safe, resilient and ever increasingly well controlled light landings. Flight will form a part of most lessons from the earliest stages. Children should already have developed a confidence about taking off and landing, but the idea of increasing the time spent in the air will be new to them. The skill and confidence necessary needs to be built up slowly and with care.

Theme 5: Pathways – a theme that emphasises 'spatial' aspects of movement

A pathway describes the path of the body or part of the body through space. Pathways can be straight, curved or twisted, as well as tracing particular patterns on the floor (and potentially on different apparatus surfaces) e.g. circles, squares, oblongs, etc. Encouraging children to use a range of different pathways rather than only the most obvious, adds much variety to their eventual work, and is also useful in helping groups to share restricted floor space and apparatus. As a much visited aspect of work from the early practices of learning to run and dodge, and learning how to use all parts of the workspace independently of each other, revisiting this theme in the later years of the primary age phase is important and will make a telling contribution to especially qualitative elements of the work produced. It is introduced again here to bring a greater variety of floor pattern to sequences, and to consider possible pathways in space when moving on, off, over and along a variety of apparatus.

Theme 6: Symmetry and asymmetry – a theme that emphasises 'body' aspects of movement

Children will have covered ideas of symmetry and asymmetry in other areas of their learning – here the concepts extend to how the body can move symmetrically and asymmetrically. Although the body itself is two-sided (bilateral) and symmetrical, few people use both sides with equal dexterity, and the majority of actions undertaken in everyday life have an asymmetrical stress. Symmetrical body movements demand control, coordination and body awareness e.g. children on the whole find it easier to roll backwards over one shoulder than to roll straight when first learning the skill. Focus on this theme can help to develop the necessary control and this clearly also contributes to asymmetrical movement which is more natural and therefore less limiting. Giving children the idea that their bodies can be divided vertically down the centre by an imaginary line, helps them to develop an understanding that the body it is said to be symmetrical if one side exactly mirrors the other. If opposite sides of the body are not moving at the same time and in the same way, or if one limb does not exactly mirror the corresponding limb, then the body is at that time asymmetrical. A strong focus for the discipline required of formal gymnastics comes from an attempt to perform agilities and to work on apparatus symmetrically. Great control and precision is demanded by this work. There is a far greater variety of movements possible when working asymmetrically. By exploring both types of movement and contrasting them in sequences, the range of work is further developed and at a level conducive to the majority of children in this age band.

Theme 7: Balance and continuity – a theme that emphasises 'body' aspects of movement

Balance is the ability to hold the body still over a comparatively small supporting base and is an area that will have been a feature of much previous work. The theme is re-focused here to further the understanding of the concept of balance and to increase skill levels through further appreciation of the techniques required to maintain a held position. The continuity aspect is to develop these balancing skills within increasingly complex linked action and movement. In essence continuity involves joining a series of movements together in such a way that one arises as a natural outcome of the previous action, implying phrasing and timing.

Balance on small surfaces and points of the body requires control but there is a danger that if balance is explored as a theme on its own the lesson can become very static and one-paced. Stillness is an aspect of movement, and the ability to achieve stillness in a balanced position is best thought of as a position to be gained following and preceding movement. In turn, the balance achieved is lost (but not the control) as the body moves again. Children will learn from this work that the greater the area supporting the body (the base of support) and the more widely distributed the parts of support, the easier it is to balance. Balance requires a certain body tension if it is to be maintained on small and varied bases without unwanted movement – the achievement of 'stillness' in body action.

Theme 8: Flow – a theme that emphasises 'body' aspects of movement

As a natural follow-on to the previous theme here is another emphasising further qualitative elements of gymnastics work. If a sequence is to contain a number of contrasting elements then punctuation (moments when movement is slow or quick, or is paused) adds significantly to the work eventually produced. This theme explores the two contrasting aspects of flow, where action can actually be stopped, and the opposite in which the emphasis is on continuity of movement. Using both will bring greater interest and variety, and therefore extra quality to movement sequences.

Theme 9: Strength and lightness – a theme that emphasises the 'body' aspects of movement

Children need to learn how to use their energy efficiently and economically. They have bodies that require activities that promote natural growth, at both levels of need for fine and gross muscular development. The degree of strength employed needs to be appropriate to the different types of movement and actions performed. Many gymnastic activities require a degree of strong muscular tension, as in maintaining a balance that entails supporting body weight on small parts of the body, or in gripping and pulling on a rope or a beam to raise the body, or in taking off for a jump. It is very rare that the body is completely relaxed, for this would naturally result in a loss of control, but some movements require light muscular tension, particularly when the body is moving through the air or when rolling. Too much muscular tension can be fatiguing and too little can mean that movements lack control. Varied and more interesting gymnastic work will show varying degrees of strength and lightness. Strong, dynamic movements, particularly when associated with variations of speed and sudden changes of direction, should be used to show exciting highlights, for example at the beginning of a sequence, during the series of movements being performed, or to bring the sequence to a marked climax.

OTHER POSSIBLE THEMES TO BUILD INTO DELIVERY

Themes emphasising the 'body' aspects of movement

Locomotion

An elementary theme, worthy of inclusion in the early years work, because it is primarily concerned with travelling and stopping skills. Such a concentrated focus will support children's exploration of different ways of moving from A to B, and service the need to gain steadily, over time, improved bodily control in the workspaces provided.

Balance

A theme worth visiting in isolation, again early on in children's exploration and experimentation stage, when children are concentrating on finding out what their bodies are capable of. Balance is the ability to hold the body over a range of large and small supporting bases and therefore teaches children about large and small body parts. The overall aim of the theme is to provide an understanding of the concept (and 'feeling') of balance and to increase levels of skill through an appreciation of the different techniques required to maintain a 'held' position for short and longer periods.

Simple linking

As a precursor for 'joining movements' (and later 'sequences') this theme develops the ability to join movements together so that they follow one another smoothly. The theme in essence establishes the concept of linked movements compared with two individual movements performed in succession, and aims to extend skill through concentration on the need to finish one movement, balanced, and in a position to follow on into a second. Clearly this is the beginning of work that will eventually result in successful sequence work much later down the line, and should be concentrated within the early work covered in gymnastics programmes.

Body awareness

Here is a theme that can add polish and enhanced quality to finished sequence work, on floor and apparatus. Its focus lies in an awareness of how any part of the body is moving and the effect that this has on the body as a whole. Ultimately awareness should be through the 'feel' of a movement without a need to rely on visual or intellectual cues. Although this is a fundamental characteristic of all movement, the theme can be very useful in improving quality of performance through emphasising the need for awareness of all body parts in order to achieve a stylish, complete, polished and finished performance.

Themes emphasising the 'dynamic' aspects of movement

Acceleration and deceleration

This theme is clearly related to that of 'speed' but with a stronger focus on more gradual changes of speed. This is also a useful area of work to engage in for improving overall control of movement and increasing the variety and aesthetic qualities to be aimed for in sequence work.

Rhythm and timing

When working as an individual work in this particular area implies a growing awareness of the timing of preparation, action and recovery, and consequently the rhythmic pattern which assists efficient performance of particular skills. At a more advanced level, the theme also involves using accent, timing, phrasing and repetition in order to compose movement sequences in pairs, threes, or in potentially larger groups. In addition to developing further a sense of phrasing and timing when composing sequences, the theme encourages members of such groups to conform to various set rhythmic patterns and to experiment with the effect of altering these in a given movement phrase.

Themes emphasising the 'relationships' aspects of movement

Relation to floor and apparatus

An elementary theme which may be useful in ensuring that all the possibilities of a situation are explored. For example, in relation to the floor the body may be facing, back to, sideways to, the right way up or upside down. With apparatus there are huge possibilities of going under, over, round, along, across, up, down, on, off, etc. Under the general theme of 'partner work' almost any work covered can be developed by combining work with a partner in some way. There are also various aspects of this theme which may be explored in their own right as detailed below.

Lawry Price

Matching actions

This is when a pair of pupils look to perform as exactly as possible the same actions, at the same time or one after the other. Further possibilities come from a choice of starting position, e.g. side by side facing the same position, side by side facing different directions, facing each other and mirroring the other's movements, back to back, one behind the other facing the same direction, etc. Some of the work here presents a greater challenge because the partner will be out of sight for shorter or longer periods during the performance of the matched actions. This theme can therefore extend skill by adapting movement to match that of a partner. This may therefore involve using for example, a different foot for take-off, or performing a movement such as a cartwheel in the opposite direction from that preferred by the individual child.

Making and negotiating obstacles (without contact)

This work will involve adapting to a partner's movement and actions so that one goes over or round the other, or through potential 'holes' formed by one for the other to negotiate. The theme requires a sound understanding of weight bearing and balance, together with an ability to assess the partner's skill when making the obstacles so that impossible tasks are not set. The composition of a sequence where both partners take both sides requires inventiveness and creativity of thinking in planning, skill performance, and good timing for smooth execution.

Partner work (with contact)

This work requires greater dependence on one another, and therefore an enhanced sense of responsibility. Joanne can help Karl to maintain a balance to achieve flight for example; Jack can provide a base of support for Amy to balance on or push off from to achieve flight. True interdependence can be achieved through work on counterbalance and countertension activities. Counterbalance involves leaning or pushing against each other with the weight adjusted in such a way that neither could retain the position without the help of the other. The supporting bases of the partners will be wide apart. Countertension is a position of similar interdependence achieved with bases close together and the partners pulling against one another.

Lifting, carrying and lowering

This is an advanced theme, related to and demanding body control, strength and skill. It is probably better suited, in the primary school setting, to work in threes rather than twos. Similar counterbalance and countertension possibilities exist here as in the theme above, but with greater potential for collaborative work to be more complex with the addition of an extra person involved. (This could also be a theme visited very much earlier in the programme of children's gymnastics work when teaching the basics of lifting, carrying and manoeuvring apparatus, particularly in terms of the cooperative nature of such activities.)

Work in threes

All aspects of partner work can also be used for work in threes. This extends the possibilities, particularly in work with contact, so that two individuals control the balance, flight and placing of a third. The theme particularly encourages cooperation in the group situation, and extends movement vocabulary and experience, especially in situations where two can help a third to perform a movement which they might otherwise be incapable of performing if left to their own efforts alone.

CONCLUSION

This chapter has provided a baseline rationale for why gymnastic activities are a crucial and therefore significant part of the learning experience for all children in the primary age range (notwithstanding related activity preschool). It has advocated an approach to teaching relevant and appropriate material that supports the natural growth and development that occurs during this period and has promoted a premise that all teachers are potentially well equipped to be effective in their teaching of such material because of how well they get to know their charges across any school year. To support practice a progressive programme of themed activity has been provided on which to base learning content with the key ideas of focusing on body, dynamics and relationships principles at the forefront of this. That these themes are intrinsically linked to the original non-statutory guidelines for teaching 'key gymnastic themes' produced for the initial introduction of National Curriculum physical education way back in 1992 is no coincidence.

As a result of such statements the *why, what, where, how* and *when* questions surrounding the teaching of gymnastic activities can be encapsulated within the statements that follow and would provide the core rationale and basis for the inclusion and importance of the activity area within well balanced physical education programmes in school settings.

The why? – To service the need for children to become increasingly controlled, motor competent, and therefore skilful in their physical movements. Gymnastics is primarily concerned with both gross and fine motor development and contributes markedly to gradual and progressive improvement in body coordination, balance, maintaining flexibility and suppleness, and supporting growth in strength and stamina (with its own unique contribution to improving cardiovascular efficiency).

The what? – To broaden and further develop children's specific abilities in jumping and landing skills, the range of rolling actions they can perform, and the ability to nurture transference of weight on different parts of the body including balance and stillness on combinations of body parts.

132

The where? – The ability to display an increasing and broadening range of skills on the floor, initially on low apparatus level surfaces and increasingly on the varied surfaces offered by a full provision of gymnastic apparatus, including apparatus that provides opportunities to work at increased heights and levels. This would also entail an acceptance that, as children grow older, are more skilful, and therefore more controlled in their movement repertoire, they should be increasingly challenged by what the apparatus presents – hence a need for older children (i.e. across Key Stage 2) particularly to have lessons that provide plenty of opportunity and therefore emphasis on apparatus work.

The how? – By the use of a full range of teaching methods and the adoption of an approach that promotes children succeeding at their own level and within the confines of their abilities without losing sight of the need to challenge further and raise expectation of performance to be aimed for. The use therefore of a teaching pedagogy that promotes the individual child's learning and therefore success in physical activity is to be advocated.

The when? – Across all periods of the physical education year, with at least one unit of work in each year from Reception upwards to provide consistency and therefore progression in learning potential. Well thought-through planned units of work building on and progressing on what has been covered previously should ultimately result in meeting the key objectives of the increasingly skilled child, with an ever-extending repertoire of skilful body actions from which to draw for a multitude of different life purposes.

The further question – *what would be the impact of children not experiencing gymnastic learning* as part of their school experiences should also be reflected on at this point. It would be pertinent to suggest that if this were the case then a vital and necessary cog in children's all round development would be missing, and as a result there would inevitably be a shortfall in their physical performance capabilities. Furthermore, the wider brief and significance of physical education would be omitted or seriously undermined by such a shortfall – the subject generally, and gymnastic activities particularly, make a specific and, without overstating it, a major contribution to speaking and listening skills, children's aesthetic and artistic appreciation and understanding, and their ability to develop problem-solving skills, as well as nurturing interpersonal and observational skills. These are all invaluable life skills and part and parcel (and therefore crucial parts) of the child's schooling as wider curriculum components.

Gymnastic activities are included in the learning experience of children in the primary age range because they are recognised as beneficial to children's development, growth and overall learning needs. It is not because 'we've simply always done it' but more because there exists amongst teacher practitioners a deep-seated understanding that such activity is good for developing bodies and contributes to the growing body's needs during this crucial period of development. Ultimately we want children to become able, competent movers, confident in their abilities to develop physical skill for healthy, active lifestyles, and learning in and through gymnastic activity contributes markedly to this set of aims if taught with confidence, understanding and knowledge.

Providing gymnastics learning experiences must take into account what each individual child brings to their learning in the area. Different starting points, ability levels, confidence and social development are all factors that will affect children's performance initially. The awareness of teachers providing the learning opportunities and visualising clearly the identifiable features of children's movement abilities and the actions they naturally perform is the key to effective teaching in the area.

So to conclude, what can children do that teachers need to build on to improve overall physical performance, helping them become more agile and skilful? By visualising a child's movement and actions in the early stages of movement development (age 1 to 4) we are in a position to know what we need to provide. In essence, what can a child physically do that helps inform possible provision – what are their unique starting points?

In essence, children:

- *Move* in different ways – walking, skipping, hopping, jumping, galloping, running;
- *Balance* on different parts of their bodies;
- *Manipulate* different objects and handholds;
- *and* given opportunity and encouragement they will climb, hang, swing and balance on equipment/apparatus which will enhance movement competence and confidence as they acquire greater athleticism and agility;
- *and* they all do these actions and movements in their own personal way, because they have unique bodies capable of doing things individually differently from anybody else;
- *and* through an exposure to gymnastic activity they will enhance these skills and motor competencies as the foundations of progressively improving their all round motor function efficiency for life as well as recreational purposes.

KEY READINGS

Many of the key ideas discussed here can be followed up in depth in such texts as Price, L. (2003) *Primary School Gymnastics – Teaching Movement Skills Successfully*, London: David Fulton Publishers. Good visual materials for both teachers and pupils have become increasingly available. Good examples of such can be found in a resource from 2004 entitled 'Primary Gymnastics' still available from http://www.mwgymnastics.co.uk/

REFERENCES

Department for Children, Schools and Families (DCSF) (2008) *Early Years Foundation Stage*, London: HMSO.
Price, L. (2003) *Primary School Gymnastics – Teaching Movement Skills Successfully*, London: David Fulton Publishers.

CHAPTER EIGHT

DANCE TEACHING AND LEARNING POSSIBILITIES WITHIN THE EARLY YEARS AND PRIMARY SCHOOL CONTEXT

Rachael Jefferson-Buchanan

INTRODUCTION

The teaching and learning possibilities in dance will be the subject of this chapter, specifically the need for distinctive yet integrated movement experiences in the early years and primary school. Dance constitutes a playful learning environment for young children in particular, since it serves to stimulate and channel their spontaneity and live- liness, offering them rich sensory experiences that are so vital for their full-bodied devel- opment and wellbeing. It is also an ideal vehicle through which a child can explore and become confident in the processes of composing, performing and appreciating, three 'key factors in determining teaching and learning programmes' (Smith-Autard, 1994: 1). Following an initial review of the place of dance in the Early Years Foundation Stage (DCSF, 2008) and the UK primary physical education curriculum, these three dance processes will be interrogated individually and Rudolf Laban's (1948) theoretical frame- works will be illuminated. As such, key dance knowledge, skills and understandings will be drawn out, highlighting the importance of nurturing children's physical dexterity and skilfulness, their creative play and dance-making, as well as their powers of description, analysis, interpretation and evaluation. This holistic approach to teaching and learning in dance is essential for children's full, embodied experiences, seeking to nurture 'thinking bodies' and 'moving minds' (Tinning, 2009). The chapter will conclude with an example of a dance idea that models previously discussed aspects, challenging the dance teacher to think beyond the boundaries of 'areas of Learning and Development' (DCSF, 2008) and traditional primary 'subjects', due to the integrated, holistic, cross-curricular nature of the teaching and learning presented.

THE PLACE OF DANCE IN THE EARLY YEARS SETTING IN THE UK

In the early years context, dance straddles all six of the 'areas of Learning and Development' that have been identified within the EYFS (DCSF, 2008). The EYFS (DCSF, 2008) is a comprehensive framework which sets the standards for learning, development and care of children from birth to 5. Each area of learning and development: *personal social and emotional development; communication, language and literacy; problem solving, reasoning and numeracy; knowledge and understanding of the world; physical development;* and *creative development* is divided into 'aspects' that are fleshed out in section 4.4 of the framework. For the purposes of this discussion, the six areas of learning and development are the focal point, and strategies to enhance and refine these through dance will subsequently be explored, with reference to a selection of EYFS (DCSF, 2008) 'aspects' as appropriate.

Personal, social and emotional development is an area to which a number of educationalists believe that dance can contribute. This is particularly evident when examining a range of dance education books with themes based on moods and emotions, each detailing how children are given an opportunity to express themselves and socially progress through movement (Davies, 2001; Harrison, 1993; Shreeves, 1990). Hall (1997: 5), for example, maintains 'feelings are expressed through body movement, as in angry stamping of feet; joyful gesturing of arms', simultaneously claiming that the partner and group work in dance lessons can lead to 'a strong sense of "togetherness": unselfish sharing of space; taking turns; demonstrating to and being demonstrated to; and being appreciated and helped by others' comments'. Similarly, Davies (2001: 144) affirms that the 'personal expressive characteristics' of children are developed in the performance process as well as through a set of relevant experiences that are precursors to this. Taking part alongside others in a physical activity such as dance is something that the majority of children seem to enjoy (YDE, 2010). Children share space, resources and ideas in a dance lesson, and there are many moments of interaction that can help to foster their social relationships. In particular, shared dance-making can also encourage children to communicate with and relate to others, giving them a sense of social cohesion, and supporting relationships between peers. This ties in well with the EYFS (DCSF, 2008) aspects of 'making relationships' and a 'sense of community'. Moreover, decision making and negotiating are prevalent in a dance lesson; such life-skill processes can help children to develop their personal and social responsibility. Children relate to their peers as they grow in confidence, and the relationships that they make are dependent on them acquiring and practising complex social skills. Dance is a medium through which they can potentially develop their personal, social and emotional abilities when guided and nurtured by the early years practitioner.

The area of *communication, language and literacy* is an interesting one when related to the dance context, for the child not only has an opportunity to use their body as a communication tool, but there is a whole new set of vocabulary for them to learn that is specific to and extends beyond dance per se. Prepositions, muscle names, dynamics, types of actions and the like are commonplace when providing directions, instructions or explaining movement qualities to children. The EYFS (DCSF, 2008) suggests that *communication, language and literacy* is made up of six aspects, and on closer inspection, explicit links can be made between these and dance learning. Non-verbal communication is referred to, as is the recreation of roles and experiences. Moreover, the use of rhyme, rhythm and alliteration is included, illuminating the need for musicality, a fundamental aspect of dance teaching and learning. However, this is merely scratching the surface in relation to the deeper learning that can be cultivated, since every literacy-related classroom topic can be 'danced' about with a sprinkle of teacher imagination, and children can be encouraged to communicate through voice, gesture and in whole-bodied ways like never before in the dance domain. Furthermore, it has been documented elsewhere how aspects such as reading, writing and handwriting (DCSF, 2008) can be successfully incorporated into the dance classroom (Cohen, 2007; Jefferson-Buchanan, 2007; Landalf and Gerke, 2004; Oussoren, 2005).

In the early years dance lesson, *problem solving, reasoning and numeracy* can be investigated in a number of ways. The EYFS (DCSF, 2008) refers to the need for children to explore 'shape, size and pattern', each of which can be progressed from the recommended 'block play' to the design of different body shapes and sizes in a dance milieu. Spatial patterns made on the floor, as well as in the air, can also be experimented with and observed; these might be recreated on paper in an ensuing art and design-based session. Shreeves (1990: 48) confirms this symbiotic nature of dance and art: 'making designs with paint or collage might well be a follow-up to a movement lesson and in turn stimulate dance ideas'. Moreover, 'distance and measures' (DCSF, 2008) can be woven into dance lessons, by children reflecting on and measuring their use of personal space (close to body) and general space (whole hall), or reviewing distances between body parts or between self and partner. Children will also use numbers and counting, as well as the concepts of adding together and taking away in compositional work, since selection and rejection of dance actions and qualities is inevitable in such problem solving processes. Some suggest that when children use their whole bodies to explore the environment (as in a dance lesson), there are important brain pathways laid down: 'self-initiated movement, exploration, interaction and physical experience for the joy and challenge of it, facilitates neurogenesis (nerve growth) for a lifetime' (Hannaford, 2005: 22). In a similar vein, Lee (2005:13) advocates a more physical approach to numeracy in the early years, making explicit references to mathematical concepts and terms: 'When children experience crouching, stretching, running, jumping, climbing and rolling, pathways are laid down in the brain and these contribute greatly to learning about position, size, shape and space'.

Within the *knowledge and understanding of the world* area of learning and development, exploration and investigation are cited as central aspects in the EYFS (DCSF, 2008). In tandem with these, designing and making, ICT, time, place and communities are delineated. Promoting a reflective approach to dance-making in focused appreciation work encourages children to question how and why things work, and to develop their understanding of change and patterns. Through prop work (e.g. scarves, ribbons, cloth, costumes), children can also investigate materials and their properties, learning and applying concepts such as gravity, momentum, forces, sending and receiving, pattern-making and more. In designing and making dance sequences, construction processes from the classroom using specific tools and techniques can be reviewed and revitalised through the physical. An additional ideal support for dance learning is ICT; children's sequences can be filmed and evaluated, simple composition diaries can be typed up, and information sources and images can be readily accessed from the internet – cross-curricular approaches such as these aim to consolidate, integrate and extend pupil learning. With carefully focused thematic work, the EYFS (DCSF, 2008) aspects of time, place and communities can also be examined through dance units of work, permitting dance to become 'the element ... that ideally bridges the gap between hall and classroom' (Slater, 1993: v).

At first sight, it is the EYFS (DCSF, 2008) area of learning and development entitled *physical development* that seems to provide the strongest rationale for dance. Indeed, its emphasis on the aspects of movement and space, health and bodily awareness, and using equipment and materials, as well as its recommendation for children to use 'all of their senses to learn about the world around them' (DCSF, 2008), reveal strong interrelationships between the EYFS and dance. Skills of 'coordination, control, manipulation and movement' are also specifically referred to here; these provide the movement building blocks from which the teacher can design and plan their dance lessons. Through frequent practice, individual parts of the child's body have to learn to work together, which becomes more challenging as movements are varied. In this way, children can be guided to move their arms and legs with contrasting dynamics or in different directions as their physical proficiency levels increase. Interestingly, Davies (2003: 54) inadvertently refers to the EYFS (DCSF, 2008) 'using equipment and materials' when she describes one of four important categories of movement: young children test themselves 'in terms of dexterity through handling and playing with objects such as rattles, balls, hoops, ropes, sticks, conkers and stones'. Moreover, through actions such as turning, spinning, twirling, and swooping – an integral part of Davies' (2003: 54) fourth movement category – it is clear that children can satisfy their appetite for movement in different spatial areas; an essential ingredient of any early years dance lesson.

Just like its predecessor, *physical development,* the aspect known as *creative development* has an obvious connection to dance. Indeed, the EYFS (DCSF, 2008) confirms that creating music and dance is one of the aspects of creative development, emphasising the need for children to experience independent and guided explorations that include matching movements to music. Once again, the senses are illuminated in creative work, as are children's abilities to 'express and communicate their own ideas, thoughts and feelings'. The importance of these aspects in dance education have been highlighted by several dance writers in the field (Bartal and Ne'eman, 2001, Davies, 2003; Smith-Autard, 1994), who encourage the promotion of sensory work and divergent thinking in dance contexts, along with originality and spontaneity. Under the umbrella of creative development, developing imagination and imaginative play are also proposed in the EYFS (DCSF, 2008), and dance is mentioned in conjunction with stories, role-plays, imaginative play, music, design, and art. Dance could also become an integral part of the EYFS (DCSF, 2008) aspect entitled 'exploring media and materials', since children are expected to find out about, think about and work with colour, texture, shape, space and form in two and three dimensions. Clearly, two- and three-dimensional work in all of these areas is possible in the dance lesson. Harrison (1993: 102–103), for example, suggests dance tasks based on group shapes and formations, whilst others investigate colour, texture, space and form through schemes of work that are highly cross-curricular in nature (Slater, 1993; Shreeves, 1990).

Rachael Jefferson-Buchanan

THE PLACE OF DANCE IN THE PRIMARY SCHOOL IN THE UK

In the Tickell Review (2011) of the EYFS, the six areas of learning and development are rearticulated to form three 'prime' and four 'specific areas' (Tickell, 2011: 27), with physical development being one of the prime areas alongside personal, social and emotional development, and communication and language. The four specific areas in which the prime skills are applied are literacy, mathematics, expressive arts and design, and understanding the world (Tickell, 2011: 27). Evidently, the argument above for raising the profile of dance in the EYFS (DCSF, 2008) is therefore well timed, since dance has long been recognised as a 'physical art form' (McFee, 1992) that seems to fit into both physical and expressive arts domains according to the context. Notwithstanding this, dance sits quite uncomfortably at times in the National Curriculum primary physical education programme of study. Indeed, there has been much debate as to whether this is its ideal location, despite the fact that it became a statutory part of physical education for Key Stages 1 and 2 in 1992 (Sanderson, 1996). For now, however, it is essential to focus on how dance is presented within the current primary physical education programme of study (PoS) in order to contextualise the discussion that follows. Dance is one of three core activities at Key Stage 1 (alongside gymnastics and games), and it retains this status in Key Stage 2. The requirements for dance at Key Stages 1 and 2 are given below in their original format; they will be investigated through the subsequent discussion of the three dance processes.

> *At Key Stage 1, pupils should be taught to:*
> - use movement imaginatively, responding to stimuli, including music, and performing basic skills (for example, travelling, being still, making a shape, jumping, turning and gesturing)
> - change the rhythm, speed, level and direction of their movements
> - create and perform dances using simple movement patterns, including those from different times and cultures
> - express and communicate ideas and feelings.
>
> *At Key Stage 2, pupils should be taught to:*
> - create and perform dances using a range of movement patterns, including those from different times, places and cultures
> - respond to a range of stimuli and accompaniment.
>
> (DfE/QCA, 1999)

THE THREE DANCE PROCESSES: COMPOSITION, PERFORMANCE AND APPRECIATION

Connections to the EYFS are evident in the above primary physical education PoS, particularly in terms of the use of the imagination, patterns, and expressing and communicating ideas and feelings. However, something that is perhaps even more noteworthy, is the way in which the primary physical education PoS is underpinned by Rudolf Laban's (1948) movement analysis, which developed into a language for interpreting, describing, visualising and notating all forms of human movement. During the late 1940s until the early 1970s, Laban principles strongly influenced dance in schools, resulting in a change to its name ('modern educational dance', 'creative dance') and its form, which became more 'free' and 'child-centred' as opposed to following sets of standardised exercises in earlier physical education syllabi (Preston-Dunlop, 1963; Smith-Autard, 1994). Due to the limitations of this chapter, it is impossible to examine Laban's work in any real depth, but it should be recognised that Laban classified movement into sixteen themes, each of which suggests a range of movement that can be explored. In Theme IV, for example, 'The awareness of the different aspects of the flow of movement is developed and used to form movement phrases' (Preston-Dunlop, 1963: xiv). Space, weight, time and flow are central to these sixteen themes, and it is concepts such as these, in tandem with other generic dance concepts, that warrant further consideration in the review of the three dance processes below.

COMPOSITION

Composition is one of the three processes that provide the conceptual framework for dance in education, and due to its inherent nature, it can help to foster children's creativity. Hawkins (1964: 30) maintains that 'the creative aspect of dance should start early and be experienced continually'. A simple way to introduce composition to young children is to explain the notion of 'dance-making'. The diagram below might help teachers to understand the processes involved in dance composition, although it should be noted that this is a guideline only, with multiple entry and exit points. For instance, improvisation occurs throughout the composition process, not merely in the initial stages before phrases and motifs are created.

> choose stimulus → investigate and respond to stimulus → improvise → select movement material → compose phrases and create motifs → vary, develop and refine phrases and motifs → use compositional devices → decide on the dance form

Choose stimulus: in the primary physical education PoS, it is clear that a range of stimuli and accompaniment is deemed essential. Stimuli to help begin the dance composition process might be ideational (topic-based, conveying a story or idea), visual, auditory, tactile or kinaesthetic in nature (Smith-Autard, 1992: 26–28). Sometimes, combinations of stimuli might influence the dance composition as it evolves.

Investigate and respond to stimulus: once stimuli have been decided upon and shared, pupils can investigate and respond to these, reflecting on what the stimulus makes them think about and how this might be developed into movement. At this stage, children could be encouraged to develop a concept-map or word bank, which could subsequently develop into an 'action concept-map' or 'action bank' when improvisation begins to take place in the primary hall.

Improvise: in this process, pupils experiment with their bodies, solving movement problems given to them by the teacher in imaginative and spontaneous ways. It is important

that they are given adequate time to go beyond their 'favourite' movements and dig deeper into new movement possibilities. Pupils can be encouraged to perform some of the basic skills in the Key Stage 1 primary physical education PoS: 'travelling, being still, making a shape, jumping, turning and gesturing'. In Laban's Theme VI (Preston-Dunlop, 1963: 37), five similar body actions are also identified: gesture, stepping, locomotion, jumping and turning. These skills and actions facilitate the extension of pupils' movement vocabulary.

Select movement material: during the improvisation process, the teacher and pupil choose which movements they wish to keep or discard, according to the style, type or intention of the dance composition.

Compose phrases and create motifs: this is the 'building' stage of the dance, wherein actions are ordered into dance phrases and potential motifs (simple movements or movement patterns that can be developed) are found.

Vary, develop and refine phrases and motifs: in this process, the building continues, but with an awareness of variation and development. Smith-Autard (1992: 40–43) suggests that a motif can be developed and refined by focusing on action, qualitative (dynamics), spatial and relationship features. Several of Laban's themes use these same possibilities (Themes II, IV, V, VII, Preston-Dunlop, 1963: xiv–xv). Moreover, the primary physical education PoS alludes to changes of 'rhythm, speed [dynamics], level and direction [space]'.

Use compositional devices: some examples of compositional devices are canon, unison, repetition, variation and development, contrast and complementary movements, highlights, climax, chance, addition and subtraction, juxtaposition, balance, proportion. These devices add colour, texture and interest to a dance composition.

Decide on the dance form: this is the structure or shape of the dance. Phrases usually bind together into sections (A, B, C ...), and these sections have transitions. The organisation of movements, phrases and sections constitutes the dance form. Dance composition often borrows from musical forms, thus 'binary' (AB), 'ternary' (ABA), 'rondo' (ABACA) and related forms are commonplace. Laban's Theme XII (Preston-Dunlop, 1963: 103–111) considers the relationship between the form and content of movement, focusing particularly on the concept of wholeness and the link between effort (dynamics) and shape in movement.

PERFORMANCE

Whilst the composition process is undertaken, pupils will inevitably develop and refine the quality of their performance skills, but it is the teacher's role to ensure that performance is an explicit part of every dance lesson. This might simply be achieved through opportunities to share dance work with one another in small group or whole-class situations, but it could also include observing performances of professional dance works and working with professional dance artists. In terms of what performance actually constitutes, 'It is generally accepted that performance skills in dance can be divided into three

141

distinct categories of technical skills, expressive skills, and movement components' (Beveridge and Jefferson-Buchanan, 2009: 3). This gives the early years and primary teacher essential ingredients to select from and subsequently design their dance lessons, thus each of these performance categories warrants discussion.

Technical skills include heightening children's awareness of their posture and alignment. Regular consideration and correction of body shapes, along with basic sitting and standing positions can be woven into the dance lesson's warm-up, main activity and cool-down. Children's ability to manage their bodies and control movements in motion and stillness is also important. Beyond this, an additional technical skill to nurture in young children is moving the whole body and parts of the body with coordination, strength, flexibility and balance, for which a flow of energy is vital. Moreover, the development of movement memory might also be classed as an important technical skill to be nurtured in the young child. In terms of the primary physical education PoS, at Key Stage 1 there is predominantly an emphasis on performing basic skills (travelling, being still, making a shape, jumping, turning and gesturing), but very little additional guidance in the area of technical skills either at Key Stage 1 or 2.

Expressive skills essentially comprise projection, focus and a sense of style. In addition, the dancer's ability to convey the compositional intention, idea, theme, story or mood is essential, as 'Children use dance movements as a form of communication, expressing what they understand through the content of their dances' (Bloomfield and Childs, 2000: 61). The development of musicality is also important for the child learning to dance. Indeed, without sensitivity to and an understanding of music, the child will be unable to respond appropriately to the rhythm, melody and mood of the accompaniment. The primary physical education PoS highlights the need for pupils to learn to express and communicate ideas and feelings, which seems to affirm the pivotal place of expressive skills in dance work.

There is general consensus that *movement components* are action (what), dynamics (how), space (where) and relationships (with whom/what) (Smith-Autard, 1992: 19). In the primary physical education PoS, pupils should be guided to change the rhythm, speed, level and direction of their movements; this draws attention to the movement components of dynamics and space in particular. Children's performance skills can effectively be sharpened throughout the dance lesson by consistently reminding them that movements have to be clear in terms of the four components. Laban's (1948) previously discussed body actions can be introduced: gesture, stepping, locomotion, jumping and turning, and in addition to these, flexion, extension, rotation, pause (stillness), isolation and weight transference can be refined. Laban's Theme VII (Preston-Dunlop, 1963: 44–59) is particularly useful when it comes to developing children's understanding of dynamics, which might be encouraged by focusing on pairs of dynamic opposites: thrusting and floating, slashing and gliding, wringing and dabbing, pressing and flicking. Dynamics essentially colour the movement, affecting its weight, flow, speed, rhythm, accent and phrasing. In the third movement component, space, the child can be guided to reflect on body shape, directions, floor and air pathways, levels (high, medium, low), size and orientation. Two of Laban's themes (Theme IX and XI, Preston-Dunlop, 1963) concentrate on the awareness of shape in movement and orientation in space respectively. Finally, in relationship work a body part to body part, movement to movement, dancer to dancer, or the inter-action and communication between dancers could become significant at various stages. It is also essential for children to develop their sensitivity to other dancers, as a result of which, complementary and contrasting relationships will arise.

APPRECIATION

Appreciation is often the most neglected of the three dance processes, yet it is through appreciation that children can learn to apply theory to their practice of composition and performance, and vice versa. Davies (2003: 172) affirms the strong relationship between *'doing* and *viewing'*, referring to them as 'interchangeable partners'. Dance appreciation is recognised as being inherently complex, involving description, analysis, interpretation and evaluation (Adshead, 1988). However, in young children it is relatively easy to culti-vate their appreciation skills by having a simple observational framework and ensuring that there is enough time in and beyond the lesson to reflect on dance works made by the children and also by professionals. For example, if the four performance movement components mentioned previously were focused on, the teacher could nurture chil-dren's appreciation in relation to the dancer's/dancers' use of action, dynamics, space and relationships in their composition. Ashley (2002: 173) confirms that 'If you under-stand more about what makes a successful dance your own work will improve', which could well be used as an argument for fine-tuning children's appreciation skills due to the positive effect that they can have on follow-up composition and performance work. Interestingly, the primary physical education PoS fails to mention appreciation skills, which seems to be rather an oversight, particularly when the former EYFS (DCSF, 2008) discussion successfully illuminated the strong cross-curricular potential between dance and communication, language and literacy.

It is essential to elaborate on the four components of dance appreciation to better under-stand how these might be developed in the early years and primary context:

Description: in its simplest form, appreciation involves observing, identifying, naming and describing movements. When young children watch each other's dance work, their descriptions might focus on a particular movement they remember, an interesting body part or shape that was used, or perhaps a moment that they found exciting, always under-pinned with reasons why such features were notable for them. They could talk, write or draw about such experiences, which highlights the intrinsic cross-curricular possibilities within appreciation. When watching a professional dance work, pupils might focus on the dance idea, or the historical and social context of the work. The style of a piece, as well as the gender, number and role of the dancers might also be investigated, and key features of the set, design, costume, and lighting could be drawn or painted.

Analysis: during this process, each small aspect of a movement can be examined in detail. For example, the young child might be encouraged to reflect on the movement they remembered from before and comment on its use of dynamics, or they could observe the previous interesting body part or shape again and consider the use of symmetry and asymmetry throughout. The four movement components (action, dynamics,

143

space, relationships) are again important at this stage of appreciation. Pupils might be encouraged to find and share words that capture the feeling, meaning or mood of the dance phrase or movement. Moreover, compositional devices such as unison, canon and climax could be analysed in small groups or as a whole class. When reviewing a professional dance work, pupils could focus on all of the above aspects, but additionally contemplate how the accompaniment, lighting, costumes or set might support the dance idea, or focus on identifying and analysing each section of the dance's form.

Interpretation: it is perhaps helpful to connect this component of appreciation with meaning-making. Hodgens (in Adshead, 1988: 61) confirms that an interpretation of a dance involves meanings or significance, but she develops this to include a dance's character and qualities as well. In the educational context, pupils need to be encouraged to make sense of what they see being danced before them, but their powers of perception and imagination require support from the teacher in this process. Central questions to consider are what they think is being communicated, and what feelings the character or qualities of the work evoke in them. Older children might be encouraged to use metaphors and analogies to clarify their viewpoints and perceptions. However, at all stages, each point made needs to be substantiated with reasoned comments that include examples from earlier description and analysis.

Evaluation: means judging or appraising the worth of the dance; the observer effectively weighs up its merits and decides what works and why it works, as well as why they like or dislike it. It should be mentioned here that although it is recognised that evaluations of dances are socially and culturally determined, comments still need to be supported by references to specific aspects of the dance. If the dance has a purpose, the worth of it might be assessed according to whether or not it has achieved this by explaining certain movements viewed. A dance might also be evaluated in terms of the experiences it engenders, for example, it might make the observer feel very happy when they are watching it due to certain aspects that are comical in nature. In the early years or primary school context the 'two stars and a wish' evaluation framework is a popular one, permitting children to describe two things they like about a dance, concurrently suggesting one thing they think could be improved. This can help to promote stimulating dialogue between the composer, performer and viewer.

THOUGHT BOX

It is common in many schools to rely on schemes or tapes to deliver part if not all of the dance curriculum elements. Consider how effective these resources are in practice in encouraging the language and learning exemplified in the three dance processes of 'composition', 'performance' and 'appreciation'.

Rachael Jefferson-Buchanan

Table 8.1 Integrated, holistic and cross-curricular ways of working: dance ideas based on 'The Tale of Mr. Jeremy Fisher' by Beatrix Potter

Stimulus/focus	Suggested activities	Examples of links to EYFS (2008) and the National Curriculum primary physical education programme of study
Text: various words from 'The Tale of Mr. Jeremy Fisher' that have movement potential: 'slippy-sloppy, enormous hops, cross-legged, wriggling, tweaked, rustle, splash, shoved, floundered, jumped, seized, dived down, bounced up, scrambled…'	**Section A:** Choose 2–3 of the text words to begin a whole class composition based on Jeremy Fisher. Focus on how the words might be interpreted through movement. Pupils learn a few examples below, and then develop their own ideas alongside these. *Examples:* 1 'tweaked' – to pinch and twist sharply (use fingers and enlarge to whole arm movements, twist arms to the side of your body and look behind you with a sudden quality). 2 'rustle' – to make a gentle sound as of dry blown leaves (lie on the floor and slide forwards whilst gently wriggling body parts, turn on tiptoes whilst performing wriggling finger movements on different levels). 3 'scrambled' – to hurriedly or anxiously clamber, crawl, climb (use low-level movements that quickly rise, incorporate legs and arms in fast coordinated patterns).	**EYFS (2008):** *personal social and emotional development* (working as a whole group, following instructions and cooperating with others in a practical context); *communication, language and literacy* (working from text, characterisation, building vocabulary from movement work); *problem solving, reasoning and numeracy* (sequential memory, adding movements together); *knowledge and understanding of the world* (frogs and their habitats/movements); *physical development* (fine and gross motor, coordination); *creative development* (imaginative play, finding novel ways of moving, interpreting words and translating them into actions, texturing these actions with frog-like qualities). **Primary Physical Education PoS:** *Key Stage 1*: use movement imaginatively, responding to stimuli, including music, and performing basic skills; change the rhythm, speed, level and direction of their movements; create and perform dances using simple movement patterns, including those from different times and cultures; express and communicate ideas and feelings. *At Key Stage 2*: create and perform dances using a range of movement patterns, including those from different times, places and cultures; respond to a range of stimuli and accompaniment.

continued overleaf

Stimulus/focus	Suggested activities	Examples of links to EYFS (2008) and the National Curriculum primary physical education programme of study
Professional dance work: DVD 'Tales of Beatrix Potter' (1971) Frederick Ashton, Dancers of the Royal Ballet.	**Section B:** Watch Jeremy Fisher's solo in the ballet 'Tales of Beatrix Potter'. Pupils learn some of the steps and actions from Jeremy Fisher's solo. 1 Take a relaxed position reading a real or imagined newspaper. 2 Jump and leap in the rain: pupils learn 1–2 different symmetrical/asymmetrical jumps and leaps, e.g. pas de chat, diamond shape with legs made from a 2-foot take-off. 3 Jump the imaginary lily pads from 2 feet to 2 feet, travelling forward to a specific space. 4 Fishing: use repeated and exaggerated arm gestures…. cast the imaginary line, then struggle with an imaginary trout, fall into the water, swim to shore and crawl out onto the bank. Explore safe and different ways of 'falling', e.g. falling to side, falling with a twist. 'Swimming' movements can be stylised, i.e. actual adapted breaststroke under the 'water' but rising from the floor to the water surface (high level). 5 Sit down and check for broken body parts: wriggle the body, flex and stretch hands, feet and limbs. 6 Finish the section by leaping and jumping energetically to the edges of the hall on indirect pathways.	**EYFS (2008):** *personal social and emotional development* (working as a whole group, performing and sharing space with others, expressive qualities); *communication, language and literacy* (named actions and their qualities); *problem solving, reasoning and numeracy* (body shape, levels, spatial patterns); *knowledge and understanding of the world* (frogs and their habitats/movements, safe practice, gravity, forces, leisure pursuits: fishing, swimming); *physical development* (locomotor skills, body management, coordination); *creative development* (moving with a range of dynamic qualities, senses, using a variety of actions, matching music to movement). **Primary Physical Education PoS:** See above: all aspects can be covered.

Stimulus/focus	Suggested activities	Examples of links to EYFS (2008) and the National Curriculum primary physical education programme of study
Compositional device: canon, unison **Motif development** **Structuring the dance form**	**Refinement of sections A and B to make a whole group composition:** 1 Everyone performs section A, working on the quality of their movements and logical transitions between actions. Set off groups of pupils in canon so that they begin to observe one another's work, and are introduced to a compositional device. 2 Narrate section B, with all pupils performing this together in unison. They can make different group formations around the hall, e.g. lines, stars, 'V' shapes, or circles. 3 Develop one of the jumping/leaping movements into a motif. Change it in two ways, through *action, space, dynamics or relationships*, to make clear starting and finishing actions/positions for the composition. 4 Add section A (text exploration) to section B (professional dance work exploration) and perform as a half class. Pupils comment on teacher-directed appreciation tasks, e.g. pairs with interesting jumps/leaps, spatial and relationship variety, imaginative motif developments, clear dynamic changes and the like. These tasks can be discussed, written about, or drawn.	**EYFS (2008):** *personal social and emotional development* (working in groups, communication, decision making, performing to others and being performed to, sharing space with others); *communication, language and literacy* (listening to and following instructions, observing and appreciating dances); *problem solving, reasoning and numeracy* (timing, rhythmical structure, dance phrases, canon, spatial areas and formations); *knowledge and understanding of the world* (respect for others' work, safe practice, kinaesthetic/sensory awareness), *physical development* (locomotor skills, body management and control, clarity of movements); *creative development* (improving quality of movements and transitions between movements, recognising and respecting variation and development in others' work). **Primary Physical Education PoS:** See above: all aspects can be covered.

continued overleaf

Stimulus/focus	Suggested activities	Examples of links to EYFS (2008) and the National Curriculum primary physical education programme of study
Extension possibilities: Cross-curricular links – animals and creatures		

■ *English*: creative and descriptive writing, discussion, debate, vocabulary, stories, songs, rhymes, poetry, myths, legends…

■ *Maths*: shape, size, number, weight, counting, graphs, symmetry and asymmetry…

■ *Science*: animal movements/habitats/habits, ourselves, body structure, life forms and cycles…

■ *ICT*: digital photos/video recordings of animal dances, collecting and recording class data, e.g. pupils' pets/favourite animals…

■ *PSHE*: animal diseases, poisonous creatures, extinction, zoos, safari parks, farms and animals, animal welfare societies…

■ *Citizenship*: what improves and harms their natural environment, pollution, how some diseases are spread from animals, quarantine, names of the main parts of the body, playing and working cooperatively, different risks in different situations…

■ *History*: prehistoric animals, mythology, famous historic animals…

■ *Geography*: changes in physical features, what places are like (e.g. pond life), making a map of the pond area or Jeremy Fisher's use of space…

■ *Religious Education*: use of symbols in dance and religions, religious stories that include animals, how religious beliefs and ideas can be communicated through dance and other arts…

■ *Art and Design*: life drawings (still and moving), painting, frieze work, printing, patterns inspired by animal colourings/markings…

■ *Design and Technology*: explore the sensory qualities of materials that draw their inspiration from the frog's natural environment (e.g. leathery material: frog skin; spring: frog jumping mechanism), how mechanisms could be used to make joints that move like a frog's legs, measure, mark, cut out and shape given materials into chosen animals…

■ *Music*: animal themes, animal noises, bird song…

■ *MFL*: memorising words and phrases related to the animals and creatures topic, using dictionaries and reference material in other languages that focus on the topic, learning animal songs, rhymes and poems in other languages…

Adapted from Jefferson-Buchanan, 2004: 10–11

CONCLUSION

Due to historical influences, there can sometimes be an emphasis on composition and creativity in dance education, at the expense of performance and appreciation. Similarly, dance can be separated out from other EYFS (DCSF, 2008) areas of learning and development or primary school subjects, rather than being seen as a medium for learning in and across the curriculum. These factors, coupled with some teachers' heavy reliance on bought schemes of work for dance, can impede holistic, cross-curricular approaches. Notwithstanding this, the above discussion offers suggestions for embedding dance within the early years and primary school context, and thereby connecting up traditionally compartmentalised methods of learning and teaching. Dance is a developmentally appropriate physical activity for young children, which can help them appreciate the joy of moving and what it can accomplish in their holistic development. Indeed, it is widely recognised that dance can make a unique contribution to children's wellbeing and general development (Bloomfield and Childs, 2000; Davies, 2003; Shreeves, 1990). An integrated, holistic and cross-curricular approach to dance teaching and learning in the early years and primary context can enhance this further, helping young children to attain their movement milestones in exciting ways en route to adolescence.

KEY READINGS

It is hard to approach this topic sensibly without an appreciation of the underpinning ideas expressed in Laban, R. (1948) *Modern Educational Dance*, London: Macdonald and Evans. Greater awareness of the field leads to few 'go to' texts for the dance practitioner. Though not primary-specific, one text however that falls into this category for its vision and implementation should be Smith-Autard, J. (1992) *The Art of Dance in Education*, London: A&C Black.

REFERENCES

Adshead, J. (ed.) (1988) *Dance Analysis: Theory and Practice,* London: Dance Books.

Ashley, L. (2002) *Essential Guide to Dance* (2nd ed), London: Hodder and Stoughton.

Bartal, L. and Ne'eman, N. (2001) *Movement Awareness and Creativity* (2nd ed), Alton: Dance Books.

Beveridge, K. and Jefferson-Buchanan, R. (2009) Improving the quality of performance skills in children and young people, *Dance Matters*, 55, Summer, 2–5.

Bloomfield, A. and Childs, J. (2000) *Teaching Integrated Arts in the Primary School: Dance, Drama, Music and the Visual Arts*, London: David Fulton.

Cohen, A. (2007) *Stories on the Move: integrating Literature and Movement with Children, from Infants to Age 14*, Westport: Libraries Unlimited.

Davies, M. (2001) *Helping Children to Learn through a Movement Perspective* (2nd ed), London: Paul Chapman.

Davies, M. (2003) *Movement and Dance in Early Childhood* (2nd ed), London: Paul Chapman.

Department for Children, Schools and Families (DCSF) (2008) *Early Years Foundation Stage,* London: HMSO.

Department for Education and Employment/Qualifications and Curriculum Authority (DfE/QCA) (1999) *The National Curriculum in England; Physical Education,* London: HMSO.

Hall, J. (1997) *Dance for Infants,* London: A&C Black.

Hannaford, C. (2005) *Smart moves: Why learning is not all in your head,* Salt Lake City, Utah: Great River Books.

Harrison, K. (1993) *Let's Dance: The Place of Dance in the Primary School,* London: Hodder and Stoughton.

Hawkins, A. (1964) *Creating through Dance,* Englewood Cliffs, NJ: Prentice-Hall.

Jefferson-Buchanan, R. (2004) Beatrix Potter boogies on down: A resource for key stage 1 and 2, *Dance Matters,* Winter 2004, 41, 10–11.

Jefferson-Buchanan, R. (2007) High Quality Primary Dance – Are Stories a 'Magic Formula'?, *Primary Physical Education Matters,* 2, 1, vi.

Laban, R. (1948) *Modern Educational Dance,* London: Macdonald and Evans.

Landalf, H. and Gerke, P. (2004) *Movement Stories for Young Children: Ages 3–6,* Portland: Smith and Kraus.

Lee, K. (2005) Body of Knowledge, *TES Teacher,* 29 April, 12–13.

McFee, G. (1992) *Understanding Dance,* London: Routledge.

Ousooren, R.A. (2005) *Write Dance in the Nursery: A Pre-Writing Programme for Children 3 to 5,* Paul Chapman: London.

Preston-Dunlop, V. (1963) *A Handbook for Modern Educational Dance,* London: Macdonald and Evans.

Sanderson, P. (1996) Dance within the National Curriculum for Physical Education of England and Wales, *European Physical Education Review,* 2, 1, 54–63.

Shreeves, R. (1990) *Children Dancing* (2nd ed), East Grinstead: Ward Lock Educational.

Slater, W. (1993) *Dance and Movement in the Primary School: A Cross-Curricular Approach to Lesson Planning,* Plymouth: Northcote House.

Smith-Autard, J. (1992) *The Art of Dance in Education,* London: A&C Black.

Tickell, C. (2011) The Early Years: Foundations for life, health and learning. Available online at http://media.education.gov.uk/MediaFiles/B/1/5/%7BB15EFF0D-A4DF–4294–93A1–1E1B88C13F68%7DTickell%20review.pdf (accessed 12 May 2011).

Tinning, R. (2009) Thinking about thinking bodies and moving minds in the context of recent HPE curriculum initiatives in New Zealand, *New Zealand Physical Educator,* 42, 2, 9–13.

YDE (2010) *Young People's Dance: A Ten Year Vision,* London: Youth Dance.

CHAPTER NINE

GETTING ATHLETICS OFF THE TRACK, OUT THE SACK AND 'BACK ON TRACK'

Gerald Griggs

INTRODUCTION

The landscape of primary athletics is a patchy affair. To date it remains a neglected area of the National Curriculum for physical education (NCPE) at this level due to reasons such as lack of training and resources (Ofsted, 2005; Warburton, 2001) and the fact that the present curriculum only requires teaching athletics in Key Stage 2 and allows schools the opportunity to drop it all together if they so wish (DfEE/QCA, 1999). Where it is delivered, for the most part, the teaching of athletics involves engaging in basic running, jumping and throwing activities which will most likely have one or more of the following aims: to teach and practise basic techniques and skills, to measure and improve individual performance (often scheme-based) or to prepare for challenges and competitions such as 'sports day'. Such aims are wholly appropriate of course and are drawn from programmes of study to be found in either the current of former curriculum documents for physical education. In addition, suggested activities to aid in delivery can be found in QCA Schemes of Work (QCA, 2000), which in many schools are embedded into their planning. However, it is evident upon close examination that the most important aim has been overlooked, namely the need to develop a fundamental understanding of how the body moves.

When technique becomes the focus for instance, it is often the case that children have insufficient strength or ability to copy advanced techniques correctly or use them to their advantage. The crouch start in sprinting used on the track is a particular case in point here where the practice is encouraged by both teachers and pupils alike but in reality most children have to use their energy just to get up again! They gain no advantage from the deep compression of the leg that an adult would and are better served by standing and merely leaning in a ready position over their front leg. In contrast, by simply 'practising for sports day' and getting little direction or getting told to bounce along in a sack, children's learning is severely restricted. Though it may be argued that understanding develops by participating in athletic activities, these two examples demonstrate it is very possible to neglect understanding entirely whilst still being consistent with planned objectives. What is illustrated here also is that a meaningful athletic experience within primary schools has been lost as it continues to be squashed between two perspectives. On the one hand the early and inappropriate adoption of adult techniques represents the leaching down of athletics most readily taught in secondary schools, which is arguably the dominant model learned by those now delivering athletics. On the other hand we merely recreate a world of participation, referred to by Placek (1983) whereby children are being 'busy, happy, and good' in which their progressive development is neglected. Clearly neither scenario is ideal and a more effective model for primary athletics needs to be found. A revisiting of Almond's (1989) framework is perhaps timely.

THOUGHT BOX

Consider how many things you deliver in athletics that might not focus on maximising pupil learning. Do they run a certain distance because that is where the lines are marked on the field? Do they do an activity because you found some equipment in the cupboard? Do they do an activity a certain way because you did it that way at secondary school or you saw it on the television?

A FRAMEWORK FOR PRIMARY ATHLETICS – REVISITING ALMOND

Almond (1989) proposes the use of a three-phase model which spans the range of the education system. These three phases are hierarchical and are comprised of:

- Phase 1 – Integrated play
- Phase 2 – The athletic form
- Phase 3 – Athletics as a sport

The integrated play element looks to immerse young children in the world of basic movement identified by Gallahue (1982) in which different actions such as walking, running, jumping and throwing are part of this vocabulary. However, there is no requirement to distinguish between games or gymnastics or athletics here, merely to engage in activities which promote and enjoy movement. Jumping off one foot and landing on two feet would represent such a building block example which in years to come could service any number of uses from landing on a springboard, to catching a netball and completing a long jump. This approach could easily slot into much current practice in Key Stage 1 which does not explicitly plan for athletics. In addition it is also in keeping with the increasing fashion to deliver versions of what are referred to as fundamental movement skills (FMS). However if a sense of progression is to occur practice must then move to Phase 2 which would most commonly occur in the upper primary years.

In this second phase, referred to as the athletic form, three clear dimensions are identified.

The first of these dimensions, that of action possibilities, frames the different action and challenges appropriate for this level. So for example trying the different actions one may use to throw an object such as slinging, trying to throw an object from different positions such as sitting or standing and using these actions for differing purposes such as

152

Gerald Griggs

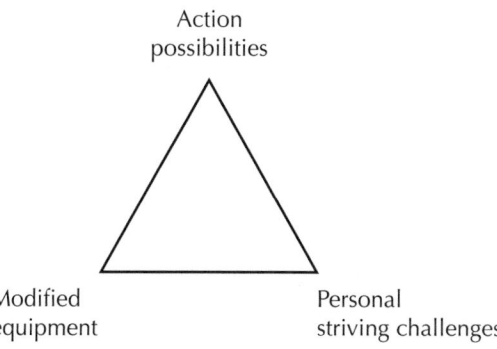

Action
possibilities

Modified
equipment

Personal
striving challenges

Source: Almond, 1989

Figure 9.1 The athletic form

throwing for distance or accuracy. In short exploring fully all the possible actions a body can perform for an athletic purpose. The second dimension is developing an environment where the focus remains on doing one's best and seeking to improve rather than resort to the perpetual need for competition and comparison. Sports days and Mini Olympics have their place in primary school cultures but if these are the sole focus of athletics during these years they appeal to the few successful ones rather than to the many. If lifelong participation in physical activity is a desirable outcome from physical education then such issues have to be given consideration. The third dimension, that of modified equipment, is the commitment to use resources that are appropriate to the maturity of the child and that do not hinder their athletic development. For example, using barriers when hurdling that are proportional to the height and leg length of the child and not just an old set of 'proper hurdles' that have been in the store cupboard for years.

It is expected that at a point within secondary schooling phase three known as 'athletics as sport' will become the focus of attention. It should not automatically be assumed that it should start on day one though! To do so neglects any appreciation that physical education is progressive and developmental in nature. That said, this phase does represent what many of us will identify as 'proper athletics'. Again the phase is illustrated by the use of three dimensions and again in the form of a triangle.

Here one can see that action possibilities have progressed into more formal practices and so the different ways of throwing explained in Phase 2 become the recognised events of javelin, discus, hammer and shot. To this end as the child gains in physical maturity their ability to use the standard equipment increases. However, having learned solid foundations of biomechanical movement in Phase 2, the child should find transition much easier to accommodate. Finally here, athletics moves towards more of the Olympic ideal of faster, higher, stronger and the recognition that athletics at its pinnacle is a competitive practice.

Recognising
competitive
events

Standard
equipment

Striving to
win challenges

Source: Almond, 1989

Figure 9.2 Athletics as sport

The importance of Almond's (1989) framework is that in essence it locates the two polar examples explained earlier of a more adult or competitive-focused athletics and one of participation or more play-focused athletics on something of a continuum. What is more, a central space between these points is clearly identified, exemplifying a progression between the two and locating a secure foundation upon which primary athletics may be based. With a hope that a form of integrated play or fundamental movement practice should find its way into most Key Stage 1 planning, it is this neglected phase of the athletic form that needs greatest attention and it is to that our focus now turns.

EXEMPLIFYING THE ATHLETIC FORM

If the athletic form is to be an effective phase then time and thought must be given to what should comprise the action possibilities, the personal striving challenges and the modified equipment. Without due care and attention the tendency would be to drift towards either of the two poles outlined earlier. It seems appropriate therefore to provide further clarification and exemplification of some key ideas. The first section here provides a comprehensive though not exhaustive list of useful action possibilities.

Action possibilities

Walking

Walk freely
Walk tall or close to the ground
Walk fast

Running

Run on the spot
Run at different speeds e.g. slow, medium and fast
Start and stop running on a signal
Run around different shapes
Run a slalom
Run in different directions e.g. forwards and backwards
Run tall
Frequently change direction whilst running
Run over barriers
Run and exchange an object
Jog with a partner or group

Jumping

Jump for height off two feet
Jump for distance, two feet to two feet (standing long jump)
Jump for distance, one foot to two feet
Hop on one foot onto the same foot
Hop on one foot onto the other foot
Try hopscotch steps from two feet to one foot and then back to two again
Use different combinations of one- and two-footed jumps in a row – 3 or 4 linked together
Jump over a low barrier – jump over it in different directions e.g. forwards or sideways
Try any of the above jumps standing, walking and then running

Throwing

Throwing a large ball up in the air with two hands
Throw a large ball underarm with two hands
Throw a large ball with two hands for distance (soccer ball throw)
Push a large ball with two hands for accuracy and then distance
Throw a small ball up high in the air
Throw a small ball underarm with one hand for accuracy
Throw a small ball with one hand for distance (a 'pull' throw)
Push a small ball with one hand for accuracy and then distance
Try all the above actions from sitting, standing and then walking
Sling a hoop or a quoit sidearm for accuracy then distance
Heave a quoit on a rope over the shoulder for distance

Personal striving challenges

When choosing the type of action possibilities for children the key aspects to consider are first how the movements learned in the integrated play phase can be combined and refined and second what formal events these activities will contribute to at a later stage. Any of the action possibilities listed can simply be turned into a personal challenge in some semblance of a 'beat your own score' activity. This, however, can be arranged according to the tastes of the teacher. With an eye towards later formal events, however, the culmination of this phase should work towards the following challenges:

Walking
- Speed
- Distance
- Running

Speed (sprinting)
- Distance
- Relays
- Hurdling

Jumping
- Standing long jump
- Long jump
- Straddle high jump
- Triple jump

Throwing
- Pulling action (overarm throw) for later javelin
- Pushing action for later shot put
- Slinging sidearm action for later discus
- Heaving over the shoulder action for later hammer

Modified equipment

Key to exploring the action possibilities and achieving success in any of the personal challenges is providing pupils with modified events or equipment. This aspect is again often overlooked as standardised forms, even unwittingly, prevail. For example all too often lanes are drawn on the school field as an annual occurrence and as such there seems to be some obligation to run all the way down them. If anyone has actually observed a small child running what might well be a 100 metre stretch, they will know they sprint at the very beginning, sometimes only as much as 20 metres and then struggle and effectively move as if swimming for the rest of the way. Effectively what this distance has done is to prevent sprinting rather than promote it. If therefore the intention is to run fast the distances chosen should enable this. Therefore a rule of thumb as a starting point would be to add a zero to the current primary year groups to ascertain a maximum

distance e.g. Year 3 = 30 metres up to Year 6 = 60 metres. Again if these are not quite right after trying them out, the distances can be adjusted up or most likely down as required. Inside this distance structure, when required, hurdles can be inserted. Again the focus should be to run over these quickly so the height of the obstacles should allow this and not turn it into a jumping exercise. The obstacles of course can be made from anything from the physical education equipment store that will not hurt if contacted. Ready-made, inexpensive packs can be bought from most stockists but if not the side of a cardboard box folded in half would do equally well. Relays too can also be slotted into this structure with changeovers (the exchanging of any object will do) occurring at the required sprint distances or the lanes being divided up into multiple turns, such as four pupils in each lane. Distance running and pacing become an issue for any child beyond the point at which they stop sprinting. So again, just because a school has a field there is no obligation to run around it – it might be too far. In this instance try multiples of the appropriate sprint distance and again adjust accordingly after seeing the pupils run.

Given the lack of specialist equipment needed for most jumping at a higher level the ability to improvise appropriate barriers here is important also. Canes, ropes or anything long can often be rested on cones to make a higher barrier. Throwing too needs thought especially if all the actions are to be covered in progression for Phase 3. If objects are heavy they are hard to lift, let alone throw. When objects are larger than the hand they are often hard to grip. That said they do need to behave in a way that facilitates the action required. Overarm throwing which develops what is known as the pull action can be completed with anything small enough to be gripped, such as a ball or beanbag. There should be no obligation to throw a stick or a javelin-like object if they cannot throw it straight and true. A better progression would be to use a shuttlecock which behaves the same way if thrown and is easier and arguably safer to use. Balls and bean-bags are also suitable for pushing or putting. For slinging, small hoops or rubber quoits held on one side are far more appropriate than asking a child to use their hand span to grip a fake polystyrene discus. Again grip is everything here. Heaving can be prac-tised by safely improving a weight on the end of a string. Most effectively this can be done by looping a skipping rope around a quoit, though a beanbag in a long sock will serve the same purpose. Given the encouragement to improvise advocated here, a note of caution must be added. In recent years the 'improvisation' of equipment has been frowned upon by some authorities and organisations and so it is always best to check that the newly created objects that you might choose to use are considered appropriate for the activity for which you wish to use them.

APPROACHES TO TEACHING ATHLETICS

As with many areas within sport or physical education a didactic approach to delivery prevails within athletics teaching gleaned from club participation or secondary school provision. This is commonly intertwined with the delivery of a list of apparently 'correct' techniques. As ever this usually neglects the needs and abilities of the child within the primary age phase and so in reality most should be judged with a healthy scepticism. In most instances of far greater benefit to both teachers and their pupils would be to engage in activities that promote personal striving whilst exploring action possibilities. In many cases these are often explored using either a multi-activity or carousel approach and developing activities that foster understanding.

A multi-activity or carousel approach

To gain further experience and practise the personal challenges set across any unit of work, the use of a carousel of activities can be a useful approach to use. It will need planning carefully not least in terms of equipment and space. For example a throwing activity is best placed aimed towards a corner or a wall rather than located in the middle of the room. Similarly in such instances beanbags must be the object of choice as they will not continue to roll unlike tennis balls. That said, with careful thought at least eight activities can be devised in even the smallest of spaces. With two pairs at any activity preferably with one performing and the other observing or recording, a class of 32 pupils can easily be accommodated. A rotation can occur at regular intervals enabling all to gain an experience of the planned activities. While such an approach does well in terms of management, activity levels and participation, efforts must be made here by the teacher to ensure learning occurs. If these activities are essentially being used as practice towards meeting personal challenges, it is recommended that some input occurs at least at the start of the session on a particular activity or that the teacher focuses on developing learning in one area, such as overarm throwing. A focus must remain on quality (of movement) and not just quantity (of success or minutes exercising).

Teaching for understanding

Teaching children to think and understand within athletics sets out to gain an understanding of how the body moves as its primary aim, which in turn provides a solid foundation for engaging in the fundamental athletic activities of walking, running, jumping and throwing. In order to enable children to develop the required understanding, problem-solving activities and focused questioning are a most effective tool to enable children to think. Below are examples of the type of problems/questions that can be set.

Running
- What helps you run quickly?
- Do you run quicker or slower with you arms behind your back? Why/why not?
- When running over hurdles, are you faster if you take off from one foot or two feet? Why?
- Is it better to hurdle with the same or a different leg each time?

Jumping
- Do you jump further/higher with your arms by your side? Why/why not?
- What do your legs do during a) take-off and b) landing?
- What happens to your body weight as you jump?

158

Throwing
- Can you throw a ball further with one hand or two hands?
- When throwing, is it better to stand sideways or face forwards?
- Can you throw as far if you sit down? Why/why not?

There is clearly no right or wrong here just choices to make. The environment, the pupils or your experience on different days will influence this choice but as long as learning occurs and pupils are guided towards increasingly efficient movement, it matters not.

THOUGHT BOX

Consider the strengths and weaknesses of these different approaches. Consider which situations might lend themselves to adopting the different approaches to delivering athletics highlighted here.

CONCLUSION

Given the neglect that athletics has suffered there is clearly a long way to go to get primary athletics back on track and towards an identifiable and meaningful focus. A revisiting of Almond's (1989) framework provides this focus with both a clarification of three distinct phases and then with a later focus on the specific issues pertaining to the second phase of the athletic form. It is hoped what this chapter has served to do is to highlight a way forward for those who wish to put meaningful activities such as walking, running, jumping and throwing back at the heart of physical education. It is felt that with such solid foundations, athletics has a greater potential to be a positive experience for all, usefully underpinning other areas of physical education and contributing to the wider remit of supporting lifelong physical activity.

KEY READINGS

To understand the underpinning concepts of primary athletics, as indicated earlier, Almond, L. (1989) *The Place of Physical Education in Schools*, London: Kogan Page is a good place to start. Key next perhaps would be to find a teaching resource to see how the guidance offered could fit into this framework. An example might be *Elevating Athletics* which has been widely circulated in schools. More details can be found online at http://www.englandathletics.org/

REFERENCES

Almond, L. (1989) *The Place of Physical Education in Schools*, London: Kogan Page.

Department for Education and Employment/Qualifications and Curriculum Authority (DfE/QCA) (1999) *The National Curriculum in England: Physical Education*, London: HMSO.

Gallahue, D. (1982) *Understanding Motor Development in Children*, New York: Jon Wiley.

Ofsted (2005) *Physical education in primary schools*, London: HMSO.

Placek, J.H. (1983) Conceptions of success in teaching: Busy, happy, and good?, in T. Templin and J. Olsen (eds), *Teaching in Physical Education*, Champaign, Il: Human Kinetics Publishers.

Qualifications and Curriculum Authority (QCA) (2000) *Physical education: a scheme of work for key stages 1 and 2*, London: QCA.

Warburton, P. (2001) A sporting future for all: fact or fiction?, *The British Journal of Teaching Physical Education*, 32, 2, 18–21.

Gerald Griggs

CHAPTER TEN

OUTDOOR AND ADVENTUROUS ACTIVITIES

From desks to dens

Nalda Wainwright

INTRODUCTION

This chapter considers the role of outdoor and adventurous activities in the primary school. It is divided into two distinct sections. The first section outlines a rationale for outdoor and adventurous activities as an integral part of children's learning. The second section looks at how schools can achieve this.

There has been much reported in the media demonstrating growing concerns in society about the lack of opportunities for children to roam and play in green spaces (*The Times*, 2007; *Daily Mail*, 2008; *Daily Telegraph*, 2010). In recent years, the ever increasing developments in technology and the loss of green spaces available for children's play in both urban and rural areas have inevitably meant that children spend more of their leisure time on electronic games, in front of televisions and computer screens (Palmer, 2006). Parental fears of children being hurt by traffic, or being snatched by strangers has increased with highly publicised cases in the press and on television resulting in a situation where children are growing up without the same opportunities for physical and free play that were experienced by past generations. Allied to this is an increasing awareness of the outdoor environment as an integral and valued resource for children's learning and development (Maynard and Walters, 2007; Louv, 2005; Garrick, 2004; Waite, 2011), in particular the natural environment, where learning incorporates increased levels of physical activity (Mygind, 2007) and improved motor development (Fjortoft, 2004).

OUTDOOR AND ADVENTUROUS ACTIVITIES, A MUST FOR PHYSICAL EDUCATION

This section explores existing research and literature that create a strong rationale for outdoor and adventurous activities being a part of all children's physical education and wider learning experiences. The field is extensive, and so for the purpose of this chapter, key themes that are particularly relevant to the primary school are considered under separate sub-headings. Although each aspect cannot be discussed in great depth, the aim of this chapter is to give the reader an understanding of the full potential of this area of the curriculum, and the possible consequences if pupils do not have opportunities for outdoor and adventurous activities.

THE IMPORTANCE OF MOVEMENT

The importance of movement in physical education is obvious, but how that early physicality affects a child later in school, in physical education and all aspects of learning, is something that not all teachers are aware of. Early movement experiences are vital for brain development. It is the motor and sensory input experienced in early childhood that 'will "mould" the neurons and interconnections to form sensory and motor processes' (Ayres, 2005: 37).

The development of balance is particularly important, children need to develop good gravitational awareness in order to be able to sit, walk, run and move with competence. This development of balance and postural control is supported by visual and motor systems. The training of these systems takes place gradually over at least seven years, but also continues through puberty and beyond (Goddard Blythe, 2005). If this system does not have the necessary stimuli and experiences to mature then children may have problems later in life. As Blythe and McGlown (1979) explain: 'Immature vestibular functioning is frequently found amongst children who have specific learning difficulties such as Dyslexia and Dyspraxia, problems of attention, language impairment, emotional problems' (cited in Goddard Blythe, 2005: 17).

The increase in the number and variety of baby gadgets available for parents has meant that busy parents are able to entertain babies with relative ease. A baby may be in a car seat, bouncy chair or buggy for much of the day, with little chance for movement, and due to the seat design the baby is supported and has no need to develop core stability and balance. The baby can only interact with its immediate surroundings; opportunities to explore the world are extremely limited. The consequences of this are becoming evident in our schools, with young children unable to sit properly on chairs and lacking the strength and stability required to develop fine motor control.

Children need rich movement experiences, involving, crawling, climbing, swinging, balancing, and inverting the body to ensure maturation of the systems required throughout life. With increasing numbers of children struggling in schools due to poor concentration, a lack of coordination and balance, and delayed speech and language many pupils follow motor programmes as an intervention. These children often find physical education particularly challenging, often missing lessons with a note, forgetting kit, or are so slow changing that they miss much of the session. Ironically, these are the pupils that desperately need good movement experiences.

Outdoor play and adventure can be a means for all pupils to experience high levels of movement in a low stress, meaningful context. Giving pupils opportunities to use the outdoors as an integral part of their learning in natural settings in particular results in improved motor development. The landscape provides dynamic and rough playscapes that challenge motor activity and obstacles that encourage a variety of bodily skills (Fjortoft, 2004). 'Outdoor playgrounds develop strength, flexibility and co-ordination due to the types of activities facilitated by play equipment such as climbing, swinging and balancing' (Munoz, 2009: 11).

Waite (2011) highlights wider benefits suggesting learning outside the classroom enables observation of children's natural behaviour that is not tied to a particular learning outcome. Teachers have opportunities to view the holistic social and emotional aspects of learning that have long been linked with outdoor education. This holistic nature of learning in the outdoors gives young children exploratory experiences in a meaningful context, enabling them to develop an understanding of the embodied self and creating 'opportunities to become risk literate and physically literate' (Maude, 2010: 113).

HEALTH AND WELLBEING

The development of physical literacy contributes to lifelong physical activity, and is defined by Whitehead as:

> Appropriate to each individual's endowment, Physical Literacy is the motivation, confidence, physical competence, knowledge and understanding to maintain physical activity throughout the life course.
>
> (Whitehead, 2010: 11)

Physical activity is an important factor in the maintenance of health, with childhood health and wellbeing constantly in the media. In recent years the particular obsession has been with obesity (*The Times*, 2010a; *Daily Telegraph*, 2011), although there are also concerns about children's mental health (*The Times*, 2010b; *Guardian*, 2006). Research shows that learning in a natural environment incorporates increased levels of physical activity helping significantly towards children achieving their recommended daily activity levels (Mygind, 2007). It also encourages greater levels of activity in girls than in normal schooling (Groves and McNish, 2008). However, it is not just physical health that is improved, contact with nature is also needed to maintain mental health. Louv (2005) highlights the increase in psychological and emotional problems in young children who have reduced contact with natural environments. He goes so far as to identify this as 'Nature-deficit Disorder [which is] the human costs of alienation from nature, among them: diminished use of the senses, attention difficulties, and higher rates of physical and emotional illnesses' (Louv, 2005: 36).

In the report *Natural Thinking*, Bird (2007) also makes a strong case for the importance of engagement with nature linked to a variety of issues. He identifies evidence that suggests nature impacts positively on children's concentration, reducing levels of stress and aggression. It can be used to treat children with poor self-discipline and ADHD (attention deficit hyperactivity disorder) as well as improve wellbeing and mental health. Louv (2005: 105) describes this restorative quality of the environment as 'Nature's Ritalin'.

RISK

Outdoor play has also been linked to the development of children's understandings of risk (Frost, 2006, cited in Munoz, 2009). This is particularly of relevance in light of the much publicised 'cotton wool' society, where children who play in parks and outdoor spaces are usually under the supervision of their parents. Children become more dependent on this supervision and, ironically, less careful (Walsh, 2004). A decrease in the amount of time children spend in free play, roaming woods and parks, results in a loss of opportunity for children to learn about risk and Gill (2007) suggests learning to be safe is about understanding risk. By seeking to protect children, parents are potentially putting them in more danger. Children inevitably seek adventure and challenge and if they have no sanctioned opportunities for this, they may seek out their own and be exposed to greater risk. Or, if as Mortlock (2009) suggests adventure in the natural environment has been replaced by adventure in the form of computer games, then children are not having the necessary real experiences from which to learn to make good judgements. Gill (2007: 16) gives a further argument for exposing children to risk: 'that children build their characters through facing up to adverse circumstances.'

THOUGHT BOX

Consider how much 'fear' impacts upon the opportunities we provide for children in outdoor environments. How real are these fears and can they be overcome?

ENVIRONMENTAL AWARENESS

Environmental awareness has also long been associated with learning in the outdoors. At a time when the Earth's resources are increasingly under pressure there has never been a greater need to develop children's understanding of these issues, and to foster in them the desire to safeguard the environment. Children engaged and learning in the outdoors develop a greater connection with nature (Tunnicliffe, 2008). This recognition is nothing new, and work by Steve Van Matre and Joseph Cornell in the 1970s focused on engaging young people with nature, through multi-sensory approaches to learning in the outdoors. The awareness of the environment does not stop with the knowledge of the biodiversity, but also encompasses students developing an awareness of humanity's impact on the landscape, both historically and in the present. Children will begin to understand their part in that landscape developing a 'sense of place'. Reading the stories of a landscape and being aware of the historical events in a place will develop understanding and empathy for all life dependent on, and linked to, the land (Stewart, 2008). This understanding shapes the view people have of the land and the environment, which influences their treatment both of that place and the people within it.

EQUAL OPPORTUNITIES

The development of empathy through engagement with the landscape is only one aspect of personal growth long associated with learning in the outdoors. The use of outdoor education to engage disaffected pupils is widely acknowledged. There are those that would argue outdoor and adventure activities should not be in the curriculum, that it is not a subject, or area of activity, but a way of experiencing learning and a means of personal growth. Perhaps this difference is a reason in itself to ensure all pupils can experience it. There is no doubt that for most schools the types of specialist experiences that outdoor centres can offer would be impossible to provide and the unique value of a residential experience should not be replaced. With growing numbers of pupils experiencing regular adventurous activities and needing to extend these experiences beyond the school curriculum, the demand for centres may even increase.

Physical education in schools has long been dominated by sport and traditional games in particular (Kirk, 2010), and although what schools are able to offer is a 'curriculum version' of outdoor and adventurous activities it is still a means to engage and motivate the many pupils for whom the traditional physical education experience lacks meaning. The unique nature of many of the challenges in outdoor and adventurous activities means that pupils of all abilities and disabilities are able to engage in the processes required for tasks. This gives an opportunity for those that are not 'sporty' to engage in physical activity and be successful, 'key in becoming and remaining intrinsically motivated' (Glover and Anderson, 2003: 11). Unfortunately it has all too often been an aspect that only takes place at a residential visit, or as occasional orienteering and problem solving around the school grounds (Williams and Wainwright, 2011). However, the opening line of the Qualifications and Curriculum Authority (QCA) definition of physical education states: *'A high quality Physical Education curriculum enables all pupils to enjoy and succeed in many kinds of physical activity'* (QCA, 2007, cited in Kirk, 2010: 13).

Outdoor and adventurous activities therefore needs to be an integral part of the physical education programme of study to ensure a broad experience with a range of activities.

21ST-CENTURY LEARNERS

The lack of emphasis on outdoor and adventurous activities may be set to change. In Wales this has already happened. The revised curriculum in 2008 saw adventurous activities become a statutory element of the physical education programme of study at Key Stages 2 and 3 and optional at Key Stage 4. Early Years and Key Stage 1 were replaced by the Foundation Phase, a play-based curriculum with a greater emphasis on learning in the outdoors. A Skills Framework was introduced to underpin the whole of the curriculum for 3–19 year olds, and requires the development of the key skills of thinking, communication, IT and number, through all aspects of learning. This change in the curriculum was brought about to suit the aptitudes and interests of learners and to meet the requirements of employers and others (DCELLS, 2008).

165

It is a well acknowledged fact that the pupils of the 21st century will not need to know information, as much as they will need to know how to find, process and use information (Henton, 1996). Teachers are acutely aware of the pressure to enable pupils to become critical thinkers and problem solvers. Research into the implementation of adventurous activities in the new physical education curriculum in Wales highlighted the strength of these activities in delivering opportunities for children to develop these key skills (Wainwright and Williams, 2011). One factor that develops metacognition is an environment that encourages pupils to take risks with their learning, developing learners who are not afraid to make mistakes when attempting new challenges, and able to reflect on their experiences.

Team-building and adventure activities have often been seen as an ideal vehicle, not only for developing leadership skills and group work, but also as a means of creating situations that enable young people to overcome challenging situations. These activities often result in raised levels of confidence and self-esteem, vital qualities in any context, and especially necessary for confronting failure (Katz, 1993). Our pupils need to develop into dynamic, active learners able to deal with the challenges of the 21st century. They will need a variety of experiences to develop the resilience and creativity to solve problems they encounter in life. Outdoor and Adventurous Activities have a significant contribution to make in helping them achieve this.

HOW DOES A SCHOOL PUT THIS INTO PRACTICE?

This section will discuss practical issues for implementing outdoor and adventurous activities in physical education and across the curriculum. Every school is unique, and one of the challenges for teachers is knowing what will work for their school. There is no easy one-size-fits-all toolbox; every local area and community is different, with a variety of needs and expectations. The individual abilities of pupils, their readiness for activities and challenges, and their perceptions of adventure may be very different in each context.

In every school, the grounds, facilities and range of staff expertise will be different. As well as considering the resources in the school, opportunities in the local community also need to be assessed. Parents, clubs and organisations may be able to support outdoor and adventurous activities and offer extra-curricular opportunities.

DEVELOPING THE SCHOOL ENVIRONMENT

There is a growing focus on the design of children's play spaces and the need to facilitate access to outdoor spaces where children can engage in outdoor activities (Munoz, 2009). Not only are the designs important, but the way in which schools use their grounds and access the local environment will impact on the quality and amount of outdoor learning available to the children. Many urban schools may not have access to the types of landscapes and wild places that Mortlock (2001) used for

Nalda Wainwright

adventurous activities when working with children and this will generally remain the role of outdoor centres. However, much of the research evidenced by Bird (2007) demonstrates the impact of nature to be so profound that even minimal exposure to nature can be beneficial (Taylor *et al.*, 2001 – cited in Bird, 2007). Much can be done with limited space and Moore and Wong (1997, cited in Munoz, 2009: 15) highlighted a wide range of benefits to pupils and staff resulting from the transformation of a tarmac yard into an 'environmental yard' with the addition of natural elements. Key to the success of most school ground developments is the involvement of the pupils. School and class councils need to be consulted about the things they want in their school grounds. Children need to be observed to see how they play, the range of activities and areas and landscapes that they prefer. Many books and websites are available to support and give ideas for school ground development such as the use of areas, zoning and resourcing outdoor spaces.

PLANNING AND PROGRESSION

Curriculum expectations in the UK require children to undertake activities that involve problem solving, cooperation, challenge and the use of the outdoors. These are usually delivered in schools in the form of team-building and problem-solving activities and orienteering. In Wales schools have also introduced campcraft and bouldering following the introduction of resources and training in the form of Outdoor Learning Cards produced by the Outdoor Education Advisors Panel (OEAP, 2008).

ACTIVITIES

Activities will be considered in turn, and mapped out from early years through to the end of Key Stage 2. This is *not* a tick list of activities, but ideas to help initiate or develop the delivery of outdoor and adventurous activities. Activities should be used only if developmentally appropriate for the child.

Campcraft/shelter building

These activities begin in their simplest form with very young children creating dens under a table or chair, or in boxes. Older Key Stage 2 children may be able to plan and carry out a camp on a school site or in the local area.

This may develop through the use of some of the following activities:

- Dens in class for child and/or toys
- Dens outside for child and/or toys
- Dens in pairs and groups
- Dens to shelter from the sun/wind/rain, etc.
- Dens/shelters to read/listen to stories/tell stories

167

- Dens/shelters for relaxing/thinking/hiding, etc.
- Dens/shelters made out of a variety of material and fabrics
- Dens/shelters made from natural materials
- Dens/shelters using purpose-made equipment, poles and bivvies
- Exploring the properties of a range of materials for shelter
- Identifying appropriate sites for shelter in a variety of weather conditions
- Becoming familiar with a variety of tents, and be able to use them
- Learning to cook safely in a camp/outdoor setting
- Knowing the range of equipment needed for camping and be able to use it safely.

Orienteering

Orienteering begins initially with young children being able to distinguish an aerial view of an object. This begins with small toys and objects in the class. Older Key Stage 2 children may be able to undertake orienteering races in and around the school site and in the local environment.

This may develop through the use of some of the following activities:

- Picking out pictures that match a view of an object
- Matching games using pictures of aerial views
- Drawing aerial views of a variety of objects
- Drawing plans of desks, table tops, objects on trays
- Drawing plans of class
- Treasure hunts
- Photo trails
- Taking photos and creating photo trails
- Drawing plans of playground/areas of the playground
- Orientation of map
- Games to learn compass points
- Identifying symbols on plans/simple maps
- Identifying and using a key
- Drawing a map of the playground
- Creating a key for a map
- Using own maps for treasure hunts to identify locations of clues
- Matching symbol games for official map symbols
- Star course orienteering activities using orienteering map
- Use of orienteering maps to find objects on school grounds
- Variety of orienteering courses on school site
- Use of compass and bearings
- Map work/orienteering in the local environment.

Bouldering

Climbing and bouldering are body management skills, and when watching an experienced climber move up or across a route, the similarities to dance and gymnastics become clear. There is fluidity to the movement, which is balanced and controlled; the climber appears to flow with a series of smooth, linked actions. For children to develop their skills for climbing, this begins with early body management, balance posture and coordination. Children are natural climbers and most will be climbing in many aspects of their play when given the opportunities. Children will start to climb on small pieces of equipment and frames in the early years, and by the end of Key Stage 2 may develop into confident climbers on a school bouldering/traversing wall.

This may develop through the use of some of the following activities:

- Climbing on and over apparatus and soft play equipment
- Climbing on small logs
- Using purpose-built frames in the hall/playground
- Climbing up steps for slides
- Climbing ladders on frames
- Moving around uneven natural terrain, with slopes and mounds
- Climbing small trees and fallen trees on woodland visits/forest schools
- Climbing on rocks and boulders in school grounds/local environment/local woodlands
- Hanging and swinging from monkey bars/similar equipment in school hall/grounds
- Climbing on and using trim trail equipment, involving balancing, and swinging
- Learning to spot for a partner on a bouldering wall
- Learning weight management using footholds on bouldering wall
- Travelling techniques for use on the bouldering wall
- Foot placement
- Hand holds
- Body positions
- Variety of games to practise and refine skills
- Visiting a local climbing wall.

Team building/problem solving

Team-building and problem-solving activities are perhaps the most used and versatile aspect of outdoor and adventurous activities. These activities are particularly relevant in the present climate with the emphasis on developing critical thinking and communication skills. Developing cooperative skills is particularly important for young children starting school, who may need to develop their social skills. By the end of Key Stage 2 pupils will be able to solve demanding challenges in creative and innovative ways, drawing on the abilities of all members of a group, such as the 'toxic waste' challenge (bucket in a rope circle, which has to be removed without anyone touching it). The challenges listed are well known team-building activities, descriptions of them can be found in books, on the internet and on the Outdoor Learning Cards.

Team-building skills may develop through the use of some of the following activities:

- Early cooperative games in circle time
- Taking circle time games to the hall and outside
- Parachute games
- Keep-up games with balloons
- Moving balloons through raised hoops
- Frozen bean game
- Travelling in pairs or small groups whilst keeping contact with each other
- Magic carpet
- Islands
- River crossing games, across hall or playground
- Bench sorting/ordering games
- Human knots
- Spider web games
- Electric fence challenges
- Obstacle courses
- Blind trails
- Robot races
- Leaky tube
- Roller ball
- Toxic waste.

There are many more examples of activities for all of the areas of activity. Many are available on the internet and in books, as well as through training and resources that have been produced to support the curriculum, such as the Outdoor Learning Cards produced by the OEAP. Schemes of work and lesson ideas for outdoor and adventurous activities exist in most local authorities, with many more available on the internet.

EXAMPLES FROM SCHOOLS

This section contains examples of how some schools have delivered outdoor and adventurous activities. These examples show a range of approaches. Every school will have different facilities and needs, but some of the strategies used by other schools may help to stimulate ideas for different contexts.

Key Stage 1

Year 1/Foundation Phase

Sessions should involve developing early orienteering skills, teamwork/problem solving and communication, mathematics, geography and literacy. Year 1 pupils have been looking at shape in mathematics and have drawn plans of the playground. The children choose simple symbols to represent aspects of the playground. The teacher hides small bags around the grounds with words in them, and marks on the children's map where the bags are hidden. The children work in groups with a map to find the bags and collect words. They then assemble the sentence from the collected words. The sentence asks them to choose a good place to listen to a story in the school grounds. The group must all agree on the place. There are many variations on this type of activity; the finding of the bags can be in a physical education lesson, as simple orienteering activity, or a way of ensuring a physical and outdoor approach to other curriculum areas, leaving the physical education lesson time still available for more physical education!

Mixed year groups, Reception, Year 1 and Year 2/Foundation Phase

With a mixed-age group the teacher needs to ensure that there is some focused input with the groups. The session should involve problem solving/teamwork, sending and receiving/ball skills, treasure hunt/orienteering and bouldering wall. The teacher has the support of a teaching assistant. The pupils are put into four groups.

Group 1 problem solving (older Year 1 and Year 2 pupils)
The children have a problem-solving task in a large construction area outside in the school grounds. The area has an assortment of tyres, logs, crates and planks, following a theme in the class the children are challenged to construct a fire engine from the materials available. The group work on this task, supervised from a distance by the teaching assistant.

Group 2 bouldering wall (older Year 1 and Year 2 pupils)
The children have been taught to spot for each other in a previous physical education session. They use the Outdoor Learning Cards to remind them what to do and practise traversing across the area in pairs.

Group 3 treasure hunt/orienteering (Reception and Year 1 pupils)
Working with the teacher, the children are given maps of the ground and are sent to find 'treasure' from marked places on the maps. The treasure is a clue, which is a mathematical problem. The children work out the answer within their pair and return to the teacher to explain their answer, before going to find the next.

Group 4 sending and receiving/ball skills (Reception and Year 1 pupils)
The children are consolidating previously learned skills, they have a variety of small equipment and balls of various sizes and weights, they devise games in pairs or small groups to practise throwing and catching. The teaching assistant supports the group.

Groups 1 and 2 swap over half way through and groups 3 and 4 swap over half way through.

Key Stage 2

Year 4

Shelter building
The pupils are using map skills learned in previous outdoor and adventurous activities sessions to collect the equipment needed for this session. The class is split into groups. Each has a map of the grounds with numbered locations. The groups find the locations and collect equipment that is there (an assortment of materials, e.g. ropes, bungees, pegs and tarpaulins). They bring all their equipment to the final location on the map and use it to construct a shelter. Once each group has finished they sit in their shelter and reflect on the activity. They have a list of initial questions to consider for reflection but may develop these. Once they have all finished, the groups inspect and evaluate each shelter to identify good aspects and areas for improvement.

Year 5

Mountain biking (capitalising on teacher expertise)
The school is in an area of social deprivation. The children do not all own mountain bikes, but have bikes that they ride on the estate, wasteland and in the park. The class teacher is a keen mountain biker. In order to engage and motivate the children, the school has recognised the need to listen to pupils and ensure the learning is relevant and meaningful to the children. Following discussion with the children, mountain biking was chosen as an adventurous activity to develop in physical education. IT sessions were used to research mountain bike trails and routes. Key features of the routes were highlighted. The children did a survey of the school grounds. They planned and designed a mountain bike route around the school grounds. During physical education sessions the class teacher worked at improving their balance and cycling skills, which the children practised doing circuits around their course.

Year 6

Problem-based learning (PBL)
Problem-based learning is a powerful tool for developing pupils' independent learning strategies. The headteacher of the school is enthusiastic about using the outdoors as an integral part of children's learning. The children are experienced in PBL. They have used their local environment throughout their time in primary school. Pupils are given a problem/scenario that they work through in groups to identify key issues.

The scenario:

> A Year 6 class from our partner school in Finland are coming to stay. The headteacher has decided it would be good for our class to take them on a walk in the local environment and camp in the school grounds. We need to plan, organise and prepare for the visit.

172

The groups identify several aspects to research and prepare/practise:

- Map reading skills for the local environment
- Areas of interest, historical, environmental, geographical
- Hazards and risk assessment
- Fitness and physical capabilities of the group
- Weather
- Clothing
- Camping area
- Camping and cooking equipment
- Food.

Problem-based learning requires careful planning. The teacher's role is more of a facilitator. Resources need to be well prepared enabling the children to research and access information and equipment independently. It may be challenging for teachers to let go and allow children to lead their learning, but this is part of the ethos of outdoor and adventurous activities.

THOUGHT BOX

Common responses heard in schools when reviewing provision for outdoor and adventurous activities are 'they do it on the residential at the top of the school' or 'we haven't got the grounds for it'. Are these acceptable positions? Which strands of the activities found in this chapter could be incorporated into most environments?

CONCLUSION

By exploring the impact of outdoor and adventurous activities on children's health, wellbeing and aptitude for learning this chapter has sought to develop a rationale for ensuring that all pupils experience this aspect of the curriculum. It is hoped that the discussion raises questions and highlights the importance of the outdoors as a vehicle for learning. The research and literature suggests that the potential impact is considerable. Changes in society, children's preschool experiences, and in their play opportunities mean it is crucial that schools act to ensure children have high-quality outdoor and adventurous activities in physical education. It is also vital that children have the chance to engage in outdoor learning opportunities across all aspects of the curriculum. The challenge is for schools to recognise this and act to ensure meaningful, challenging outdoor experiences for all pupils, helping to equip them for life in the 21st century.

REFERENCES

Ayres, J. (2005) *Sensory Integration and the Child*, LA: Western Psychological Services.

Bird, W. (2007) *Natural Thinking*, A report by Dr William Bird for the Royal Society for the Protection of Birds, Investigating the links between the Natural Environment, Biodiversity and Mental Health, London: RSPB.

Blythe, P. and McGlown, D. (1979) *An Organic Basis for Neuroses and Educational Difficulties*, Chester: Insight Publications.

Daily Mail (2008) Parents risk creating 'battery farm children' by not letting them play outside, 5 February.

Daily Telegraph (2010) Don't cosset children in 'cotton wool' says commissioner, 8 June.

Daily Telegraph (2011) Obesity crisis half a million children have liver disease, 3 July.

DCELLS (Department for Children, Education, Lifelong Learning and Skills) (2008) *Skills Framework for 3–19 year olds in Wales*, Cardiff: DCELLS.

Fjortoft, I. (2004) Landscape as playscape: the effects of natural environments on children's play and motor development, *Children, Youth and Environments*, 14, 2, 21–44.

Garrick, R. (2004) *Playing Outdoors in the Early Years*, London: Continuum.

Gill, T. (2007) *No Fear. Growing Up in a Risk Averse Society*, London: Calouste Gulbenkian Foundation.

Goddard Blythe, S. (2005) *The Well Balanced Child: Movement and Early Learning*, Gloucestershire: Hawthorn Press.

Glover, D. and Anderson, L. (2003) *Character Education*, Leeds: Human Kinetics.

Groves, L. and McNish, H. (2008) *Baseline Study of Play at Merrylee Primary School, Glasgow*. Forestry Commission Scotland.

Guardian (2006) Ads blamed for childhood stress, 12 December.

Henton, M. (1996) *Adventure in the classroom*, Iowa: Kendall/Hunt Publishing.

Katz, L. (1993) All about me, *American Educator*, 17, 2, 18–23.

Kirk, D. (2010) *Physical Education Futures*, Oxon: Routledge.

Louv, R. (2005) *Last Child in the Woods: Saving Our Children from Nature Deficit Disorder*, London: Atlantic Books.

Maude, P. (2010) Physical literacy and the young child, in M. Whitehead (ed.), *Physical literacy throughout the lifecourse*. Oxon: Routledge.

Maynard, T. and Waters, J. (2007) Learning in the outdoor environment: a missed opportunity?, *Early Years*, 27, 3.

Moore, R.C. and Wong, H.H. (1997) *Natural learning: creating environments for rediscovering nature's way of teaching,* Berkeley: MIG Communications.

Mortlock, C. (2001) *Beyond Adventure,* London: Cicerone Press.

Mortlock, C. (2009) *The Spirit of Adventure: Towards a Better World,* Kendal: Outdoor Integrity Publishing.

Munoz, S.A. (2009) *Children in the outdoors: a literature review,* Forres, Scotland: Sustainable Development Research Centre.

Mygind, E. (2007) A comparison between children's physical activity levels at school and learning in an outdoor environment, *Journal of Adventure Education and Outdoor Learning, 7, 2.*

OEAP (2008) *The Outdoor Learning Handbook,* Perthshire: Harvey Pub.

Palmer, S. (2006) *Toxic childhood, How the modern world is damaging our children and what we can do about it,* London: Orion.

Stewart, A. (2008) Whose place, whose history? Outdoor environmental education pedagogy as 'reading' the landscape. *Journal of Adventure Education and Outdoor Learning, 8, 2, 79–98.*

Taylor, A., Kuo, F. and Sullivan, W. (2001) Views of nature and self-discipline: evidence from inner city children, *Journal of Environmental Psychology, 21, supp.*

The Times (2007) How many adults does it take to let children play outside?, 4 August.

The Times (2010a) Obesity damages children's hearts, 3 October.

The Times (2010b) Can children as young as three be depressed?, 4 September.

Tunnicliffe, S. (2008) Children's understanding of the natural world – pond, *Environmental Education,* Summer, 16–18 and 27–28.

Wainwright, N. and Williams, A. (2011) *Camping on concrete: professional development for adventurous activities in Wales,* AIESEP Conference, Limerick.

Waite, S. (ed.) (2011) *Children learning outside the classroom: from birth to eleven,* London: Sage.

Walsh, D. (2004) Frog Boy and the American Monkey: The Body in Japanese Early Schooling, in L. Bresler, (ed.) *Knowing Bodies, Moving Minds,* Netherlands: Kluwer Academic Publishers.

Whitehead, M. (2010) *Physical literacy throughout the lifecourse,* Oxon: Routledge.

Williams, A. and Wainwright, N. (2011) Changing times and a new opportunity for outdoor learning in Wales – Outdoor Learning Cards, adventurous activities and physical education, *Horizons,* Spring, 53, Cumbria: The Institute of Outdoor Learning.

Part 3

ISSUES IN PRIMARY PHYSICAL EDUCATION

CHAPTER ELEVEN

ADDRESSING TRAINING AND DEVELOPMENT NEEDS IN PRIMARY PHYSICAL EDUCATION

Jeanne Keay and Jon Spence

INTRODUCTION

This chapter explores the issue of teachers' training and development needs in primary physical education through an examination of past and contemporary research and identifies improving the professional development of primary teachers as the main solution to the problem of raising attainment for pupils in primary physical education. Specific challenges are identified in relation to the curriculum, initial teacher education (ITE), professional development, managing specialist support and subject leadership. We present the main constraints in these areas, identify specific learning needs and make suggestions for overcoming barriers to professional learning in this subject. Throughout the chapter we encourage the adoption of a reflective, reflexive and continuous approach to professional development.

THOUGHT BOX

Before you read on, take a moment to reflect on your own training. Is it or was it effective in preparing you for the delivery of primary physical education? What changes might you suggest to improve its effectiveness?

TEACHING PRIMARY PHYSICAL EDUCATION

For some time criticisms have been made about the ineffective delivery of primary physical education and more generally about pupils' experiences in this stage of learning (Ofsted, 2000, 2004, 2009; Physical Education Association, 1998, 2000; Central Council for Physical Recreation, 2004). In recent years some progress has been made, however, achieving high-quality physical education remains a challenge and, while there is some evidence of improvement, pupils' achievement in physical education remains a concern. Reports of cancelled lessons or lessons providing physical activity opportunities rather than focusing on physical education learning

179

opportunities are still in evidence and clearly a cause for concern. Ofsted (2009: 8) found that pupils enjoyed physical education, were participating in more competitive activities and that schools had increased the time allocated to physical education. However, while there was evidence of rising standards, with two-thirds of pupils achieving 'good' standards, 'outstanding' achievement was rare. A less positive picture is painted by a report on the impact of professional development opportunities provided by local delivery agencies (LDA) within the government-funded Physical Education, School Sport and Club Links (PESSCL) and Physical Education, School Sport and Young People's (PESSYP) strategies on outcomes for pupils. It states that by the time they leave primary school, many pupils do not reach the standards in physical education of which they are capable.

Published research focusing on primary physical education provides evidence of the longevity of problems identified within primary physical education (Kirk *et al.*, 1988; Tinning and Hawkins, 1988; CCPR/NAHT, 1992; Davies, 1999). The earlier articles cite teachers' lack of skills or knowledge to deliver the curriculum and describe approaches where physical education lessons became merely fitness sessions. In more recent articles, reporting research drawn from across the world, little seems to have changed and there is consensus about the barriers to effective primary physical education. A range of international writers agree that teachers' attitudes are the main 'problem', together with lack of subject knowledge, resulting in low levels of competence and confidence (Sloan, 2010; Petrie, 2010; Morgan and Bourke, 2005; Morgan and Hansen, 2008; Kasale and Mokgwathi, 2010). Most primary teachers are expected to teach physical education to their pupils, but the vast majority have little or no experience in the subject (Green, 2008). Compounding this issue are teachers' prior experiences of the subject, which have often been negative. Prior experience of physical education as a pupil and the importance of secondary physical education, in particular, in forming attitudes to teaching physical education, have been highlighted by Morgan and Bourke (2008), Spence and Haydn-Davies (2011) and Pickup (2006a, 2006b). If teachers have had a poor experience of physical education as pupils, it is unlikely that they will be positively disposed to promoting the subject. Therefore, while this chapter focuses on supporting primary teachers, it is also important to acknowledge the influence of all school experiences and the need to improve all stages of physical education.

The writers cited above highlight class size, poor facilities and low time allocation for physical education as barriers to high-quality physical education, however, the main issues raised relate to teachers' confusion about curriculum expectations, their ITE, which has almost certainly been limited in scope and time, few professional development opportunities and poor or negative subject leadership. Improving teaching is therefore key to raising attainment in physical education and the following sections explore these four issues, together with a more recent concern, the use of subject specialists such as coaches to deliver the curriculum, and propose ways to overcome barriers in these areas.

TEACHER DEVELOPMENT: THE KEY TO IMPROVING PRIMARY PHYSICAL EDUCATION

The primary phase of physical education should provide the building blocks for all children to achieve physical competence and, as a result, become confident in a range of movements in order to be able to lead active lives. The foundations provided in this age phase should help children to achieve their true potential both in sporting terms as competitors or participants and more generally in enjoying a healthy lifestyle. There must be progression in the teaching of physical education if children are to achieve these aims and teachers must have increasingly complex expectations of their pupils. Teachers are clearly central to the provision of high-quality learning experiences and the quality of teachers is vital to the education system as a whole and to the delivery of the curriculum (Barber and Mourshed, 2007; Alexander *et al.*, 2009). Therefore, providing a progressive and developmentally appropriate curriculum, which provides a positive learning experience for all, should be the result of appropriate and effective professional development for teachers.

The suggestions presented in the sections below are based on a definition of professional development which encompasses all learning opportunities and through which unplanned learning experiences become part of the learning process through reflecting on action, in action and making changes as a result of reflection (Keay and Lloyd, 2011). Such a learning process is deliberate, planned, includes a range of activities and is personally relevant. Professional learning should be clearly linked to children's learning and teachers should be able to identify the impact of their new learning through the identification of evidence of children's learning, a task which should take place before professional development activities are selected and undertaken. Professional development is a continuum of learning, starting with ITE and continuing throughout a teacher's time in the profession. However, as mentioned earlier, the influence of prior experience cannot be ignored as it contributes to professional development through the development of a 'subjective warrant' (Lawson, 1983), during which the requirements of teaching are developed through the views of significant others (e.g. parents, family, peers and teachers), involvement in sport, and school physical education experiences. As will be explored within several of the following sections although a teacher's 'subjective warrant' is a major influence, ITE and school culture can also affect teaching behaviour and professional beliefs (Keay, 2006).

There are a range of measures we advocate to support teachers in their delivery of physical education but key to the successful development of teachers is progressive and continuous support, which caters for the needs of beginning teachers through to those with many years of experience. These measures include a clear understanding of the curriculum, appropriate ITE, personalised professional development, managing subject support within a professional learning community and effective subject leadership. Professional development on such a continuum must be personally and contextually relevant because teachers in primary schools are not a homogeneous group, their prior experiences at school, selected training route, ITE course content and professional context all contribute to the need for differentiated professional development. All the elements of teacher development cited above combine to produce a range of philosophical views about the subject and inevitably affect levels of confidence and competence to deliver the physical education curriculum. For example, teachers' different personal experiences of schooling constrain or enhance physical education opportunities and affect their teaching practices and the attitudes they adopt towards the subject. Different ITE training pathways also affect teaching practice and professional development, for example, a three- or four-year undergraduate route provides different, and some might say, less restricted professional learning opportunities in comparison to a one-year postgraduate route. Some teachers are trained as specialist physical educationalists within a primary course but most teachers are trained through a generalist primary education course, which covers all core and foundation subjects in varying degrees of depth. Within these courses trainee teachers often specialise in a particular age phase, which also contributes to different professional knowledge and development needs. A third initial preparation route, employment-based, presents significantly different challenges from university-based routes and many of the cultural issues identified later in this chapter can be seen in this type of ITE. When teachers graduate they are employed in different schools and contexts and therefore face different challenges in terms of meeting the physical education needs of their pupils. All of these prior experiences and contextual differences emphasise the need to identify ways to personalise professional development in order to meet individual needs.

UNDERSTANDING THE CURRICULUM

In England, physical education has recently been named as one of four compulsory subjects for all children (DfE, 2011) and its status as a statutory subject provides evidence that the subject is now seen as important by politicians and consequently may help to ensure that teachers are provided with the necessary support both at the ITE stage and in the provision of professional development in order to meet curricular expectations. However, clarity about the subject and its intended outcomes and getting the 'right' curriculum to achieve those outcomes are also important.

One of the biggest challenges for primary teachers is being able to define physical education and to articulate what it is aiming to achieve; National Curriculum descriptions do not currently help to do this and consequently teachers make assumptions about the content based on their own experiences at school, which are often sport-based and frequently negative. Teachers lack confidence because of their beliefs about the specialist nature of the curriculum and the seemingly expert focus on formal activities. Perceptions that there is a lack of subject knowledge and resulting lack of confidence have been highlighted through investigations of both trainee teachers (Haydn-Davies and Spence, 2010) and more experienced teachers (Spence and Haydn-Davies, 2011) working at Key Stage 1. A lack of clarity regarding, or misconceptions surrounding, the aims, values and purposes of primary physical education is a significant factor (Wright, 2002; Lee, 2003; Kay, 2004; Evans and Penney, 2008). Marsden and Weston (2007) suggest that the esoteric nature of physical education knowledge causes confusion, conflict and counterproductivity within the early years curriculum and this observation could easily apply across the primary curriculum. The use of the word esoteric to describe the curriculum provides a clear image of a subject that is understood by a small number of people in the teaching profession but is largely misunderstood or misinterpreted by the broader community, for example by, government ministers, parents, some teachers and the sporting community.

There is also confusion about the aims of physical education and its relationship to the achievement of physical activity targets and some writers (Birtwistle and Brodie, 1991; Gard and Wright, 2001) see physical education as the opportunity for pupils to be active but not necessarily learning. Obesity and health issues are high on the agenda for governments and indeed anyone concerned about children's health, however, this focus does sometimes create challenges for teachers when the focus of physical education becomes physical activity and not physical education. The subject is vulnerable to pressures from a societal understanding of what it is, as well as national areas of concern and interest, which include obesity, health and sporting success (Marsden and Weston, 2007). For example, the current government in England is promoting competition through the funding of competition managers and is driving children's involvement in competitive activities both in and outside the curriculum at all key stages.

Primary teachers not only need to understand the content and aims of the subject within the age phases they teach but they also need to be aware of progressions across the whole physical education curriculum. They need to understand their roles in providing a curriculum, which enables pupils to develop the basic movement competence and understanding required to later apply their skills and knowledge to sporting, health and leisure contexts, which should lead to increased physical confidence.

Providing a solution to these issues is not a simple task, however, we would suggest that the physical education profession, that is those specialists who may be teaching and working in schools, further or higher education, advisors and consultants and those who hold positions in membership organisations and other groups interested in the subject, should stop making the subject complex. Physical education in primary education must be demystified and teachers must believe that they have the generic pedagogical skills, which can be applied within any subject. Curriculum documents and other resources must be presented in a way that all involved understand; technical terms should be avoided or clearly explained. Clarifying the curriculum is an overarching responsibility for those providing ITE and professional development, for all involved in providing physical education and possibly most importantly for those holding subject leader posts in primary schools.

INITIAL TEACHER EDUCATION (ITE)

ITE in primary physical education has been reported as a poor experience and a poor professional preparation by a number of studies (Caldecott et al., 2006; Jacklin et al., 2006; Haydn-Davies et al., 2007; Carney and Winkler, 2008) and most of them point to a lack of time allocation within ITE programmes as a key factor. It is acknowledged that there is a considerable range of knowledge required to teach the elements of physical education (Ofsted, 2009) and lack of subject knowledge results in teachers' low confidence levels and anxieties which can lead to reticence about teaching the subject and the use of inappropriate pedagogy, therefore time within ITE programmes is a concern. However, as suggested in the section above, it is also important for ITE providers to consider how the curriculum is presented to the trainees and whether the content is appropriate for generalist students. More time within a programme does not necessarily mean that the outcomes will be of a higher quality unless the content and pedagogy of the programme are appropriate.

There are also issues relating to deficiencies in school experience and, in particular, the lack of opportunity for trainee teachers to practise teaching physical education (Haydn-Davies, 2008). An investigation into trainee teachers' opportunities to teach physical education during their training, carried out in our own institution, in collaboration with two other universities, confirmed that opportunities to practise teaching physical education and observe others teaching were not offered or possibly taken by a significant number of trainees. The investigation was undertaken with both undergraduate and postgraduate trainees in the three institutions and we found that between 26 per cent and 51 per cent of trainees on placement did not teach more than one lesson of physical education. In fact, on average, a quarter of trainees did not teach any physical education while on placement. The reasons provided by trainees for these situations included coaches and other specialists being employed to cover teachers taking planning, preparation and assessment (PPA) time and cancelled lessons. The same pattern emerged in relation to observation of physical education lessons, with similar reasons given for not undertaking observation as a development activity. These figures would suggest that there is a lack of enthusiasm to teach physical education in too many primary schools, poor mentoring of trainees in relation to physical education, a lack of good teaching examples and too few opportunities to observe good practice.

While physical education ITE programmes are frequently given too little time, there is a need to consider trainees' individual needs. The results of research by Haydn-Davies and Spence (2010) suggest that ITE needs to take account of prior experience of trainees and any pre-conceptions they bring to their course in order to meet their individual needs. This means reviewing the content of courses in order to address trainee needs and working in partnership with schools to extend their learning experiences. They examined perceived levels of confidence and competence to teach primary physical education in students on a primary education programme. In order to gain an understanding of how trainee teachers perceive the subject, they identified how students attribute importance to various factors affecting their overall confidence and competence in the subject. They identified typologies of students (enthusiasts, engaged, undecided, worriers and avoiders) in order to demonstrate the range of factors impacting on perceptions of the subject during training and how they changed after school experience and physical education modules. The project tracked the changes in these typologies through the trainees' ITE programme and found that it could have a positive effect on feelings of confidence and competence. However, despite the fact that the number of students in the 'enthusiasts' and 'engaged' groups increased from 24 per cent at the start of their ITE to 64 per cent at the end of their programme, 36 per cent of the cohort entered the teaching profession as 'undecided', 'worriers' or 'avoiders'. The results of the study showed how, due to prior experiences, students enter training with differing perceptions and that ITE providers need to meet individual needs and recognise individual preconceptions during training. Experiences of teaching physical education in school are not always available to students and, where available, not always positive and therefore the research report recommends that ITE providers need to work with schools to develop mentoring arrangements, ensure progression for training teachers and help teachers already in the profession to continue to develop their teaching of physical education.

Using the findings of this research, progress has been made by the ITE provider in addressing these objectives within their programme. Students are required to identify themselves against the descriptions outlined in the trainee typologies at the start of the course and then training is provided which is tailored to meet their specific needs. The focus of the ITE is on developing an appropriate philosophy and understanding of the subject and on building confidence to deliver a child-centred, developmental curriculum. The education provided aims to build confidence and competence and to support trainee teachers towards becoming 'enthusiasts' or 'engaged'.

Although ITE learning experiences are frequently constrained, it is possible to address the following objectives within a primary physical education ITE programme:

- Promote understanding of the values of physical education
- Provide experiences to teach physical education
- Increase enthusiasm to teach physical education
- Address prior experience and its influences and outcomes
- Demystify the subject
- Provide some support to develop subject knowledge and understand its application.

However, in order to address these objectives ITE providers have a responsibility to ensure that the right people are teaching on the programmes; lecturers must be physical educationalists and not merely activity specialists. They must ensure that trainees have time to develop and above all they must work in close partnership with schools to ensure that the most appropriate support and learning opportunities are available for all trainees.

Professional development for teachers in partnership schools is also necessary in order to promote the right people undertaking mentoring roles, to help them to understand the philosophy underpinning the work of the students and to help schools and teachers to develop an appropriate curriculum and appropriate teaching strategies. Other examples adopted by ITE providers include approaches to influence the experience of their trainees when in school, ranging from professional development courses to the production of exemplar videos designed to help educate teachers about the subject and the requirements of the trainees.

In summary, appropriate and developmental ITE must provide sufficient time for trainees to develop confidence and competence in the subject through experiences in training and during school experience, through appropriately staffed programmes. School experience must provide regular teaching, both solo and team, and observation opportunities, with time to discuss professional practice and be given feedback by appropriately trained mentors.

PROFESSIONAL DEVELOPMENT

The ways in which primary teachers' professional development needs in physical education are met replicates many teachers' attitudes and approaches to professional development across all subjects and age phases. Teachers often have a limited view of what professional development means in practice and many see it as going on a course; Pedder *et al.* (2008) found that the type of activity teachers take part in most frequently reflects passive forms of learning such as listening to a lecture or presentation. However, as Armour (2010) points out, such experiences are likely to be disconnected from previous learning and it is therefore not surprising that although they consider such activities as professional development, in practice they seek 'pre-packed' answers to their concerns and teaching challenges. Hence, a ready-made curriculum, lesson plans and easy to follow resources, for example, are very popular with teachers in primary education in particular, where there are pressures of having to be an expert in a broad range of subjects. Unfortunately, this approach to development does not take into account their specific contextual needs and the teaching approaches promoted are welcomed and used unquestioningly by teachers. While resources, and the associated professional development, that provide 'ready-made' answers are not the best solution there is evidence that they do support teachers in the absence of any other help. For example, Harris *et al.* (2011) found that Top Programmes, which are activity-specific training courses with supporting resources, increased confidence, however, there was a heavy reliance on resource cards promoting a specific activity focus and this was seen as a limitation because the diverse needs of teachers and pupils were not being met.

A further challenge to meeting teachers' learning needs can be seen where headteachers will only agree development time if the focus relates to the school plan and targets. Therefore, unless physical education is included in the organisation's strategic priorities or indeed it becomes an area of the curriculum on which teachers are required to report, releasing them for professional development in physical education will not be a priority. Headteachers show a clear preference for professional development that focuses on school-based and classroom-based opportunities as they are seen to provide more value for money (Pedder *et al.*, 2008). While this broader view of development opportunities is to be welcomed, it will only be effective if there are teachers in the school who have the subject knowledge and expertise to support colleagues. Unfortunately, as will be discussed below, in relation to physical education this is often not the case.

While we see professional development as a continuum, which includes induction into the teaching profession, it should be acknowledged that this period presents specific challenges for new teachers as they begin their careers and therefore deserves to be considered separately. The first year of a teacher's career presents many challenges and this is not a new situation, it has been a long-standing problem (Tickle, 1994; Simco,

2000); one of the main concerns has been that ITE and induction have not been linked or complementary. Statutory induction has gone some way towards addressing the problems faced by new teachers but they are often isolated and not provided with sufficient or appropriate support. The relationship between ITE and continuing professional development provision can be affected by different forms of professionalism played out within a school, which may strongly influence practice. For example, while democratic professionalism will encourage teachers to adopt a collaborative and critically reflective approach to professional development, in a school where managerial professionalism is enacted, professional development will be related to compliance and self-interest and practice will be slow to change (Keay and Lloyd, 2011). Experienced colleagues are highly influential and if their attitudes to physical education are negative or restricted, new teachers are unlikely to challenge the status quo during their induction year. In fact, for most new teachers who have concerns about teaching physical education, a culture where the subject is not valued may be a relief and, consequently, poor, or indeed non-existent, practice will be perpetuated.

The previous paragraphs paint a very gloomy picture, however, through the PESSCL and PESSYP strategies, a great deal has been undertaken, with some success (Ofsted, 2009), in order to improve primary physical education. The professional development element of these strategies offered support to primary teachers in the form of traditional courses and they were well received by teachers and seen to have a positive impact. They contributed to primary teachers' development, increasing their enthusiasm for physical education and their confidence to teach it, enhancing subject knowledge and the competence to teach. A more recent project, funded by the Top Foundation (Youth Sport Trust), has examined the professional development needs of teachers in Key Stage 1 classes with a view to improving primary physical education. Following an extensive research and consultation process, the final report proposes three main actions: changes to the curriculum to simplify the content and pedagogy; the need for advocacy aimed at persuading parents and school leaders of the importance of physical education; and the need to develop local professional learning communities which would involve anyone supporting teaching physical education, including coaches, local ITE providers and secondary colleagues (Keay, 2011). Sponsorship has now facilitated the extension of this project and the targets will be addressed in schools from 2011–12 onwards.

One of the research projects (Spence and Haydn-Davies, 2011), which contributed to the Key Stage 1 project, asked teachers what support they needed to help them to be able to deliver high-quality physical education. Discussions with teachers relating to teaching approaches in physical education demonstrated a lack of knowledge and confidence in teaching physical education. They felt that they did not have sufficient subject knowledge or understanding of the breadth of activity areas needed to cover the National Curriculum requirements and in particular they felt that they lacked knowledge of how to develop children's physical skills and many felt that they lacked understanding of what children should be able to do at different stages and how to set appropriate activities which would help children learn and develop. Many teachers attributed this to not receiving sufficient depth in ITE in preparation to teach physical education. The teachers also highlighted that they lacked confidence in assessment in physical education and it was clear that both the use of an 'assessment for learning' approach and mechanisms for recording assessments are areas that challenged these teachers. The teachers involved in the study clearly feel insecure in their understanding of what children should be able to do, how to recognise 'next steps' and what they should be recording about their pupils.

The teachers involved in the investigation suggested some specific solutions to their professional development needs such as the provision of materials with linked training/courses and the need for materials to be made available, online, which show children moving and performing in order to help them to understand what they are trying to achieve with their pupils. However, they also recognised the benefits of coaching and mentoring arrangements to support them in teaching physical education and while this approach is one we fully support, it also needs to be recognised that in order to provide such individualised support we will need to increase the number of confident practitioners in primary schools. The final two sections of this chapter address this issue though an exploration of the development of a professional learning community and strengthening subject leadership.

In summary, our suggestions for supporting teachers to improve primary physical education relate to the definition of professional development stated earlier in this chapter. Any development activity should be developmental and progressive and primary teachers should to be encouraged to utilise the pedagogical skills they demonstrate in the classroom. Professional development should be planned and use an appropriate range of methods and one-off sessions, which often have little impact on practice, should only be used where a specific need has been identified and which requires this form of learning activity. In particular, attendance at sport-specific courses should be minimal as many of them have little or no relevance for the primary school teacher.

MANAGING SPECIALIST SUPPORT

The debate about whether we should employ physical education specialists in primary schools has been long running and is played out in most publications analysing the experiences of teachers in primary schools and some make reference to coaches filling the need for specialist support. Some writers (Petrie, 2010; Tsangaridou, 2008) acknowledge that while primary generalists with a good understanding of child development and pedagogy should be able to meet the needs of the curriculum and the children, the broad range of subject knowledge, as well as negative attitudes and lack of confidence mean that physical education specialists may be a better solution. However, there is also acknowledgement within the physical education profession that specialist support in the form of primary physical education teachers is an expensive option and one unlikely to be met without a large input of funding from the government. It is therefore important to consider alternative scenarios to a specialist teacher and how classroom teachers might best use and manage such support.

There is a growing tendency for primary schools to employ different groups of people to take responsibility for teaching physical education or providing extra-curricular activities. In 2004 Sportscoach UK indicated a growing trend (138,000 at that time) of coaches working in primary schools delivering sports sessions and more recently the number of adults other than teachers in primary physical education has increased significantly (Sportscoach, 2004) (Lavin *et al.*, 2008). While many of these sports sessions will be delivered during out-of-school-hours learning (OSHL), Griggs (2010) also found that 75 per cent of the coaches he interviewed were actually delivering the curriculum. Blair and Capel (2008a, 2008b) report that coaches who demonstrate that they can be trusted in OSHL are being asked to deliver within the curriculum and therefore we must consider how these adults, who are not teachers but who are providing this service, are used and managed.

These arrangements are often found where teachers have no particular interest in physical education, or where they perceive themselves to lack expertise and consequently confidence, or simply must take statutory PPA time. In these situations other people take their classes; they may be local coaches provided through a national governing body, a local organisation or business, a classroom assistant or may indeed be a colleague from a local secondary school. While the reasons for such situations may be attributed to teachers' lack of enthusiasm for physical education, Griggs (2010) suggests that the use of coaches is sometimes a management strategy to reduce costs; coaches are used as a cheap alternative to qualified teachers for PPA cover. Unfortunately, while these people may have more specific subject knowledge and subject confidence, many do not have an education background or sound knowledge of the aims of the physical education curriculum and often have little experience in, or understanding of, teaching children. While coaches may be trusted to 'deliver' the curriculum, they do not always meet full expectations of assessing pupils, reporting on levels of attainment and helping them to make progress. This clearly exemplifies the difference between the 'delivery' of a curriculum and the provision of high-quality learning experiences for children. While employing a sports coach does not in itself mean that the pupils' physical education experience is poor, if the class teacher is abdicating responsibility for the learning of the pupils and the assessment of their progress it does constitute a major deficiency. Teachers are responsible for the education of their classes and therefore, if other adults are contributing to the provision of learning experiences, they should be answerable to the teacher. Unfortunately, the employment of other specialist adults not only removes the responsibility of teaching physical education from the class teacher but it also has the long-term effect of de-skilling teachers whose confidence is progressively diminished. This, of course, will have long-term impact on the outcomes of physical education in primary schools.

Primary teachers must take responsibility for carefully selecting the specialist support they need to deliver high-quality learning experiences for their pupils and should match the support to the curriculum they have planned and not simply accept random offers of help. Rather than coaches, for example, coming to promote their particular activity within the curriculum, primary teachers should be pro-active in planning learning activities and carefully selecting and securing specialist support. Within recent partnership arrangements in England, secondary teachers have been employed to support primary colleagues in physical education and in OSHL. However, while these arrangements have helped some schools and teachers there is also the view that secondary trained teachers do not have the expertise to teach primary age children. Therefore, it is important to note that, while secondary physical education specialists may support their primary counterparts, they should not replace them but work alongside them. Secondary teachers may have subject knowledge but class teachers have knowledge of their children and their particular needs, which should influence what is taught and how the children learn.

In order to make best use of available specialist support, we suggest the development of a professional learning community, in which all interested and involved in the physical education of primary age children collaborate. Providing opportunities for professional dialogue and peer support will encourage teachers to develop their knowledge in a non-threatening and supportive environment. The purpose of a professional learning community is to ensure an organisational focus on learning, however, Day and Qing Gu (2010) take this analysis further and suggest that a successful learning community also demonstrates 'collective efficacy', that is, the belief by the members in the success of the community. If this is achieved in primary physical education, we will see all involved in providing physical education learning experiences working towards the same vision. Wenger's (1998) analysis of teacher learning connects the individual, the community and related organisations and this provides a useful basis for explaining how a professional learning community in primary physical education might work.

- Individual: engaging in and contributing to the practices of the community, bringing specific skills and knowledge of physical education.
- Community: together individuals work to refine and improve physical education practice, ensuring that developments are sustainable for the following generations.
- Organisations: different organisations remain linked to the professional learning community and connected to each other, therefore ensuring that a shared vision for physical education is developed and maintained.

This analysis highlights the importance of sharing practice in order to ensure community progression and effectiveness.

THOUGHT BOX

In developing a professional learning community, identify what you believe to be the different strengths and weaknesses of each individual or role holder. What are the key aspects that each need to learn in order to become a more effective practitioner?

SUBJECT LEADERSHIP

The findings of the Key Stage 1 investigation (Keay, 2011) and previous research into leadership and management (Bush, 2008) would suggest that strong and informed leadership of the subject will help to ensure that curriculum design and delivery provides children with appropriate learning opportunities and will support teachers in their subject knowledge and pedagogical development. Training of appropriate staff to work with colleagues to support their development is a key aspect of leadership in primary physical education, as is the mentoring of colleagues, modelling of best practice and the development of the subject within whole school policy. These are the tasks of a subject leader and clearly demonstrate the importance of this role; unfortunately, Ofsted (2009) has reported poor or negative subject leadership in primary physical education. However, while this section highlights the specific role of the subject leader, we cannot underestimate the influence of the headteacher as a leader and how s/he enables or constrains opportunities in the subject. In a school where a headteacher promotes a collaborative culture professional development will be encouraged and effective (McCormick *et al.*, 2008; Day and Qing Gu, 2010; Day, 2000) and a subject leader will be enabled to provide relevant learning opportunities for other members of staff.

There are ITE programmes that prepare teachers for the subject leader role in physical education and they help teachers to develop the required leadership and management skills. The national physical education professional development programme introduced as part of the PESSYP/PESSCL strategy attempted to meet the needs of primary school teachers appointed as Primary Link Teachers (PLT) but many did not access the training or, having been trained, subsequently moved away from these roles. It is evident that many subject leaders lack the experience and training to carry out the role and would benefit from further support to maximise their impact. Helping teachers to become leaders is an essential element of support, which will help to improve teaching across a school and provide a better experience for all pupils.

CONCLUSION

This chapter has presented the case for primary teacher development to be seen as the key to achieving higher-quality learning experiences and raising achievement in primary physical education. We have proposed that in order to improve primary physical education changes are necessary in ITE and in the provision on professional development opportunities for all teachers employed in primary schools. There is clearly a need for clarity about the aims, objectives and curriculum content of physical education and in order to achieve consensus about a vision for primary physical education all those making a contribution must work together. A professional learning community in which teachers take responsibility for developing appropriate partnerships is one way to achieve this outcome. Effective leadership, and in particular subject leadership, will be essential to the development and maintenance of such partnerships.

REFERENCES

Alexander, R., Armstrong, M., Flutter, J., Hargreaves, L., Harrison, D., Harlen, W., Hartley-Brewer, E., Kershner, R., Macbeath, J., Mayall, B., Norther, S., Pugh, G., Richards, C. and Utting, D. (2009) *Children, Their World, Their Education: Final Report and Recommendations of the Cambridge Primary Review*, London: Routledge.

Armour, K. (2010) The physical education profession and its professional responsibility … or … why '12 weeks paid holiday' will never be enough, *Physical Education and Sport Pedagogy*, 15, 1, 1–13.

Barber, M. and Mourshed, M. (McKinsey Report) (2007) *How the world's best performing school systems come out on top*, McKinsey. Available at http://www.mckinsey.com/AppMedia/reports/SSO/Worlds_School_Systemss_Final.pdf.

Birtwistle, G.E. and Brodie, D.A. (1991) Children's attitudes towards activity and perceptions of physical education, *Health Education Research*, 6, 465–78.

Blair, R. and Capel, S. (2008a) The use of coaches to cover planning, preparation and assessment time – Some issues, *Primary Physical Education Matters*, 3, 2, ix–x.

Blair, R. and Capel, S. (2008b) The use of coaches to cover planning, preparation and assessment time – Some issues, *Primary Physical Education Matters* 3, 3, v–vii.

Bush, T. (2008) From management to leadership: semantic or meaningful change?, *Educational Management Administration and Leadership*, 36, 2, 271–288.

Caldecott, S., Warburton, P. and Waring, M. (2006) A survey of the time devoted to the preparation of primary and junior school trainee teachers to teach physical education in England, *Physical Education Matters*, 1, 1, 45–48.

Carney, P. and Winkler, J. (2008) The Problem with Primary Physical Education, *Physical Education Matters*, 3, 1, 13–5.

Central Council for Physical Recreation (CCPR)/National Association of Head Teachers (NAHT) (1992) *National Survey of Physical Education in Primary Schools, A Sporting Chance?*, CCPR/NAHT, London.

Central Council for Physical Recreation (CCPR) (2004) *CCPR Challenge 2004–05,* London: CCPR.

Davies, H. (1999) Standards in Physical Education in England at Key Stage 1 and Key Stage 2: Past, Present and Future, *Physical Education and Sport Pedagogy*, 4, 2, 173–190.

Day, C. (2000) Teachers in the twenty-first century: time to renew the vision, *Teachers and Teaching: Theory and Practice*, 6, 1, 101–115.

Day, C. and Qing Gu (2010) *The New Lives of Teachers*, Abingdon: Routledge.

Jeanne Keay and Jon Spence

Department for Education (DfE) (2011) Review of National Curriculum. Available at http://www.education.gov.uk/inthenews/inthenews/a0073152/michael-gove-announces-major-review-of-national-curriculum.

Evans, J. and Penney, D. (2008) Levels on the playing field: the social construct of physical 'ability' in the physical education curriculum, *Physical Education and Sport Pedagogy,* 13, 1, 31–47.

Gard, M. and Wright, J. (2001) Managing Uncertainty: Obesity Discourse and Physical Education in a Risk Society, *Studies in Philosophy and Education,* 20, 535–549.

Green, K. (2008) *Understanding Physical Education,* London: Sage.

Griggs, G. (2010) For sale – primary physical education. £20 per hour or nearest offer, *Education 3–13,* 38, 1, 39–46.

Harris, J., Cale, L. and Musson, H. (2011) The effects of a professional development programme on primary school teachers' perceptions of physical education, *Professional Development in Education,* 37, 2, 291–305.

Haydn-Davies, D. (2008) What do we need to know about as teachers of primary physical education? Big benefits from working with little learners, *Primary Physical Education Matters,* 3, 2, v–vi.

Haydn-Davies, D. and Spence, J. (2010) The importance of goats in primary initial teacher education: a case study in physical education, paper presented at the British Educational Research Association annual conference, Warwick University, September 2010.

Haydn-Davies, D., Jess, M. and Pickup, I. (2007) The Challenges and Potential within Primary Physical Education, *Physical Education Matters,* 2, 1, 12–15.

Jacklin, A., Griffith, W. and Robinson, C. (2006) *Beginning primary teaching: moving beyond survival,* Maidenhead: Open University Press.

Kasale, L. and Mokgwathi, M. (2010) Primary School Teacher Perceptions towards the Physical Education Component of Creative and Performing Arts Curriculum in Botswana, *Asian Journal of Physical Education and Recreation,* 16, 2, 58–64.

Kay, W. (2004) Are mentors and trainees talking the same language? *British Journal of Teaching Physical Education,* 35, 3, 19–22.

Keay, J. (2006) What is a physical education teacher's role? The influence of learning opportunities on role definition, *Sport, Education and Society,* 11, 4, 369–383.

Keay, J. (2011) *Supporting Key Stage 1 Physical Education,* Phase 1 Report for Top Foundation, February, YST.

Keay, J. and Lloyd, C. (2011) *Linking Children's Learning with Professional Learning: Impact, Evidence and Inclusive Practice,* Rotterdam: Sense.

Kirk, D., Colquhoun, D. and Gore, J. (1988) Generalists, specialists and daily physical education in Queensland, *The ACHPER National Journal,* 122, 7–9, 36.

Lavin, J., Swindlehurst, G. and Foster, V. (2008) The use of coaches, adults supporting learning and teaching assistants in the teaching of physical education in the primary school, *Primary Physical Education Matters,* 3, 1, ix–xi.

Lawson, H. (1983) Toward a model of teacher socialisation: entry into schools, teachers' role orientations, and longevity in teaching (Part 2), *Journal of Teaching in Physical Education,* Fall, 3–15.

Lee, M.J. (2003) Values in physical education and sport: a conflict of interests?, *British Journal of Teaching Physical Education,* 35, 1, 6–10.

Marsden, E. and Weston, C. (2007) Locating quality physical education in early years pedagogy, *Sport, Education and Society,* 12, 4, 383–398.

McCormick, R., Banks, F., Morgan, B. Opfer, D., Pedder, D., Storey, A. and Wolfenden, F. (2008) *Schools and continuing professional development in England: State of the Nation research project (T34718),* Report for the Training and Development Agency for Schools: London: TDA.

Morgan, P. and Bourke, S. (2005) An investigation of pre-service and primary school teachers' perspectives of physical education teaching confidence and physical education teacher education, *ACHPER Healthy Lifestyles Journal*, 52, 1.

Morgan, P. and Bourke, S. (2008) Non-specialist teachers' confidence to teach physical education: the nature and influence of personal school experiences in physical education, *Physical Education and Sport Pedagogy*, 13, 1, 1–29.

Morgan, P.J. and Hansen, V. (2008) Physical education in primary schools: Classroom teachers' perceptions of benefits and outcomes, *Health Education Journal*, 67, 3, 196–207.

Office for Standards in Education (Ofsted) (2000) *Annual report of Her Majesty's chief inspector of schools, 1998–99*, London: HMSO.

Office for Standards in Education (Ofsted) (2004) *Physical Education in Maintained Primary and Secondary Schools in England*, London: HMSO.

Office for Standards in Education (Ofsted) (2009) *Physical Education in Schools 2005/2008: Working towards 2012 and beyond*, London: HMSO.

Pedder, D., Storey, A. and Opfer, D. (2008) *Schools and continuing professional development in England: State of the Nation research project*, report for TDA.

Petrie, K. (2010) Creating confident, motivated teachers of primary physical education in primary schools, *European Journal of Physical Education*, 16, 1, 47–64.

Physical Education Association of the United Kingdom (1998) *PEA UK position statement on physical education at Key Stage 1 and 2 national curriculum in primary schools*, London: PEA UK.

Physical Education Association of the United Kingdom (2000) *Support statement. University of Birmingham and Westhill conference proceedings, positive action for primary physical education*, Reading: PEA UK.

Pickup, I. (2006a) Love it or hate it you have to teach it: Accounts of trainee primary teachers' experiences in, and perceptions of, Physical Education. Paper presented at the 13th Commonwealth International Sport Conference, Melbourne, 12 March 2006.

Pickup, I. (2006b) Telling tales from school: Trainee primary teachers' experiences in physical education. Paper presented at the British Educational Research Association annual conference, Warwick University, 8 September, 2006.

Simco, N. (2000) *Succeeding in the Induction Year*, Exeter, Learning Matters.

Sloan, S. (2010) The continuing development of primary sector physical education: Working together to raise the quality of provision, *European Physical Education Review*, 16, 3, 267–281.

Spence, J. and Haydn-Davies, D. (2011) *Teacher Perceptions Research Report*, for Key Stage 1 Project (Top Foundation).

Sportscoach UK (2004) *Sports Coaching in the UK: Final Report*, London, Sportscoach UK.

Tickle, L. (1994) *The Induction of New Teachers: Reflective Professional Practice*, London: Cassell.

Tinning, R. and Hawkins, K. (1988) Montaville revisited: a daily physical education programme four years on, *The ACPHER National Journal*, 121, 24–29.

Tsangaridou, N. (2008) Trainee primary teachers' beliefs and practices about physical education during student teaching. *Physical Education and Sport Pedagogy*, 13, 2, 13–152.

Wenger, E. (1998) *Communities of Practice*, Cambridge: Cambridge University Press.

Wright, L. (2002) Rescuing primary physical education: and the values that matter most, *British Journal of Teaching Physical Education*, 33, 1, 37–38.

CHAPTER TWELVE

TOWARDS A MORE INCLUSIVE PROVISION

Richard Medcalf

INTRODUCTION

In recent years, there has been an increasing level of attention paid to the nature of special educational needs (SEN) in National Curriculum physical education (NCPE). Much of this consideration has been upon the inclusion of (and planning for) children and young people with a physical disability of some kind. This focus somewhat lacks an appreciation of the wider concept of 'need' in NCPE. A focus upon 'need' in the physical domain has negated the full range of difficulties which can be ascribed the label of SEN (i.e. profound and multiple learning difficulties; behavioural, emotional and social difficulties; and speech, language and communication needs). Each of these categories is born out of distinct variations of 'need', and, subsequently, the requirement for pedagogic and policy differentiation is apparent. This chapter will consider inclusive provision in primary physical education, highlighting the need for a range of 'core learning' opportunities for all children and young people who are considered as being on the spectrum of special educational need.

VIEWING THE CURRENT LANDSCAPE

Within the context of the primary school National Curriculum, this chapter highlights issues relating to the concept of inclusion when considered in regard to the variances in 'need' which teachers are faced with. It discusses how these issues transcend both moral and pedagogic issues, and how they are enacted within the multi-faceted and complex educational environment of physical education. The interactional nature of such environments often causes a wide spectrum of polarised experiences, which are reasonably considered as being a product of the visible manifestation of 'need' which participation can evoke. The varying didactic challenges in meeting individual and diverse learning needs, are testament to the complexities inherent in ensuring that the rights of all pupils are accommodated. The rights of the child are both many and varied; for the purpose of this chapter, the foremost right of all learners is that of being included in an equitable experience of physical education.

There is a general consensus that, in providing effective learning opportunities for all pupils and consequently including all learners in inclusively orientated environments pro-active strategies and mechanisms that support children and young people to succeed are necessary. This pro-activity is especially necessary when considered in light of the challenges associated with the delivery of quality physical education in the primary sector. Booth and Ainscow (2002) contend that schools should concern themselves with increasing both the participation, and the broad educational achievements, of all students. These are clear moral and ethical foregrounds to the provision of equitable educational opportunities, which allow all pupils to progress irrespective of their relative abilities.

Before discussing issues within the physical education context, it is worth noting the important differences between what is commonly termed 'integration' (whereby the child fits into a predisposed system), and 'inclusion' (whereby the system itself is adapted to suit the child). Despite the clarity of this distinction, inclusion itself is a term more difficult to define. The term is widely understood to mean different things to different people, and subsequently is a challenge to define in any succinct way. Broadly speaking, Ainscow and Cesar (2006: 233) describe the over-arching necessity in 'working together to address barriers to education experienced by some learners … within a particular context'. However, they go further by highlighting a typology of five different ways in which inclusion could be defined (see Ainscow et al., 2006). The variance in how this term is interpreted, and the subjective nature of inclusiveness itself, are complications that are more adequately described by Ainscow and Cesar (2006).

There are clear philosophical justifications for the proliferation of inclusive practices in education. In contemporary research, these justifications are most commonly underpinned by internationally recognised policy documents such as the *Convention on the Rights of a Child* (United Nations, 1989). A further landmark publication is the *Salamanca Statement* on inclusive education (United Nations Educational Scientific and Cultural Organisation, 1994), which outlines guidelines in principles, policy and practice in special needs education, re-affirming the right and commitment to education for all, in schools of 'inclusive orientation'.

These are further grounded by the commitments made by education curricula (at a national level). The legislative drive for an inclusive ethos in NCPE is also substantiated by research which has resulted in a critical mass of papers that offer weight and credibility to the fundamental argument of the aforementioned rights of the child. In meeting these rights, there is the need for physical education to provide effective and positive learning opportunities which reflect a differentiated level of support in regard to the fundamental movement skills of participants, especially so as 'Students learn in different ways … and enter physical education with different levels of movement experience. This precipitates different learner needs and aspirations' (Byra, 2006: 449). The subsequent potential for physical education to 'include', and the ease with which it is possible for it to 'exclude', is testimony to the common variance in affinity towards the subject.

Irrespective of what form it takes, there are often many pre-conceived ideas of the subject, especially in regard to the fear associated with teaching a curriculum for which most have had very little training for through primary initial teacher training. Such

196

Richard Medcalf

perceptions are naturally exacerbated when faced with a diverse group of learners who display great variance in their physical and emotional states. Whether this be a perception or an actuality, the very nature of physical education leads to a variance in 'need', to which the teacher must respond. Natural variances in cognitive and physical abilities are at their most visible when participating in physical education, and thus the very visible requirement for differentiation is magnified by the performative nature of the outcomes which define the perceived success of any individual task accomplishment.

In light of these variances in ability and 'need', there is the requirement to ensure the application of pedagogies which respond to the individualised needs of all learners (both in a physical and educational sense). In the planning of inclusive physical education lessons, the adaptation of activities to meet these needs is an imperative, if the subsequent alternative perception of feeling 'othered' is to be avoided. The importance of particular cultures, policies and practices of inclusion are further exacerbated in a number of ways, when learning in a physical context, through NCPE in the primary context.

INCLUSION IN PHYSICAL EDUCATION

The contested nature and purpose of physical education is often dominated by wider educational and philosophical agendas. Historically, the inclusion of physical education as a curriculum subject has been justified on the basis of broad and diverse goals of physical, social, and moral development (Sallis and McKenzie, 1991). These are goals that many other subjects cannot lay claim to. Despite the relatively active characteristics of other practical subjects, including drama and the arts for example, active participation in physical education involves learning that is unique to the physical domain. The distinctive nature of physical education has been postulated, therefore, to result in a range of outcomes that are not seen as being inherently possible in other curriculum subjects.

Values generally related to the ethical principles of fairness and honesty have long been internal, built-in, logically constitutive features of the games and sports, which feature prominently in the familiar primary physical education curriculum (Reid, 1997). As a consequence, rather than an emphasis on the benefits resulting from participation in physical education, the subject is seen by many as having value in its own right (Whitehead, 2000). Despite the often overlooked and sometimes marginalised position of physical education in schools (Hardman and Marshall, 2009), the subject is one that is often advocated as being a source of many positive developmental characteristics through adolescence. As a statutory 'core' subject area, it offers a niche within curriculum time in which multiple personal, physical and social qualities can develop if complemented by teaching, learning environments, and lesson content, which the individual finds facilitative to his or her long-term development.

> Physical education helps pupils develop personally and socially. They work
> as individuals, in groups and in teams, developing concepts of fairness
> and of personal and social responsibility. They take on different roles and

responsibilities, including leadership, coaching and officiating. Through the range of experiences that physical education offers, they learn how to be effective in competitive, creative and challenging situations.

(QCA, 2007b: 189)

Without claiming too much in the name of physical education, there remains an important role for the subject to play in providing young people with a holistic knowledge, understanding, and social skills to ensure physical activity (of some kind) becomes a regular aspect of their daily life (Fairclough and Stratton, 2005). Children and young people experiencing physical education are encouraged, by the nature of the subject, to potentially engage in acts that are physical and often cooperative by design. The possibility of physical education to produce profound affective gains in individuals has, as such, been widely researched. Researchers have recognised physical education as a site that is well suited to the promotion of young people's social development (Lawson, 1999). Miller *et al.* (1997) cited how responsibility and cooperation were key features of their socio-moral programme through physical education. Moore (2002) has built upon this further by discussing how physical education has the potential to develop personal qualities such as self-esteem, self-confidence, empathy, and compassion.

Within the wider curriculum, there have long been claims of the multiple discourses at play in physical education and, more specifically, the breadth of learning that it is invariably claimed that the subject develops, or is concerned to develop, in pupils (Penney, 2000). physical education is indeed one of few curriculum subjects whose inherent motives, structures, pedagogies and content lend themselves to the opportunity for a holistic and developmental programme of activities, which go some way in fostering a range of positive attributes. Physical education lends itself to the development of physical skills, team building, character development, responsibility, creativity and imagination.

The effects of physical education are no longer seen as being merely part of the relatively short-lived curriculum for children of school age. Its unique contribution to life-long learning and education has been acknowledged by Doll-Tepper (2005), who spoke of the indispensable role of physical education in the education process. Kay (2003) highlights the long-term aims of participation including not only continued engagement in activities throughout life, but also now with an appreciation of a wide variety of considered, holistic and interdisciplinary benefits. It is also appreciated more widely as playing an important role in achieving broader educational objectives such as whole school improvement, community development and effecting personal behavioural and attitudinal change among pupils (Houlihan and Green, 2006).

The subject area is in a relatively distinct position, from which it can assume a level of responsibility to in some way address many issues in the life of a school. As such, the specificities of physical education, in regard to its place within curricula in comparison to other subjects, are worthy of interrogation in relation to how this affects the children and young people. These varied effects should be considered as being dependent upon the characteristics of the learner, in context, and dependent on the situational environment of their class. The implementation of pedagogies which seek to plan for the full and active participation in learning is vital in this regard. The uniqueness of this co-creation of experience means that there are also particular barriers to inclusion, within a subject of relative uniqueness in the curricula of physical education.

Vickerman *et al.* (2003) highlight four key principles when contextualising issues of inclusion to NCPE. They argue for entitlement, accessibility, integration, and integrity as being the cornerstones of inclusive practice in the subject. These are only possible because of the breadth of learning that can take place within physical education. According to Penney (2002), such breadth is seen in 'extending the range of skills, knowledge and understanding that are incorporated in descriptions of learning in physical education extends the potential for the subject to be inclusive of the varied educational needs, abilities and interests of all pupils' (Penney, 2002: 124).

In providing opportunities which cater for the needs of all pupils, irrespective of their practical ability or competencies, it is an expectation that physical education can provide positive and inclusive outcomes through active participation and engagement. Such opportunities to experience success in learning are possible regardless of gender, race, ethnicity, cognitive aptitude or physical ability. Moreover, an educational provision which meets the needs of all pupils is widely expected to meet the needs of those deemed to experience a special educational need.

VARIANCES IN 'NEED'

Inclusive provision in physical education is most commonly focused within the context of pupils deemed to experience a form of special educational need (SEN). Prior to discussion of the specificities of this term, it is worth acknowledging the growing body of legislation that supports the fundamental right to an inclusive education for all pupils with any form of SEN (Vickerman *et al.,* 2003). In England and Wales, there is an excess of such legislative and non-statutory guidance, which has pursued this agenda. The Green Paper on *Excellence for All* (DfEE, 1997), *The Special Educational Needs and Disability Act* (DfES, 2001a), *The Special Educational Needs Code of Practice* (DfES, 2001b), and, in relation to physical education, the *Planning for Inclusion* statement within the National Curriculum (QCA, 2007a), have each contributed in the most recent past. The issues, which surround students with SEN in the National Curriculum, have, hence, received noticeable recent attention within both academia and in policy. Whilst it is not the task of this chapter to provide an overview of the historical developments within this field, Smith (2004) indicates that the aforementioned contemporary developments are part of a process, which 'can be traced back as far as the mid 1800s', and points to the 'long term social process' in his conceptualisation of current physical education provision for pupils with SEN (p.40).

The definition for special educational needs used in the Department for Education and Skills (2001b) *Code of Practice*, is actually that contained within the *Education Act* (DfEE, 1996). This describes a child having SEN if he (or she) 'has a learning difficulty which calls for special educational provision to be made for him' (or her) (section 312). Despite remaining current in the main, this definition has been somewhat supplemented first by the introduction of *The Special Educational Needs and Disability Act* (DfES, 2001a), and, more recently, by Department for Children, Schools and Families (2008) guidance. The consistent feature of such guidance is that children and young people who are deemed to experience a special educational need, do so as they are faced with particular barriers to learning and participation.

Despite this, localised interpretations of ideological statements, and subsequent national policies, are notoriously challenging to benchmark. In the UK, the decentralised nature of SEN assessment has been legislated through documents which discuss the requirement for such a delivery of these principles to take place at a local level (DfEE, 1996). The SEN Green Paper *Excellence for all Children* (DfEE, 1997) drew attention to the regional dimension in SEN provision, which led to variation amongst the quality and nature of the provision being offered. It has been shown that such disparities continue to occur in regard to prevalence and support for SEN (Lewis *et al.*, 2010). Such a localised emphasis serves to perpetuate the differences between the extents to which pupils are included in relation to matters of their education. The variance within processes associated with identifying, assessing, and making provisions for those with additional needs, are further exacerbated when considered alongside individual provisions which respect the variable developmental maturity of pupils.

SEN AND 'CORE LEARNING OPPORTUNITIES' IN PRIMARY PHYSICAL EDUCATION

As mentioned previously, physical education has the potential to make significant contributions to the education and development of all children and young people in many ways, most of which are not reproducible through other areas of the curriculum, or through other sporting or physical activities (Bailey and Dismore, 2004). In this regard, Wright and Sugden (1999: 16) cite how, for all pupils, but especially those with SEN, 'physical education is not simply education of the physical, but also involves education through the physical of other naturally developing attributes such as language, cognition, socialisation, and emotions'. The subject's ability to offer such contributions is, nevertheless, mediated by the wider social cultures that can manifest themselves in curriculum physical education. Arguably, in countries where emphasis is 'placed upon sport and team games within the physical education curriculum [it] appears to do rather more to exclude, than include, some pupils from particular learning situations in physical education' (Smith, 2004: 51). These experiences are, hence, heavily framed by individuals' special educational needs, or lack thereof. The great ranges of difficulty, which can attest to the label of SEN, are most regularly spoken about, within physical education, alongside literature discussing inclusive practice. In meeting any inclusion statements in physical education curricula, 'teachers need to actively review the pedagogical practices in order to ensure they meet … requirements to facilitate entitlement and accessibility to inclusive activities for all pupils, including those with SEN' (Vickerman, 2007: 58).

Richard Medcalf

Inclusive physical education for pupils with SEN is concerned with a recognition of
the philosophical basis of inclusion, as well as a commitment and desire to support its
implementation through both the execution of policy and a desire to change practice
(Vickerman *et al.*, 2003: 50). This point serves as a reminder that central to all processes
occurring in their classrooms are the pedagogic and didactic behaviours of educators.
Consequently, the role of the educator as a facilitator to these processes must, of course,
not be forgotten. In this regard, Morley *et al.* (2005) discussed how physical education
teachers conceptualised the subject as one which is significantly different from other
subject areas. Their research highlighted the perceived difficulties in teaching children
with behavioural difficulties more so than other manifestations of SEN.

In working with pupils who might present difficulties across the special needs spectrum, it is imperative that those leading physical education lessons have the confidence
to anticipate barriers to learning (both physical and otherwise), to consequently minimise or reduce the likelihood that they might affect the individuals' progression. The
organisational, social and physical barriers to participation (see JRF, 2009) which might
cause such difficulties necessitate that staff modify the tasks to suit the developmental
stage of the pupil. This is of great importance if opportunities for pupils to achieve and
demonstrate successes are to be utilised – occasions which might not be so readily available in other aspects of their curriculum. It is worth considering the opportunities which
physical education provides to encourage confidence in the performance of fundamental
movement skills, through giving assurances of freedoms within age-appropriate tasks. As
learners progress through the national curriculum level descriptors, and judgements are
made as to their progress, the nature of their participation and the demands placed upon
their teachers increase. It is at this point that need for highly imaginative content which
emphasises the social and communicative aspects of participation, in consciously using
physical education as the opportunity to develop wider psycho-social characteristics.

The claimed and/or perceived benefits of active participation in physical education are
reconciled by individuals' reciprocity to the subject. Their affinity will undoubtedly be
affected by the provisions made to address the additional needs of individuals who
either excel, or experience difficulty, with the physical and visible nature of participation. Studies have highlighted how secondary physical education teachers have, in the
past, recognised the pragmatic and conceptual difficulties that such inclusion can pose
(Robertson *et al.*, 2000). This can be seen as a reflection of what Smith and Green
(2004: 605) describe as the long-established disposition of a 'pre-eminence of a sporting
ideology in [physical education teachers'] views'. These issues highlight the difficulties

201

in what Smith and Thomas (2006b) perceive as being the diametrically opposed policies of inclusion in its broadest sense, alongside the emphasis within physical education on raising standards of practical achievement. There is a clear dichotomy between an ethos of performance, (born out of a concentration on physical abilities and measures), and a desired inclusive philosophy. The corollary of such a culture is described by Morley *et al.* (2005) as being the inherent 'conflict' within physical education, which seeks to promote equity and excellence simultaneously.

Such contradictions are potentially magnified through 'needs' that are physical in nature. In turn, the challenges facing inclusive discussions in physical education are most often spoken about within the remit of a physical need. Coates and Vickerman (2008: 170) re-affirm that the majority of research that examines the physical education perspectives of children with SEN do so from the perspective of a physical disability, and 'as such may not prove representative of the full sphere of special educational needs'. Studies of those with such physical difficulties reveal a range of contrasting experiences, including a spectrum of feelings from difference and estrangement, self-doubt, acceptance, discrimination, to the enjoyment gained from socialising whilst strengthening their physique. However, when considering issues of inclusion in physical education, it is important not to solely focus on the subject as a physical domain. The relative importance of this lack of attention of other SEN subsets is exacerbated in that Smith and Thomas (2006a) highlight the fact that, actually, teachers often find it especially difficult to include pupils who have social, emotional and behavioural difficulties.

CONCLUSION

This chapter has sought to highlight issues regarding the changeable and highly individual nature of inclusive practice in NCPE. The inclusion of all children and young people within an environment that is practical in nature, is both a moral and pedagogic matter which is a challenge that is hugely dependent upon the 'need' of the student. In creating space for positive experiences to occur, physical education in the primary school has a responsibility to include all learners, so that they can engage with participation at their most appropriate skill level and learn to appreciate the value of movement. Hence, enabling choices which are facilitative to the individual needs of all learners requires recognition of the changeable landscape of physical education and the challenge that this poses to primary educators.

The environment in which the child is asked to learn and behave is a critical factor to consider, when discussing the causes of, and responses to, their school experiences. This is particularly magnified in primary physical education, where the rhetoric and policies of inclusive education intersect with the intrinsic physicality of the environment. The importance of maintaining pupil confidence in this environment, when participating in developmental activities, is central to the experiences which will result. The subsequent embodied responses are most likely to be a product of socially constructed perceptions of the subject, which have developed over time. The polarised nature of such experiences, and the variance in experience and perception of physical education, are befitting of the overarching effect of context when educated through the physical domain (Eldar, 2008). As such developing the confidence to participate may take some time, and may be a process which calls for astute management of expectation and peer comparisons.

Participation (and experience) has been shown by previous literature to be circumscribed in a variety of ways by gender, social class, and the school (Smith *et al.*, 2007). Furthermore, people's actions and participation in physical education are both enabled and constrained by the complex networks of inter-dependent people in schools (Smith *et al.*, 2007). Factors that contribute to experiences and task adherence are multiple and interrelated to such extent that exhaustive description and differentiation are complex (Medcalf *et al.*, 2006). It is impossible to state, to any firm degree of conclusion, the relative importance of such interdependencies. It is one of, or a combination of, physical education's curricular structures, lesson content, didactic practices, and the environmental structures inherent and consistent in any physical education class, which contribute in some way to the varying perceptions of inclusive practice in physical education.

In reflecting upon what Ainscow *et al.* (2003) highlight as the importance of 'learning from difference' in the development of inclusive practice, there is worth in recognising that perceptions of (and experiences in) physical education are circumscribed by an individual's differing past experiences. Consequently, participation has a number of contrasting effects, which we should learn from. Florian (2005) suggests that 'Special and inclusive education are stuck in the dilemma of difference ... new understandings about how to respond to those who experience difficulties in learning are needed' (Florian, 2005: 97). These differences cannot be delineated by label, location, pedagogy or activity. It is only by allowing time and opportunities for truly inclusive practice, that it is possible to appreciate the complex precursors and wide-ranging variables which contribute to the experiences of children and young people. Physical educationalists should consider such variance, and the subsequent inconsistencies in their pupils' experiences, to be a matter of the individualities which define social, emotional and behavioural difficulties.

It is hoped that this chapter has provoked thought, and a re-consideration of the variances in need that can be experienced within physical education. The TDA (2009) provide a useful tool for those interested in conducting a 'self audit' for inclusive practices within the subject.

KEY READINGS

For an extensive overview of the topic see Coates, J. and Vickerman, P. (2008) Let the children have their say: a review of children with special educational needs experiences of physical education, *Support for Learning*, 23, 4, 168–175. As a way forward for practice regardless of context, many sources often cite the *Index for Inclusion* (see Booth, T. and Ainscow, M. (2002) *Index for inclusion: developing learning and participation in schools* (2nd ed), Bristol: Centre for Studies on Inclusive Education).

REFERENCES

Ainscow, M., Booth, T., Dyson, A., Farrell, P., Frankham, J., Gallannaugh, F., Howes, A. and Smith, R. (2006) *Improving schools, developing inclusion,* London: Routledge.

Ainscow, M. and Cesar, M. (2006) Inclusive education ten years after Salamanca: Setting the agenda, *European Journal of Psychology in Education,* 21, 3, 231–238.

Ainscow, M., Howes, A., Farrell, P. and Frankham, J. (2003) Making sense of the development of inclusive practices, *European Journal of Special Needs Education,* 18, 2, 227–242.

Bailey, R. and Dismore, H. (2004) SpinEd: The role of physical education and sport in education; Project Report. 4th International conference of ministers and senior officials responsible for physical education and sport (MINEPS IV), Athens, Greece.

Booth, T. and Ainscow, M. (2002) *Index for inclusion: developing learning and participation in schools* (2nd ed), Bristol: Centre for Studies on Inclusive Education.

Byra, M. (2006) Teaching styles and inclusive pedagogies, in D. Kirk, D. Macdonald and M. O'Sullivan (eds) *Handbook of Physical Education,* London: Sage, 449–466.

Coates, J. and Vickerman, P. (2008) Let the children have their say: a review of children with special educational needs experiences of physical education, *Support for Learning,* 23, 4, 168–175.

Department for Children Schools and Families (2008) *The Education of Children and Young People with Behavioural, Emotional and Social Difficulties as a Special Educational Need,* London: HMSO.

Department for Education and Employment (1996) *The Education Act,* London: HMSO.

Department for Education and Employment (1997) *Excellence for All Children: Meeting Special Educational Needs,* London: HMSO.

Department for Education and Skills (2001a) *Special Educational Needs and Disability Act,* London: HMSO.

Department for Education and Skills (2001b) *Special Educational Needs: Code of Practice,* London: HMSO.

Doll-Tepper, G. (2005) The UK in the world of physical education, National Summit on Physical Education, London.

Eldar, E. (2008) Educating through the physical – behavioural interpretation, *Physical Education and Sport Pedagogy,* 13, 3, 215–229.

Fairclough, S.J. and Stratton, G. (2005) Physical education makes you fit and healthy: Physical education's contribution to young people's activity levels, *Health Education Research,* 20, 1, 14–23.

Florian, L. (2005) 'Inclusion', 'special needs' and the search for new understandings, *Support for Learning,* 20, 2, 96–98.

Hardman, K. and Marshall, J. (2009) *Second World-wide Survey of School Physical Education,* Berlin: ICSSPE.

Houlihan, B. and Green, M. (2006) The changing status of school sport and physical education: explaining policy change, *Sport, Education and Society,* 11, 1, 73–92.

Joseph Rowntree Foundation (JRF) (2009) *Inclusion of disabled children in primary school playgrounds,* York: Joseph Rowntree Foundation.

Kay, W. (2003) Physical Education R.I.P.? *British Journal of Teaching Physical Education,* 34, 4, 6–9.

Lawson, H.A. (1999) Education for social responsibility: preconditions in retrospect and prospect, *Quest,* 51, 2, 116–149.

Lewis, J., Mooney, A., Brady, L.M., Gill, C., Henshall, A., Willmott, N., Owen, C. and Evans, K., Statham, J. (2010) *Special Educational Needs and Disability: Understanding Local Variation in Prevalence, Service Provision and Support (Extended Summary),* London: DCSF.

Medcalf, R., Marshall, J.J. and Rhoden, C. (2006) Exploring the relationship between physical education and enhancing behaviour in pupils with emotional behavioural difficulties, *Support for Learning,* 21, 4, 169–174.

Miller, S.C., Bredemeier, B.J.L. and Shields, D.L.L. (1997) Sociomoral education through physical education with at risk children, *Quest,* 49, 1, 114–129.

Moore, G. (2002) In our hands: the future is in the hands of those who give our young people hope and reason to live, *British Journal of Teaching in Physical Education,* 30, 2, 26–27.

Morley, D., Bailey, R., Tan, J. and Cooke, B. (2005) Inclusive physical education: teachers' views of including pupils with special educational needs and/or disabilities in physical education, *European Physical Education Review,* 11, 1, 84–107.

Penney, D. (2000) Physical education, sporting excellence and educational excellence, *European Physical Education Review,* 6, 2, 135–150.

Penney, D. (2002) Equality, equity and inclusion in physical education and school sport, in A. Laker (ed.) *The Sociology of Sport and Physical Education: An Introductory Reader,* Abingdon: Routledge, 110–128.

Qualifications and Curriculum Authority (2007a) *National Curriculum for Physical Education: Planning For Inclusion,* London: Qualifications and Curriculum Authority.

Qualifications and Curriculum Authority (2007b) *Physical education: programme of study for key stage 3 and attainment target,* London: Qualifications and Curriculum Authority.

Reid, A. (1997) Value pluralism and physical education, *European Physical Education Review,* 3, 1, 6–20.

Robertson, C., Childs, C. and Marsen, E. (2000) Equality and the inclusion of pupils with special educational needs in physical education, in S. Capel and S. Piotrowski (eds) *Issues in Physical Education,* Abingdon: RoutledgeFalmer, 47–63.

Sallis, J.F. and McKenzie, T.L. (1991) Physical education's role in public health, *Research Quarterly for Exercise and Sport,* 62, 2, 124–137.

Smith, A. (2004) The inclusion of pupils with special educational needs in secondary school physical education, *Physical Education and Sport Pedagogy,* 9, 1, 37–54.

Smith, A. and Green, K. (2004) Including pupils with special educational needs in secondary school physical education: a sociological analysis of teachers' views, *British Journal of Sociology of Education,* 25, 5, 593–607.

Smith, A. and Thomas, N. (2006a) Including pupils with special educational needs and disabilities in national curriculum physical education: a brief review, *European Journal of Special Needs Education,* 21, 1, 69–83.

Smith, A. and Thomas, N. (2006b) Inclusion, special educational needs, disability and physical education, in K. Green, and K. Hardman (eds) *Physical Education: Essential Issues,* London: Sage, 220–237.

Smith, A., Thurston, M., Lamb, K. and Green, K. (2007) Young people's participation in national curriculum physical education: A study of 15–16 year olds in north-west England and north-east Wales, *European Physical Education Review,* 13, 2, 165–194.

Training and Development Agency for Schools (TDA) (2009) *Including pupils with SEN and/or disabilities in primary physical education,* Manchester: TDA.

United Nations (1989) *Convention on the rights of the child.* Available at http://www.unicef.org/crc/index_30177.html (accessed 15 September 2006).

United Nations Educational Scientific and Cultural Organisation (1994) *The Salamanca Statement and Framework for Action on Special Needs Education.* Available at http://www.unesco.org/education/pdf/SALAMA_E.PDF (accessed 15 September 2006).

Vickerman, P. (2007) *Teaching Physical Education to Children with Special Educational Needs,* Oxon: Routledge.

Vickerman, P., Hayes, S. and Whetherly, A. (2003) Special educational needs and the national curriculum physical education, in Hayes, S. and Stidder, G. (eds) *Equity and Inclusion in Physical Education and Sport: Contemporary Issues for Teachers, Trainees and Practitioners,* London: Routledge, 47–64.

Whitehead, M. (2000) Aims as an issue in physical education, in S. Capel and S. Piotrowski (eds) *Issues in Physical Education,* Oxon: RoutledgeFalmer, 7–21.

Wright, H. and Sugden, D. (1999) *Physical Education for All: Developing Physical Education in the Curriculum for Pupils with Special Educational Needs,* London: David Fulton Publishers.

Richard Medcalf

CHAPTER THIRTEEN

PLACING AN IMPORTANCE ON HEALTH AND PHYSICAL ACTIVITY

Kristy Howells

INTRODUCTION

Within the primary school and in particular within physical education, children's atti-tudes and interests in physical development and physical activity can be fostered and an understanding of the importance of not only activity, but also diet and the concept of healthy lifestyles can be imparted. Physical education according to Howells (2011: 119) 'should encompass individual physical development, health and wellbeing' and has a crucial role in primary school education as it is much more than just simply providing exercising opportunities for every child. Yet sometimes it appears that, if newspapers, television and some academic research are to be believed, all the world's problems can be put down to our lack of physical activity, or if not all problems we are assured that the growing incidences in the Western world of cancer, type 2 diabetes, heart disease and obesity are due to its insufficiency. But what is physical activity exactly, how much is enough to stave off these impending disasters and when should we start?

WHAT IS PHYSICAL ACTIVITY?

Physical activity has been defined in numerous ways. It is, however, a 'complex behav-iour variable' which can vary 'from day to day, in intensity, frequency and duration and consists of both unavoidable activity and variable activity' according to Winsley and Armstrong (2005: 65). These suggestions follow Armstrong's (1998: 9) previous work, where he stated that 'physical activity is a complex behaviour and the accurate assess-ment of young people's physical activity patterns is extremely difficult'. Meanwhile Booth *et al.* (2001) suggested that any changes in this complex behaviour are dependent on different influences. Recently national TV adverts and local campaigns have focused on encouraging us individually and in groups to be more physically active to help benefit our health and wellbeing. There is a substantial body of evidence on the benefits to health for adults, however the physical activity levels of children have not been so extensively explored, a time when habits, likes and dislikes are being formed.

The World Health Organisation (WHO) (2010: 7) defined physical activity for chil-dren aged 5–17 as activities that include: 'play, games, sports, transportation, recrea-tion, physical education or planned exercise, in the context of the family, school and community activities'. Plasqui and Westerterp (2007: 2371) agree in their review of the ability of different accelerometers, an objective measurement tool, to assess daily physical activity and suggest that physical activity is a complex behaviour and includes 'sports as well as non-sports activities'. However, Sirard and Pate (2001: 440) provide a more specific definition of physical activity as 'any bodily movement produced by skeletal muscle that, results in energy expenditure'. It has also been defined earlier by Caspersen et al. (1985: 127) who regarded physical activity to be composed of three elements: 'Movement of the body produced by the skeletal muscles. Resulting energy expenditure which varies from low to high. A positive correlation with physical fitness'. Armstrong (1998) defined physical activity in a very similar way to Caspersen et al. (1985: 126) who also state that 'physical activity can only occur as a result of skeletal muscle activity that is supported by energy expenditure'. In a more recent study, Pearce et al. (2008) explored American rural middle school children's own understanding of physical activity and found that children defined physical activity in a compatible way to Caspersen et al. (1985: 178) as 'body activity: if you're moving'. They also went on to ask the children what they believed exercise is, to which the response was that exercise 'is when you mean to do physical activity'. They also reported that children found it difficult to understand and articulate what is meant by intense or vigorous physical activity. Although Pearce et al. (2008) did acknowledge that the results were limited due to only using one school, however their study did highlight an important factor, that of considering how children themselves understand what is meant by physical activity. This is key. If the children and primary school setting are not able to achieve the recommended targets for physical activity, it could be reasonable to ask whether this is because the children do not understand what physical activity is or how they are supposed to achieve it. Indeed, Oliver et al. (2007: 47) stated that the amount of physical activity required for very young children was not clear 'and the types of activities that are important are yet to be determined'. They also placed value upon both family and early years learning settings such as parental encouragement, motivation to get the children to be physical active, the parents' own levels of physical activity as important factors in influencing both the physical activity and health of young children (Oliver et al., 2007). The implementation here is that early years and primary educators need to be supported to promote physical activity, in particular the importance of physical activity and health with their children, and also the social promotion of physical activity.

Research into the levels of children's physical activity is important as the actual level achieved of physical activity is difficult to judge visually, because moderate to vigorous levels of physical activity are not easily seen. Mulvihill et al. (2000) defined moderate intensity as an activity which leaves the participant feeling warm and a little out of breath, whereas vigorous physical activity will leave the participant out of breath and sweaty. Children's physical activity is sporadic in nature (Waring et al., 2007) and therefore physical activity levels are difficult to identify instantly or to record without the use of specific measurement tools, such as pedometers, heart rate monitors or accelerometers. It is not easy to question or to examine whether a child is actually achieving the recommended levels of physical activity. Therefore teachers and parents may not know whether the children are reaching the recommended targets, whether the initiatives that are introduced within school are benefiting the children, nor what physical education provision contributes (if any) to any increased physical activity. Howells (2011: 121) suggested that it is important to educate in particular primary aged children who are still forming their likes and dislikes, on not only 'physical development, but also in the importance of being physically active and how diet and nutrition will impact on their individual health and wellbeing'. Obtaining knowledge and understanding of children's physical activity within the school day can help the children to understand what they are achieving and to improve children's physical activity participation. It will also help primary educators, teacher training educators, and ultimately policy-makers to offer suggestions and strategies to provide opportunities for physical activity within the school day and to share the importance of health and physical activity. Without knowing this information schools cannot reasonably take or be given responsibility for children's physical activity.

Targets for children's physical activity were recommended by Department of Health (DofH) in 2005, by the WHO in 2010 and by the NHS in 2011. These recommendations should be achieved during the day in terms of physical activity for health. Children should be physically active at a moderate to intense level for 60 minutes a day (or over 60 minutes according to the NHS (2011)). When day is referred to, this is the whole 24 hours of the day, not the waking day, nor the school day. The 60 minutes of physical activity can accumulate throughout the day (Gilson *et al.*, 2001; WHO 2010). However other levels of recommendations have been suggested such as Anderson *et al.* (2006) who stated that children aged 9 may need 120 minutes of moderate to vigorous physical activity to reduce cardiovascular disease. NICE (2009) suggested that the accumulation had to be within 10 minute bouts as a minimum, yet Gilson *et al.* (2001) and WHO (2010) do not stipulate this. According to Owens *et al.* (2000) children sleep for 10.16 hours ±44.48 minutes, the child is therefore awake for approximately 14 hours within a whole day, of which they spend 7 hours within the primary school day. Therefore school life has the potential to have a significant impact on primary aged children's lives in terms of placing an importance on health and physical activity. This only leaves 5–7 hours outside school while they are still awake (Breus, 2008). It is not surprising that the responsibility of physical activity levels could seem to fall within the school responsibility. However should only half of the physical activity levels, for example 30 minutes of the recommended target be achieved within the school day and be the responsibility of the school?

Kolle *et al.* (2009: 1368) suggested that 'children's physical activity has provided serious measurement challenges for researchers'. They proposed this was challenging due to the nature of the children's behaviour in that children tend to find it difficult to estimate their own behaviour when self-reporting, and they also find it difficult to recall in detail their physical activity patterns. Therefore it is important to educate primary aged children on the different types and levels of physical activity, so they are able to recognise these. Children's physical activity participation is rarely lengthy and is more often made of intermittent and spontaneous patterns (Kolle *et al.*, 2009). Zeigler (1994) suggested school physical education lessons provide a more regular context for structured physical activity participation which will ultimately aid children's health. Fairclough and Stratton (2006) agreed and suggested that a physical education lesson could be considered as being a pure opportunity to get children physically active, and therefore important in terms of health. They describe elements within physical education lesson such as motor, cognitive and social development as being hindrances in the achievement of this physical gain. Yet Doherty and Brennan (2008: 6) argued against these ideas and state that there is much more to school physical education lessons than just being physically active. physical education is about the whole education process of the child 'that is concerned with lifelong physical, intellectual, social and emotional wellbeing that accrues through experiencing physical activities in a variety of contexts'. By using this whole education process approach within school the child's attitudes and interests in physical development and physical education can be fostered and an understanding of the importance of not only exercise, but diet and healthy lifestyles can be imparted, rather than just simply providing exercising opportunities for every child. However, it is important for school, class teachers, the children and teacher educators to know how physically active the children's 'existing physical activity levels are prior to suggesting any solutions or strategies for primary schools' (Howells et al., 2009: 24). Children's physical activity and experience of physical education in school can help determine their engagement in lifelong physical activity, therefore it is essential for primary class teachers to ensure that physical education lessons are a positive experience for all children.

THE ROLE OF PHYSICAL EDUCATION AND PHYSICAL ACTIVITY ON HEALTH AND WELLBEING

'Today's generation of children will be the first for over a century for whom life expectancy falls' (Hills et al., 2007: 533). The prediction that obese children are likely to become obese adults is suggested by Department of Health (2006), with a forecast of one in five children (1 million, in England) by 2010 being obese, representing an increase of 9.6 per cent in boys and 10.3 per cent in girls in England in the last 15 years. According to the Health Survey for England (2008, reported by NHS, 2009) 30 per cent of children are overweight or obese and it was projected that if this trend continues, by 2050 9 out of 10 adults would be overweight or obese (Government Office of Science, 2007). Leake (2011) recently reported that obesity rates according to the National Health Service research have tripled in the past two decades. He also reported on the levels of obese adults and found that the number of adults in Kent who are obese now exceeds 30 per cent and they found that 28.6 per cent of children aged 10–11 years in Westminster were obese. The global problem of obesity is now a prominent feature within society. Consequently, increasing pressure has been placed upon the education system to rectify this serious problem (Waring et al., 2007) and in particular upon primary schools, to prevent children from becoming obese at an early age. Trudeau et al. (1999) emphasised the importance of daily physical education for primary school children and suggested that this had long-term effect on physical activity throughout not only the school day but also later on in life (Howells, 2011).

Aicken et al. (2008: 2) agreed with Waring et al. (2007) and suggested that rising rates of obesity are of widespread concern not only in the UK but also internationally. However,

the 'concern is not yet matched by either a clear map of interventions provided for children and young people or a robust evidence base on the effectiveness of interventions'. Yet Kirk (2006: 121) has argued prior to Hills et al. (2007), Waring et al. (2007) and Aicken et al. (2008) that the obesity crisis we are experiencing 'is almost entirely without foundation', whilst at the same time acknowledging that it is 'increasingly difficult to resist calls for physical education lessons to be held accountable for children's health'. Kirk (2006: 122) reflects on Johns' (2005) work and suggests that 'when children are mentioned in the obesity crisis discourse, school physical education lessons are implicated immediately, both as a source of and as a possible solution to the problem'. Pate et al. (2011) also suggest that it is often claimed that physical education lessons can provide 'important benefits to public health' as the WHO (2008) suggested that increases in children's physical activity levels could be enhanced by increasing the number of physical education lessons within school time. However Pate et al. (2011) also suggest that further research is needed to examine what physical activity is actually occurring within a physical education lesson, regarding which Harrington and Donnelly (2008: 66) argue within their research that 'before any strategies to increase physical activity can be employed, the activity levels of children need to be known'.

McMinn et al. (2010: 68) provide support for the argument that schools are the best place for physical activity for children to occur, by suggesting that 'school settings have been identified as key social establishments in which to promote physical activity, particularly through the medium of school clubs and physical education lessons'. Cox et al. (2010: 46) echo this suggestion that schools may be 'attributed responsibility for children's physical activity', in a number of ways due to the school being able to provide 'access to equipment / facilities, number of PE hours, time outdoor, trained / supportive staff'. Trost (2006: 1) also agreed and suggested that 'schools serve as an excellent venue to provide students with the opportunity for daily physical activity', though he highlights that this is often not the case and that 'most children get little or no physical activity in school'. Dale et al. (2000: 240) investigated the activity of pupils throughout the school day and stated that the 'opportunities for children to be physically active during school time are sparse and becoming increasingly so'. Yet Green (2002: 97) emphasised the importance of physical education lessons for enhancing health and physical activity and suggested that the physical education lesson is 'the most suitable vehicle for the encouragement of a lifestyle which is both healthy and physically active'. Tremblay et al. (2005) found that children's physical activity levels may decline over time and Rowlands et al. (2008: 26) suggested that this decline in physical activity levels has 'led to an increased focus on the quantity and quality of physical activity that children experience in school physical education lessons'. They go on to highlight however that there has also been a decline in the amount of timetabled physical education lessons due to increased pressures from other curriculum areas. This has meant that there has been an increased pressure on the physical education lessons to deliver the 'optimal opportunity for participation in physical activity' (and to also encourage 'physical activity outside of class time' (Rowlands et al., 2008: 26)).

Jennings-Aburto et al. (2009; 141) found in primary schools in Mexico City the only opportunities for children to participate in physical activity were in playtimes and physical education lessons, however physical education lessons only occurred once a week. They acknowledge physical education lessons as a place for physical activity to occur, yet questioned the inclusiveness of the physical education lessons that were observed and worried about whether all children would be able to access vital physical activity opportunities. They suggested that school should be increasing both the 'quantity and quality of physical activity especially during playtime'. Cardon and De Bourdeaudhuij (2002: 5) also suggested that school and in particular physical education lessons and playtimes are responsible for promoting physical activity for health and can promote an 'active lifestyle', yet limited physical education time or 'limited promotion of physical activity outside' the physical education lesson means that children may not reach the daily recommended physical activity targets. The research described has shown how potentially important school can be as a vehicle for increasing the opportunities of physical activity for health, as Green (2002) previously emphasised. Yet Wang et al. (2005) found conflicting evidence to Jennings-Aburto (2009) in that less than 70 per cent of total time of a physical education lesson had been used when assessed by heart rate monitors. They found that only on average 14.4 minutes of a 45 minute physical education lesson was spent in moderate to vigorous physical activity and with 6.7 minutes of the same lesson being at a vigorous physical activity level, so a total of 21.1 minutes of 45 minutes spent at moderate or above physical activity. They suggested improvements were needed in physical education lessons, with more emphasis upon encouraging children to engage in more physical activity, including speeding up getting changed into physical education kit to allow more time for physical activity opportunities to occur during the physical education lesson. This suggestion, however, is difficult to implement with very young children within a primary school setting, who are also in need of learning life skills, such as how to dress and undress. Sit et al. (2007) also suggested that improvements in the frequency and intensity of physical education lessons were needed when they examined the physical activity levels of children within special schools. They also suggested more physical activity opportunities within break times and lunch times to help the children reach recommended physical activity levels.

Kirk (2006: 122) in his critical examination of the obesity crisis, highlights the range of competing factors and suggests it is 'manufactured not through a conspiracy of scientists and politicians but instead through a complex process of social production of knowledge. In other words, any research exploring physical activity needs to be mindful of the multiple ways in which physical activity is, in fact, constituted. This has bearings upon how physical activity is investigated. For instance, Mallam et al. (2003) found in their comparative research of physical activity levels measured by accelerometers in three different schools that the amount of physical activity does not depend on how much physical education is timetabled and suggested that children compensate for this with the physical activity they complete outside school. Cawley et al. (2007: 1287) in contrast to Mallam et al. (2003) researched children in America and found that by increasing the amount of physical education lessons completed by the children, did increase the physical activity of girls, but they found no evidence that physical education lessons 'lowers BMI or the probability that the student is over-weight' and felt that physical education should not be used as part of an 'anti-obesity initiative'. Awareness of such contrasting ideologies regarding the purpose of the primary physical education lesson and the value given to the lesson for health and physical activity is therefore critical in exploring the realities of using physical education lessons to solve the obesity crisis. Consequently key questions that surround primary physical education relate to what is the role of primary physical education and what are the perceptions and understandings that primary school teachers have of the role of physical education? Yelling *et al.* (2000: 62) within their case study investigation suggested that physical activity is 'only one consideration of physical education lessons and the National Curriculum of physical education'. Learning about the benefits of physical activity helps aid a 'positive attitude towards a healthy and active lifestyle' beyond the school gates, which is important to extend into later adulthood (Yelling *et al.*, 2000: 62). Therefore is it really the responsibility of physical education lessons to get children fit and active or is it an important tool in developing children's skill acquisition and life skills? Kirk (2006) emphasises the need to define terms and importantly he poses the question of what is the difference between obesity and overweight. As Evans (2003: 123) suggests, there has been a 'slippage' between the use of the terms overweight and obesity but each 'refer to a different phenomenon'. Obesity was defined as excess of fat, whilst overweight was defined as body weight in excess of fixed standard. Evans (2003: 123) felt that the slippage in the meanings in relation 'to health was imprecise and contested yet regularly used unproblematically within health and scientific communities'.

THOUGHT BOX

If increased levels of physical activity become a feature of physical education lessons, what are the implications on providing for an holistic focus? Can the educational demands of physical education still be delivered effectively in such an environment?

ADDRESSING CHILDREN'S HEALTH AND THE OBESITY CRISIS

Kirk (2006: 123) states that it is 'widely reported in the media that levels of fitness and physical activity in children is low and declining'. However Harris *et al.* (2004: 123) stated that 'fitness test data provides no evidence that children's aerobic fitness is low or that fitness has declined'. This is, however, partly due to the difficulties in measuring children's aerobic fitness and consequently data on children's fitness should be used with caution. Green (2004b: 124) argues against the media's view and states that evidence since 1980s has shown an increase in opportunities for participation in physical activity and high proportions of children willingly taking up opportunities when activities are offered. The evidence and policies since the 1980s have also been produced by a variety of different government departments, which have contrasting agendas, including the obesity focus of health, Physical Education

213

in Education and Sport within the DCMS (Department for Culture, Media and Sport). These contrasting agendas make for difficult interpretation of the evidence and make it difficult to implement effectively in e.g. a primary school setting. Trost (in press) goes on to confirm Green's (2004a) viewpoint and suggests that a large proportion of children and adolescents meet the accepted guidelines for daily participation. However, this data set was produced through a large population self-reporting survey. Thus the accuracy of this data could be questioned, as it is known that populations tend to respond in a positive or media-influenced manner. Yet in 2004, contrary to Green's views of the same year 'the UK government identified obesity as a policy priority and set targets to halt the year-on-year rise in childhood obesity by 2010' (Aicken et al., 2008: 2). This policy priority however took almost four years to get underway and in 2008, the Government recognised 'obesity reduction as a national priority and set out an aim to reverse the current obesity trend' to reduce the number of obese children by 2020 to the same level as that of 2000 (Kalra and Newman, 2009: 1). Even though the Government had now set obesity reduction as a priority, costing £372 million for Healthy Weight, Healthy Lives: A cross-government strategy for England, designed to help everyone lead a healthier life, two years on since the start of the strategy the obesity rates are still too high, but the prevalence of obesity and overweight children is beginning to level off (Cross Government Obesity Unit 2008). Templeton (2010: 1) has recently suggested that 'children as young as ten are showing early signs of heart disease due to obesity' and suggested that children's BMI be measured twice during primary school, once at four or five and again at ten or eleven with the idea of helping 'families reverse it if required'. However, she does not suggest how this reversal can be assured. Kalra and Newman (2009: 1) further suggested research is still required to understand the 'dynamics of weight gain amongst young people ... to design effective policy solutions'. Rather than just setting obesity reduction as a priority, this understanding would ensure that effective solutions could be sought and implemented for all school aged children.

Interestingly Biddle et al. (2003: 124) argue that active and sedentary behaviour would seem 'possible and even commonplace in the same individual'. Craig et al. (2008: 5) suggest that sedentary behaviours are 'associated with increased risk of obesity and cardiovascular disease'. However Metcalf et al. (2010) suggested from their longitudinal research that 'physical inactivity is the result rather than the cause of obesity'. Hill et al. (1994) also discuss the conflicting affect that physical activity has on some people. They state that physical activity 'helps prevents moderate obesity in some individuals and inactivity contributes to development of obesity in some also'. Marshall et al. (2004: 124) agree with the dilemma over the ultimate effect of physical activity with this in their statement 'that the relationship media has placed on body fatness and physical activity in children' has 'little evidence to support the frequency and commonplace claim that there is a strong conclusive relationship between inactivity, sedentary behaviour and increased levels of body fatness'. They feel that this lacks clinical relevance and that factors affecting body fatness are complex and increases in body fat cannot be accounted for by a single factor. There is the need to consider other factors for example whether women and men eat and drink different food or at different times of the day and do these affect body fatness.

BEING HEALTHY

From the research described in this chapter there is great focus in terms of 'Be Healthy' not only on being overweight or obese and also on maintaining high physical activity levels. A target and success indicator of the Be Healthy outcome (of the ECM agenda, DCSF 2003) is a reduction in under-11s' obesity levels, yet there are no regularly measured statistics of this target which could be analysed to determine whether it is being achieved. If all ages are considered, the latest UK statistics from the Child Health Promotion Programme (Cross Government Obesity Unit, 2008: 10) suggest that only obesity is comparable with smoking in terms of its significance and scale of the problem, stating 'under 10 per cent of under nineteen-year-olds are obese and 20 per cent are overweight. Around 25 per cent of adults are obese and 40 per cent are overweight' the Cross Government Obesity Unit (2008) said that 'if no action is taken, by 2050 it is suggested that 25 per cent of children will be obese and 30 per cent will be overweight'. Yet Leake (2011) as mentioned earlier is already reporting that 28.6 per cent of children in Westminster are obese, a worrying report occurring 39 years before the predicted results. The Cross Government Obesity Unit (2008: 10) goes on to suggest that 'children who are obese in childhood are likely to remain obese into adulthood', although currently there has not been any longitudinal study to confirm this relationship. The paper continues and suggests that a staggering 'only 3 per cent of overweight or obese children have parents who are not overweight or obese'. They also suggest that a whole family approach to the problem should be used. This is an important point, it is all very well trying to encourage our children to engage in healthy lifestyle and becoming increasing physically active, whilst in school, but if within their home life this support does not continue, the children are still potentially at risk. This may mean that education is also needed for parents and carers, yet this has to be approached sensitively so as not to imply blame.

One way to ensure the whole family is involved in 'Being Healthy' was suggested by the Football Association (Malvern, 2010) which has called for clocks to move an hour forward to give lighter evenings to encourage more opportunities for exercise and physical activity. This could enable all children and parents to get involved and continue to be involved in physical activity throughout the whole year. NICE (2009: 16) suggested that school facilities should be made available outside school time, e.g. after the school day, at weekends and during school holidays 'to provide physical activity programmes and opportunities for physically active play'. However, it was not suggested who should be responsible to run these programmes or opportunities. Cleland et al. (2008) looked at physical activity levels over a 20-year period to consider whether overweight and physical activity levels in school compared to those in adulthood. They questioned whether patterns in childhood do actually continue into adulthood and they explored this by identifying the category of levels of physical activity levels and compulsory physical education the child was exposed to within school. Their results were revealing. They found that the prevalence of being overweight in childhood and in adulthood were similar across all groups of physical activity levels, indicating that the amount of physical activity or physical education experienced within school was not associated with the levels of overweight adults. They suggest that there are other factors that 'override any effects of school physical activity provision' (Cleland et al., 2008: 10), though they do

215

not discuss what these factors may be nor how to overcome them to help prevent adults becoming overweight.

THOUGHT BOX

What would happen if the focus of physical education was shifted so that 'Being Healthy' was its sole concern?

CONCLUSION

Overall this chapter has identified placing an importance on health and physical activity, not only for the children, but also as a lifelong learning process. It has examined not only the opportunities within the school day such as physical education lessons and play times to increase physical activity levels, but also explored the holistic development of the child (Doherty and Brennan, 2007) and in particular that of the primary aged child, to ensure positive experiences to improve children's overall wellbeing. By using this whole education process the primary school child's attitudes and interests in the importance of health can be fostered at this early age and an understanding of not only exercise, but diet and healthy lifestyles can be imparted rather than physical education lessons simply existing to provide exercise opportunities (Howells, 2011). It is important to ensure that action and education from a young age within primary school occurs and this is also passed onto families, parents and carers. By raising the influence and importance of such topics as obesity, physical activity, health and wellbeing will help to reduce not only the predicted obesity levels (Cross Government Obesity Unit, 2008) but the actual obesity levels (Leake, 2011) and will have an ultimate impact on health and the services (KNOSR, 2006). This chapter has also examined how children's health can be addressed through a whole school approach and offered suggestions to aid physical activity levels.

KEY READINGS

In an area that causes much conjecture, it is hard to find a clear way forward. To that end it seems of supreme importance to understand both the global and national landscapes pertaining to both physical education and the primary age phase. Two readings that should help here are Waring, M., Warburton, P. and Coy, M. (2007) Observation of children's physical activity levels in primary school: Is the school an ideal setting for meeting government activity targets? *European Physical Education Review* 13, 1, 25–40, and then more recently Pate, R.R. and Mclver, K.L. (2011) Physical Activity and Health: Does Physical Education Matter? *Quest,* 63, 1, 19–35.

Kristy Howells

REFERENCES

Aiken, C. Arai, L., Roberts, H. (2008) *Schemes to promote healthy weight among obese and over-weight children in England report*, London: EPPI Centre, University of London.

Anderson, L.B., Harro, M., Sardinha, L.B., Frobergd, K., Ekelund, U., Brage, S. and Anderssen, S.A., (2006) Physical activity and clustered risk in children: a cross-sectional study, The European Youth Heart Study, *Lancet*, 368, 9532, 299–304.

Armstrong, N. (1998) Young people's physical activity patterns as assessed by heart rate monitoring, *Journal of Sports Sciences*, 16, 9–16.

Biddle, S.J., Gorely, T., Marshall, S.J., Murdy, I. and Cameron, N. (2003) (p.124) in D. Kirk (2006) The 'obesity crisis' and school physical education, *Sport, Education and Society*, 11, 2, 121–133.

Booth, S.L., Sallis, J.F., Ritenbaugh, C., Hill, J.O., Birch, L.L., Frank, L.D., Glanz, K., Himmelgreen, D.A., Mudd, M., Popkin, B.M., Rickard, K.A., St. Jeor, S. and Hays, N.P. (2001) Environmental and Societal Factors Affect Food Choice and Physical Activity: Rationale, Influences, and Leverage Points, *Nutrition Reviews*, 59, 3, 21–36.

Breus, M.J. (2008 reviewed) How Much Sleep Do Children Need? Available online at http://www.webmd.com/parenting/guide/how-much-sleep-do-children-need?page=5 (accessed August 2009).

Cardon, G.M. and De Bourdeaudhuij, I.M.M. (2002) Physical Education and Physical Activity in Elementary Schools in Flanders, *European Journal of Physical Education*, 7, 5–18.

Caspersen, C.J., Powell, K.E., Christenson, G.M. (1985) Physical Activity, Exercise, and Physical Fitness: Definitions and Distinctions for Health-Related Research *Public Health Reports*, 100, 2, 126–131.

Cawley, J., Meyerhoefer, C., Newhouse, D. (2007) The impact of state physical education requirements on youth physical activity and overweight, *Health Economics*, 16, 2, 1287–1301.

Cleland, V., Dwyer, T., Blizzard, L. and Venn, A. (2008) The provision of compulsory school physical activity: Associations with physical activity, fitness and overweight in childhood and twenty years later, *International Journal of Behavioural Nutrition and Physical Activity*, 5, 14, 1–9.

Cox, M., Schofield, G. and Kolt, G.S. (2010) (p.46) Responsibility for children's physical activity: Parental, child and teacher perspectives, *Journal of Science and Medicine in Sport*, 13, 46–52.

Craig, R. Mindell, J. and Hirani, V., (2008) (eds) A Survey Carried Out on Behalf of the National Health Service Information Centre for Health and Social Care (2008), Health Survey for England, Physical activity and fitness, Summary of key findings. Available online at http://www.ic.nhs.uk/webfiles/publications/HSE/HSE08/HSE_08_Summary_of_key_findings.pdf (accessed September 2010, last updated 2008 no month).

Cross Government Obesity Unit (2008) cited in Children Health Promotion Programme (2008) DCSF and the Department of Health. Pregnancy and the first five years. Available online at http://www.dh.gov.uk/en/Publicationsandstatistics/Publications/PublicationsPolicyAndGuidance/DH_083645?IdcService=GET_FILE&dID=162747&Rendition=Web (accessed 11 September 2008, last updated March 2008).

Dale, D., Corbin, C.B., Dale, K.S. (2000) Restricting opportunities to be active during school time: do children compensate by increasing physical activity levels after school? *Research Quarterly for Exercise & Sport*, September, 71, 3, 240–248.

Department of Health (2006) *Forecasting Obesity in 2010*, London: Department of Health.

DCSF (Department for Children, Schools and Families) (2003) Every Child Matters Green Paper. Available online at http://www.everychildmatters.gov.uk/_files/EBE7EEAC90382663 E0D5BBF24C99A7AC.pdf (accessed 10 January 2008, last updated 19 November 2007).

Doherty, J. and Brennan, P. (2007) *Physical education and development 3–11: a guide for teachers*, Oxon: Routledge.

Evans, J. (2003) (p.123) in Kirk, D. (2006) The 'obesity crisis' and school physical education, *Sport, Education and Society,* 11, 2, 121–133.

Fairclough, S. and Stratton, G. (2006) Effects of Physical Education Intervention to Improve Student Activity Levels. *Physical Education and Sport Pedagogy,* 11, 1, 29–44.

Gilson, N.D., Cooke, C.B. and Mahoney, C.A. (2001) A comparison of adolescent moderate-to-vigorous physical activity participation in relation to a sustained or accumulated criterion, *Health Education Research* 16: 335–341.

Government Office of Science (2007) Tackling Obesities: Future Choices – Key Messages. Available online at http://www.bis.gov.uk/assets/bispartners/foresight/docs/obesity/20.pdf (accessed September 2010, last updated October 2007).

Green, K. (2002) Physical Education and 'the Couch Potato Society' – Part one, *European Journal of Physical Education* 7, 95–107.

Green, K. (2004a) Physical education, lifelong participation and 'the couch potato society', *Physical Education and Sport Pedagogy* 9, 1, 73–86.

Green, K. (2004b) (p.124) in Kirk, D. (2006) The 'obesity crisis' and school physical education, *Sport, Education and Society,* 11, 2 121–133.

Harrington, D.M. and Donnelly, A.E. (2008) *Physical Activity Levels of Adolescent Females Using Accelerometry: Preliminary Findings,* Engaging Young People in Physical Activity and Sport, Proceedings of Third Physical Education, Physical Activity and Youth Sport Forum, University of Limerick.

Harris, J. Cale, L. and Bromell, N. (2004) (123–124) in Kirk, D. (2006) The 'obesity crisis' and school physical education, *Sport, Education and Society.* 11, 2, 121–133.

Hill, J.O., Drougas, H.J. and Peters, J.C. (1994) Physical activity, fitness, and moderate obesity, in C. Bouchard, R.J. Shepherd and T. Stephens (eds) *Physical Activity, Fitness, and Health,* Leeds: Human Kinetics, 684–695.

Hills, A., King, N. and Armstrong, T. (2007) (p.533) The Contribution of Physical Activity and Sedentary Behaviours to the Growth and Development of Children and Adolescents: Implications for Overweight and Obesity, *Sports Medicine* 37, 6, 533–545.

Howells, K., Wellard, I. and Woolf-May, K. (2009) Do Physical Education Lessons Increase Physical Activity Levels of Primary Aged Children? – Preliminary Findings, in MacPhail, A and Young, A. (eds) (2009) *Promoting Physical Education Across Schools and Communities, Proceedings of the Fourth Physical Activity Physical Activity and Youth Sport Forum, University of Limerick,* 23–31.

Howells, K. (2011) *An Introduction to Physical Education,* in Driscoll, P., Lambirth, A. and Roden, J. (eds) (2011) *The Primary Curriculum: A Creative Approach,* London: Sage.

Jennings-Aburto, N., Nava, F., Bonvecchio, A., Safdie, M., González-Casanova, I., Gust, T. and Rivera, J. (2009) Physical activity during the school day in public primary schools in Mexico City, *Salud Publica de Mexico,* 51, 2, 141–147.

Johns, D. P. (2005) cited in Kirk, D. (2006) The 'obesity crisis' and school physical education. *Sport, Education and Society,* 11, 2, 121–133.

Kalra, N. and Newman, M. (2009) A systematic map of the research on the relationship between obesity and sedentary behaviour in young people, Technical report, in Research Evidence in Education Library, London: EPPI-Centre, Social Science Research Unit, Institute of Education, University of London. Available online at http://www.education.gov.uk/research/data/upload-files/DCSF-RBX–09–151.pdf (accessed online September 2010, last updated November 2009).

Kirk, D. (2006) The 'obesity crisis' and school physical education. *Sport, Education and Society,* 11, 2, 121–133.

KNOSR – Kent NHS Overview and Scrutiny Report (2006) Tackling Obesity NHS Overview and Scrutiny, Joint Select Committee Reports Parts I and II. Retrieved from https://shareweb.kent.gov.uk/Documents/Council-and-democracy/select%20committees/tackling-obesity-jan08.pdf (accessed September 2009, last updated December 2006).

Kolle, E., Steene-Johannessen, J., Klasson-Heggebó, L., Andersen, L.B., Anderssen, S.A. (2009) A 5-yr Change in Norwegian 9-yr Olds' Objectively Assessed Physical Activity Level, *Medicine and Science in Sports and Exercise,* 41, 7, 1368–1373.

Leake, J. (2011) Flabby Kent bulks out obesity league, *Sunday Times,* 11 September.

Mallam, K.M., Metcalf, B.S., Kirkby, J., Voss, L.D., Wilkin, T.J. (2003) Contribution of timetabled physical education to total physical activity in primary school children: cross sectional study, *British Medical Journal,* 327, 7415, 592–593.

Malvern, J. (2010) FA leads call for clocks to move hour forward, *Sunday Times,* 25 September.

Marshall, S.J., Biddle, S.J.H., Gorely, T., Cameron, N. and Murdy, I. (2004) (p.124) in Kirk, D. (2006) The 'obesity crisis' and school physical education, *Sport, Education and Society,* 11, 2, 121–133.

McMinn, D., Rowe, D.A., Stark, M., Nicol, L. (2010) (p.68) Validity of the New Lifestyles NL–1000 Accelerometer for Measuring Time Spent in Moderate-to-Vigorous Physical Activity in School Settings, *Measurement in Physical Education and Exercise Science* 14, 67–78.

Metcalf, B.S., Hosking, J., Jeffery, A.N., Voss, L.D., Henley, W., Wilkin, T.J. (2010) Fatness leads to inactivity, but inactivity does not lead to fatness: a longitudinal study in children (EarlyBird 45) *Arch Dis Child,* 1–6.

Mulvihill, C. Rivers, K. and Aggleton, P. (2000) A qualitative study investigating the views of primary-age children and parents on physical activity, *Health Education Journal* 59: 166. Available online at: http://hej.sagepub.com/content/59/2/166 (accessed 22 March 2011).

NHS Information Centre for Health and Social Care (2011) Statistics on obesity, physical activity and diet: England 2011. Available online at http://www.aso.org.uk/wp-content/uploads/downloads/2011/04/StatisticsonObesityPhysicalActivityandDietEngland2011.pdf (accessed 22 August 2011, last updated 24 February 2011).

NICE (2009) NHS National Institute for Health and Clinical Excellence, NICE Public health guidance 17, Promoting physical activity, active play and sport for pre-school and school-age children and young people in family, pre-school, school and community settings. Available online at 2010 http://www.nice.org.uk/nicemedia/pdf/PH017Guidance.pdf (accessed November 2009, last updated January 2009).

NHS Health and Social Care Information Centre (2009) Health Survey for England 2008: Physical Activity and Fitness, Leeds: NHS Information Centre.

Oliver, M.O., Scholfield, G.M., Kolt, G.S., McLachlan, C. (2007) Physical Activity in Early Childhood: Current State of Knowledge, *New Zealand Research in Early Childhood Education Journal,* 10, 47–68.

Owens, J.A., Spirito, A., McGuinn, M., Nobile, C. (2000) Sleep habits and sleep disturbances in elementary school aged children, *Developmental and Behavioural Paediatrics,* 21, 1, 27–34.

Pate, R.R. and McIver, K.L. (2011) Physical Activity and Health: Does Physical Education Matter? *Quest,* 63, 1, 19–35.

Pearce, P.F., Harrell, J.S. and McMurray, R.G. (2008) Middle-School Children's Understanding of Physical Activity: 'If You're Moving, You're Doing Physical Activity'. *Journal of Pediatric Nursing,* 23, 3, 169–182.

Plasqui, G. and Westerterp, K.R. (2007) Physical Activity Assessment with Accelerometers: An Evaluation Against Doubly Labelled Water, *Obesity,* 15, 10, 2371–2379.

Rowlands, A.V., Esliger, D.W., Pilgrim, E.L., Middlebrooke, A.R. and Eston, R.G. (2008) Physical Activity Content of Motive8 PE Compared to Primary School PE Lessons in the Context of Children's Overall Daily Activity Levels, *Journal of Exercise Science and Fitness*, 6, 1, 26–33.

Sirard, J.R. and Pate, R.R (2001) Physical Activity Assessment in Children and Adolescents, *Sports Medicine*, 31, 6, 439–454.

Sit, C.H.P., McManus, A., McKenzie, T.L., Lian, J. (2007) Physical activity levels of children in special schools, *Preventive Medicine*, 45, 6, 424–431.

Templeton, S.K. (2010) Obesity damages children's hearts, *Sunday Times*, 3 October.

Tremblay, M.S., Barnes, J.D. Copeland, J.L. and Esliger, D.W. (2005) Conquering childhood inactivity: is the answer in the past? *Medicine and Science in Sports and Exercise*, 37, 7, 1187–94.

Trost, S.G. (in press) in Kirk, D. (2006) The 'obesity crisis' and school physical education, *Sport, Education and Society*, 11, 2 121–133.

Trudeau, F., Laurencelle, L., Tremblay, J., Rajic, M. and Shepherd, R.J. (1999) Daily primary school physical education: effects on physical activity during adult life, *Medicine and Science in Sports and Exercise*, 31, 1, 111–117.

Wang, G.Y., Pereia, B. and Mota, J. (2005) Indoor physical education measured by heart rate monitor. A case study in Portugal, *Journal of Sports Medicine and Physical Fitness*, 45, 2, 171–177.

Waring, M., Warburton, P. and Coy, M. (2007) Observation of children's physical activity levels in primary school: Is the school an ideal setting for meeting government activity targets? *European Physical Education Review*, 13, 1, 25–40.

Winsley, R. and Armstrong, N. (2005) Physical Activity, Physical Fitness, Health and Young People, in K. Green and K. Hardman (eds) *Physical Education Essential Issues*, London: Sage, chap. 4.

WHO (2008) School Policy Framework, Implementation of the WHO Global Strategy on Diet, Physical Activity and Health. Available online at http://www.who.int/dietphysicalactivity/SPF-en–2008.pdf (accessed online October 2010, last updated 2008).

WHO (2010) Global Recommendations on Physical Activity For Health. Available online at http://whqlibdoc.who.int/publications/2010/9789241599979_eng.pdf (accessed October 2010, last updated 2010).

Yelling, M., Penney, D. and Swaine, I.L., (2000) Physical Activity in Physical Education: A Case Study Investigation, *European Journal of Physical Education* 5, 45–66.

Zeigler, E. (1994) Physical education's 13 principal principles, *Journal of Physical Education, Recreation and Dance*, 65, 4–5.

CHAPTER FOURTEEN

CREATIVE PHYSICAL EDUCATION

There is always another way!

Jim Lavin

INTRODUCTION

> The creative process invites the unexpected, the unusual, a deviation from the norm. It is the uniqueness of the response that merits the distinction creative.
>
> (Mosston and Ashworth, 2008)

During the last decade there has been a growing awareness of the need for creativity in the primary curriculum. This has been prompted by a range of developments at both national and local levels. A key feature in this process was the report 'All Our Futures: Creativity, Culture and Education' (1999) published by the National Advisory Committee on Creative and Cultural Education (NACCCE). The report stated that it was 'essential to provide opportunities for young people to express their own ideas, values and feelings'. The review of the primary National Curriculum for physical education in England and Wales implemented in 2000 further reinforced the need for creativity. In dance pupils were asked 'to create and perform dances' at both Key Stages 1 and 2. In Key Stage 1 games pupils should be taught to play 'games that they and others have made'. At Key Stage 2 they were required to 'play and make up small-sided and modified' games. In gymnastics at Key Stage 1 pupils were asked to 'create and perform short linked sequences' which led to being taught to 'create and perform fluent sequences' at Key Stage 2.

In 2003 the DfES published the document 'Excellence and Enjoyment' for primary schools. Amongst other aspects, teachers were encouraged to develop creative approaches and to plan and respond to pupils' creative ideas and actions. It stated 'promoting creativity is a powerful way of engaging pupils with their learning'. Furthermore teachers were exhorted to 'take ownership of the curriculum … teachers have much more freedom than they often realise to design the timetable and decide what and how they teach'.

The Office for Standards in Education (Ofsted) carried out a survey identifying good practice in the promotion of creativity in schools (Expect the Unexpected: Developing Creativity in Primary and Secondary Schools, Ofsted, 2003). They found that there was generally high quality in creative work. The Qualifications and Curriculum Authority (QCA) initiated a creativity project, which focused on Key Stages 1, 2 and 3 and worked with 120 schools to investigate how they could develop pupils' creativity. The results of the project were published as *Creativity, find it, promote it* (QCA, 2004). This provided practical materials and examples for developing creativity in schools including physical education. These initiatives have been further extended by the report 'Nurturing Creativity in Young People' (Roberts, 2006). This followed the Creativity in School Review and was jointly commissioned by Department of Culture, Media and Sport (DCMS) and the Department for Education and Skills (DfES). The importance of creative approaches was recognised in the launch of the revised Key Stage 3 National Curriculum in July 2007. One of the four key concepts in the physical education curriculum was creativity; the other three being competence, performance and healthy, active lifestyles. The importance of creativity in the primary curriculum is acknowledged in the Welsh educational system. In 2008, a new learner-centred physical education curriculum was implemented in Welsh schools. The physical education programme of study at Key Stages 2 and 3 has four areas of activity: health, fitness and wellbeing, adventurous activities, competitive activities and creative activities. This focus on creative activities allows schools to be more flexible in meeting the unique needs of their communities.

Thus primary teachers are being urged to be more creative across the curriculum. However, many primary teachers are non-specialists in physical education and their training and experience are rooted in a traditional, narrow approach to physical education. This has meant that their teaching has been limited to a focus on skill development and accurate replication of actions (Armour and Duncombe, 2009). There is a need therefore to discover ways of developing a creative approach to the teaching of primary physical education using the teachers' existing subject knowledge, teaching expertise and most importantly, knowledge of the children. Kirk (2010) argues that multi-activity, sport-based forms of physical education have been dominant in schools since the mid-twentieth century and that this approach has been highly resistant to change. He sees the focus of physical education as 'focused on the transmission of de-contextualised sport-techniques to large classes of children who possess a range of interests and abilities, where learning rarely moves beyond introductory levels.' Kirk and Macdonald (2009) suggest taking a constructivist approach in order to counter this over-reliance on instructional learning. In this model learning is an active process in which the pupil seeks out information to the task in hand and also takes into account the prevailing environmental factors. Learning is also related to the social and cultural context. The teaching of creative approaches to primary physical education relates to this model extremely well. In the creative process pupils are challenged to use imaginative ways to express and communicate ideas and overcome challenges. They are asked to explore and experiment with techniques, tactics and compositional ideas to produce something that is their unique take on the learning task they have been asked to undertake.

THE BENEFITS OF A CREATIVE APPROACH

The 'Creativity, find it, promote it' (QCA, 2004) document found that creativity in schools had the distinct characteristics of promoting imagination, providing purpose, developing originality and placing value on the children's work. It found that taking a creative approach promoted the following aspects of children's knowledge and understanding:

- Questioning and challenging conventions and assumptions.
- Making inventive connections and associating things that are not usually related.
- Envisaging what might be, imagining, seeing things in the mind's eye.
- Trying alternatives and fresh approaches, keeping options open.
- Reflecting critically on ideas, actions and outcomes.

If these qualities are applied to the teaching of physical education it is possible to assert that high quality physical education would result from this approach. Mosston and Ashworth (2008) provide a compelling argument for creative approaches to physical education. 'The discovery of new movements can modernize many traditional activities/sports; it can innovate new activities/sports; it can provide opportunities for more people with different levels of physical proficiency to become increasingly involved in activities/sports; it can emphasize the cognitive adeptness that is needed to perform many physical activities/sports; it can offer learners a personalised experience to initiate physical content.'

Taking a creative approach has the potential to transform the teaching of many non-specialist teachers who have been teaching the same physical education lessons for a number of years because it does not rely on subject knowledge or specialist expertise. For the teacher the focus is much more on their knowledge of the children as individuals. There is also an emphasis on their own personal teaching skills. For the children the benefits are that they become 'emotionally, cognitively and socially secure to move beyond memory to risk producing alternative ideas' (Mosston and Ashworth, 2008). They learn to accept other people's ideas. They can experience the genuine elation that sharing ideas and concepts can bring.

THE ROLE OF PLAY IN THE CREATIVE PHYSICAL EDUCATION CURRICULUM

The danger of a traditional skills-based curriculum is that children are taught techniques and skills in a range of disciplines such as swimming, games, athletics and gymnastics without reference to the wider context of children's play. The importance of play to children's physical and cognitive development in the Early Years Foundation Stage is well accepted (Cooper, 2004). However, even at Key Stage 2 children still love to play (Lavin, 2008). The time allocated to physical education could be seen as a time to play and explore. However, all too often it is a time for children to be instructed and judged on their physical performance. One of the great benefits of taking a creative approach to physical education is that often children need to play with the equipment/task/each other before starting to understand the constraints of the situation. The joy of moving is something that can be taken away from children. In creative approaches the children are given the freedom to explore their playful side.

Pellegrini (1991) cited in Cooper (2004) developed a model that provides a basis for describing play activities. In play children are motivated; they make choices; they are disposed to explore, to be flexible and are actively engaged. All of these qualities are present in the creative approach to physical education. In the creative continuum children use their imagination. Vygotsky (1978) in Cooper (2004) provides an authoritative explanation of the role of imaginative play. Children's play, he suggests, is imagination in action. Children enjoy play so much they learn to abide by the rules of the imaginary situation. Play, he says, is a leading factor in physical, social and cognitive development and a child's greatest self-control occurs in play. These are all convincing reasons to allow the element of play into the physical education curriculum. One of the greatest assets of the creative continuum is that it allows this play element to happen.

PROMOTING CREATIVITY

Griggs (2007) and Nickerson (1999) provide a most useful overview of how creativity can be promoted within the primary physical education curriculum:

- Supporting domain-specific knowledge with good basic skills
- Rewarding curiosity and exploration by giving value to the process by which ideas and approaches are developed
- Building motivation, particularly internal motivation. Creativity develops if pupils see their learning as meaningful and that they have ownership and control of the process
- Encouraging responsible risk taking by educating children about the environment in which physical education occurs
- Having high expectations of the children. This will move them beyond mere participation and open up the possibilities for higher-order thinking and learning
- Giving opportunities for choice and discovery
- Developing pupils' self-management skills by allowing them to make their own choices, manage their time and select resources.

THOUGHT BOX

Reflect on the above points and their related readings and consider what simple adjustments you could make to your practice in order to make it more creative.

TEACHING STYLES AND THE CREATIVE APPROACH TO PHYSICAL EDUCATION

A possible teaching style to use when taking a creative approach to physical education has been identified by Mosston and Ashworth (2008) as the Divergent Discovery Style. Within this style the learners are asked to engage in discovering and producing ideas and concepts within the subject matter set by the teacher. It invites learners to go beyond the norm and to expand their boundaries of the subject matter.

224

Jim Lavin

The fields of physical education, sports and dance are rich in opportunities to discover, design and invent. There is always another possible movement or another combination of movements, another way of passing the ball, another strategy, another dance choreography, or an additional piece of equipment. The variety of human movement is infinite – the possibilities for episodes in Divergent Discovery are endless.

(Mosston and Ashworth, 2008)

THOUGHT BOX

Do you feel confident with allowing moments of divergent discovery, whereby pupils can arrive at their own solutions? How prevalent is this within your practice? What are the constraints in allowing this to happen more frequently?

Within this style the role of the teacher is to present the focus of the learning and provide a justification for the activity. The relevant logistic parameters are given and the learners' responses are valid and valued. The question of leadership needs to be addressed here and the composition of the groups must be carefully considered. The learners must be given enough time to inquire, explore, move, and assess the alternative designs. The teacher must wait for the learners' responses to emerge. As the responses appear, the teacher circulates and offers neutral feedback (it is very important here not to 'judge' an activity at this stage). This signals to the learners that they can carry on the process of discovery. Mosston and Ashworth (2008) state that in this kind of class climate many designs/solutions/ideas are produced; some are exciting, others are not. The teacher should maintain the flow of ideas by avoiding corrective or value-laden feedback. However, the responses must fit within the parameters of the question; it is not 'anything goes'. In this process students are willing to take risks, they understand that certain problems have more than one solution; they trust the teacher not to embarrass them and finally the students learn to tolerate solutions and ideas presented by peers. An example of how a creative approach could be taken with regard to an area of the primary National Curriculum for physical education is provided below.

APPROACHES TO CREATIVE LEARNING IN A GAMES CONTEXT

Resource-initiated games

1   It is possible to challenge the children to be creative using 'standard' games equipment by giving them equipment that is not normally paired together, for example: a kwik cricket bat and a size 4 football; a parachute and skipping ropes; unihoc sticks and beanbags; rugby balls and hoops. The children would have to devise a game

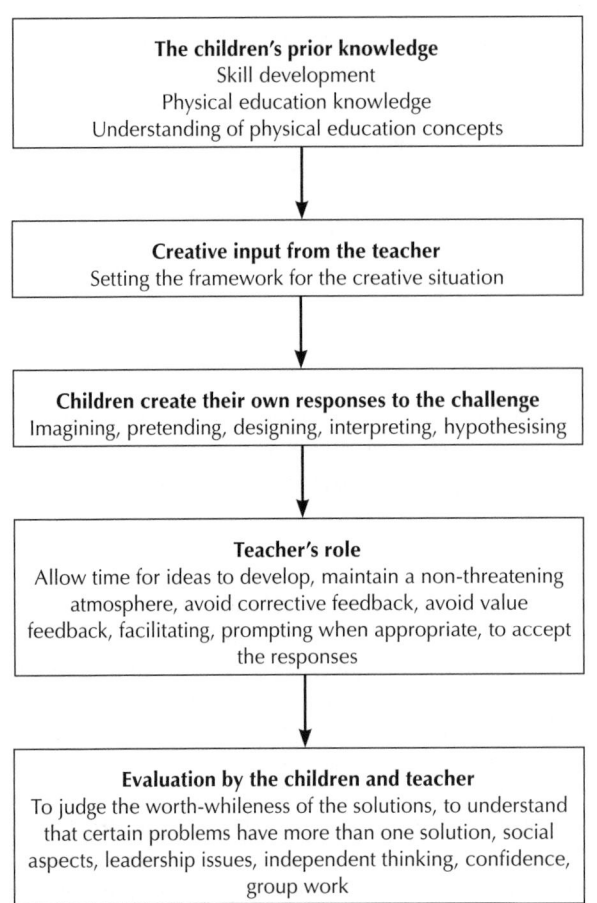

The children's prior knowledge
Skill development
Physical education knowledge
Understanding of physical education concepts

Creative input from the teacher
Setting the framework for the creative situation

Children create their own responses to the challenge
Imagining, pretending, designing, interpreting, hypothesising

Teacher's role
Allow time for ideas to develop, maintain a non-threatening atmosphere, avoid corrective feedback, avoid value feedback, facilitating, prompting when appropriate, to accept the responses

Evaluation by the children and teacher
To judge the worth-whileness of the solutions, to understand that certain problems have more than one solution, social aspects, leadership issues, independent thinking, confidence, group work

Adapted from Mosston and Ashworth, 2008

Figure 14.1 The creative continuum in primary physical education

that utilised the very different properties of each pairing. If the teacher judged that an additional piece of equipment would be useful, this could be introduced.

2 Provide the children with 'standard' equipment normally used for traditional sports-based games. Ask them to devise another way of using the equipment in order to develop a game that has its own district rules and characteristics. An example of this would be to provide a group with a football and two goals but explain that they cannot play football! They have to devise another way of using the football and goals. Likewise the children could be given a netball and two netball posts. (When I did this with the children they developed a game very similar to touchball).

3 The starting point could be a recognised game such as netball, cricket or tennis. Ask the pupils to 'add' to the game whilst keeping its essential character. An example of this would be to have a football area with four goals and perhaps two balls! The learning intention here is that participants begin to appreciate the original game

by developing variations of the game. They would begin to realise that all games/ sports have developed in this way by making rule changes over a period of time in response to perceived improvements.

4   Provide the children with equipment that they may not have used before in the game lesson context. This might be frisbees, tri golf, handball, quicksticks or even pop lacrosse. Ask them to develop a game using the equipment in different ways. For example, with tri golf the children would not be asked to hit a tri golf ball into a target in the least possible number of strokes; they would have to find another game objective and set of rules.

Skill-initiated games

Prepare a series of laminated cards, each with a games skill printed onto it. These could include catching, throwing, kicking, striking, aiming, fielding, bowling, passing, dribbling, shooting, travelling with, receiving.

Ask the group to choose cards at random without the children seeing what was on each card or alternatively allow the pupils to select the cards that appeal to them.

The number of cards allowed for each group could depend on the creative and physical ability of the group. The pupils then have to develop a game or games using these games skills only.

Tactic- or strategy-initiated games

In the classroom discuss a range of tactics or strategies with the pupils. These might include:

▪   Balance in defence and attack – does everyone attack and everyone defend (as in basketball)?
▪   Positions – should players have specific roles/positions within a game (as in netball and football)?
▪   Inclusion – how can we make sure that everyone is included within the game whatever their ability?
▪   In a base running game (as in rounders or cricket) where should the fielder throw the ball?
▪   Where should the striker hit the ball?
▪   In the hall/playground/playing field ask the groups to choose a tactic and then devise a game that has this tactic as a major factor in the game.

LINKED LEARNING

The way in which learning can be linked between subjects can allow creativity to flourish. Combining units from different subjects helps pupils to make connections and

227

transfer their learning from one subject to another. These connections make learning more coherent and allow them to see the relevance of what they do. Many subjects have common and complementary knowledge, skills and understanding. For example, the link between dance and music is a powerful one that can lead to deep learning about both forms of expression. However, if the teacher takes a more adventurous approach to linking aspects of physical education to other subjects of the curriculum, it is possible to develop both creative teaching on the part of the teacher and creative cognition on behalf of the learner. The link between geography and outdoor and adventurous activities is one that many teachers have already implemented but how about geography and games? The playground could have a world map painted onto it and games developed that allow children to learn physical geography or aspects of economic geography. The combinations of blended learning are endless and the mantra of 'education through the physical' is still an appropriate approach.

CREATIVE PHYSICAL EDUCATION AND TECHNOLOGY

The importance of technology in the lives of children should not be ignored. The technical expertise that children have can open up a wide range of possibilities in terms of creativity. Robinson (www.thepegeek.com) has developed an impressive portfolio of ways in which technology can be used to enhance the learning experience of the pupil in the physical education context.

Mobile phones

Many pupils in Key Stage 2 now have mobile phones and they play an increasingly important part in the way they communicate with their parents and peers. Most mobile phones have an array of features and these can be used in physical education lessons to encourage and develop creativity. The stopwatch facility can be used to allow the pupils to time their creative activities. The time an activity takes is often a key component of the learning process; an idea may be rejected because it takes too long to organise or implement. SMS messages allow the teacher to send bulk messages to phones from a laptop. This allows instant communication to the class and could be very useful in setting challenges in an outdoor setting such as athletics and outdoor and adventurous activities. Most mobile phones now have camera/video camera technology. Pupils could film creative activities and review them either immediately in the lesson or at a later time. Given that most creative activities develop over time going through a reflection/development process, this application could be very useful in evaluating progress and worth-whileness.

Video cameras

Video cameras have been part of the technology available in physical education lessons for many years now. However the latest flip video cameras are relatively cheap and

easy to use. As with mobile phones creative activities could be filmed and up-loaded. An interesting idea is for the pupils to upload a video on their 'new' game or dance to YouTube and receive feedback from viewers across the world.

Skype

The pupils could make contact with other teachers and children in relation to their creative ideas. They could teach their 'new' activity to another class in another country. They could also receive ideas/stimulus from other cultures or societies.

Geocaching

Geocaching is a treasure hunting game. Players try to locate hidden containers called geocaches using GPS-enabled devices. This could be a starting point for a creative activity by asking the pupils to devise and set appropriate geocaches for another set of pupils to find.

Nintendo Wii

Whilst most simulation sports on the Nintendo Wii require the participant to follow instructions and replicate actions, it is possible to use these games as a starting point to get the pupils to develop their own activity.

CREATIVE TEACHING IN PHYSICAL EDUCATION: PART OF THE FUTURE FOR PHYSICAL EDUCATION?

Over the past few years, the Physical Education, School Sport and Club Links (PESSCL) has provided an unprecedented level of funding for primary schools (Ofsted 2011). The use of coaches to deliver some of the physical education curriculum has allowed some teachers to become less than fully involved in the teaching of physical education to their pupils. The changes in school sport funding mean that teachers are now challenged to develop their own approach to the delivery of the physical education curriculum. Creative approaches to teaching physical education can allow teachers to use their professional judgement and general teaching skills without having to rely on an extensive subject knowledge base. There is a meaningful and cogent link between high-quality physical education and creative approaches. Chedzoy (2005) states this very well: 'Children who are experiencing high-quality physical education have confidence in their ability. They are not afraid to show others what they can do; they volunteer questions and answers, ask for help and talk positively about their achievements, whatever their level of attainment. They explore and experiment with new activities without worrying about failing'.

Simple strategies can have dramatic effects in terms of developing creativity in physical education lessons.

- Activities can be 'blocked' by timetabling the same creative activity two or three times a week for several weeks. Schools could provide half days, whole days or full weeks on an activity or focus.
- Providing equipment that is 'different' can provide a new stimulus to creativity. Children can get very used to the same equipment they have used each year of their primary school career.
- Allowing pupils opportunities to use specialist equipment away from the school can open up a wide range of possibilities for creative play.
- Use of teaching and learning strategies that meet the needs of visual, auditory and kinaesthetic learners.
- Link learning in different aspects of physical education. Can a forward roll be used in games lessons? How can the elements of running, jumping and throwing found in athletics be used in dance or games? How can a 'new' game be developed in a swimming context?
- Develop peer-mentoring systems to aid learning. Can constructive feedback be given on the worth-whileness of an idea or approach? What criteria will the peer use?
- Group pupils by ability, gender or ethnic background if this encourages creativity.
- Promote the notion that pupils can take on the role of referee, coach, trainer or teacher in creative activities.

CONCLUSION

A number of factors can be seen to be to driving the focus on the creative agenda. Craft (2011) defines these as being economic, social and technological. Both knowledge and creativity are seen as essential ingredients in responding to the changing demands of business success. Thorne (2007) points out that many of our primary children currently in schools will have to take their place in industries that do not even exist at the moment. The key to success is therefore a capacity to innovate and respond flexibly to changing economic developments. By its very nature, physical education has much to offer in terms of developing such attitudes. Its potential to help individuals work together in a practical and physical way, to learn experientially, to cope with success and failure is unique within the curriculum.

230

REFERENCES

Armour, K. and Duncombe, R. (2009) Teachers' continuing professional development in primary physical education: Lessons from present and past to inform the future, in Bailey, R. and Kirk, D. (eds) *Routledge Physical Education Reader*, London: Routledge.

Chedzoy, S. (2005) Children, Creativity and Physical Education in Wilson, A. (2005) *Creativity in Primary Education*, Exeter: Learning Matters.

Cooper, H. (2004) *Exploring Time and Place Through Play*, London: David Fulton.

Craft, A. (2011) *Creativity and Education Futures: Learning in a Digital Age,* Stoke-on-Trent: Trentham Books

DfES (2003) *Excellence and Enjoyment: A Strategy for Primary Schools*, London: DfES.

Griggs, G. (2007) Maximising Creativity in Primary Physical Education, *Physical Education Matters*, Winter, ii-iii.

Kirk, D. (2010) *Physical Education Futures*, London: Routledge.

Kirk, D. and Macdonald, D. (2009) in Bailey, R., and Kirk, D. (2009) *The Routledge Physical Education Reader*, London: Routledge.

Lavin, J. (ed.) (2008) *Creative Approaches to Physical Education*, London: Routledge.

Mosston. M. and Ashworth, S. (2008) *Teaching Physical Education*, First ebook: Spectrum Institute for Teaching and Learning.

NACCCE (1999) *All Our Futures: Creativity, Culture, Education*, London: DfEE.

Ofsted (2003) *Expecting the unexpected: Developing creativity in primary and secondary schools,* London: Ofsted

Ofsted (2011) *Learning Lessons from School Sports Partnerships*, London: Ofsted.

Qualifications and Curriculum Authority (2004) *Creativity, find it, promote it,* London: QCA.

Roberts, P. (2006) *Nurturing Creativity in Young People*, London: DCMS and DfES.

Robinson, J., *The PE Geek website*. Available at www.thepegeek.com.

Thorne, K. (2007) *Essential Creativity in the Classroom*, London: Routledge.

INDEX

235